PREMIERE
WITH A
PASSION

MICHAEL FEERER

PEACHPIT PRESS
BERKELEY, CALIFORNIA

PREMIERE
WITH A
PASSION

Contents

2

PLACING CLIPS IN YOUR PROJECT

3

EDITING THE SEQUENCE, PART I

4

EDITING THE SEQUENCE, PART II

5

PREVIEWING & PRINTING YOUR PROGRESS

ADDING VISUAL TRANSITIONS

Working with Transitions

Transitions in Review

Transition Acrobatics

APPLYING DIGITAL FILTERS

Filter Techniques

Filters in Focus

8 FLYING WITH MOTION SETTINGS

9 CREATING TITLES & GRAPHICS

10 SUPERIMPOSING CLIPS

11 OPTIMIZING YOUR OUTPUT

Compiling the Final Movie

A Potpourri of Output Issues

Getting Ready for More

12 CAPTURING VIDEO & SOUND

The Digitizing Process

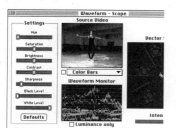

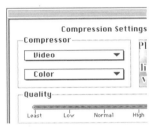

APPENDICES

Introduction

If you picked up *Premiere with a Passion*, chances are you've already felt some of the excitement of using Adobe Premiere. It's a breakthrough movie-editing and video production tool, especially in its 3.0 incarnation. The software is powerful, yet fairly approachable. So why would anyone want this book?

The answer is simple: Premiere is deceptively *deep*. There are countless nooks and crannies to explore—each brimming with creative potential. In fact, you can accomplish so many amazing things with Premiere that there's not enough time to discover them all for yourself.

This book can be a friendly shortcut for you—a partner to ease your Premiere travels. In one handy, compact source, you'll find:

• helpful guidance to *every* aspect of Premiere, including mysteries the manual touches on only lightly or ignores

• step-by-step techniques that pull everything together for a variety of creative (and mundane) tasks

• reference charts and visual comparisons to help you choose at a glance the right path for your project

• numerous movie examples and screen images (after all, Premiere users are visually-oriented)

• loads of time-saving tips and tricks—so you can make that deadline *and* do other things with your life, too

There's one other reason to keep this book in reach. All of the help is delivered to you in an unusual way—*with a passion*. I wrote this book because I'm crazy about Premiere. Learning about Premiere wonders (and warts) should be as appealing and fun as using the software.

The passion also means these pages reflect well over a thousand hours of intensive testing, everyday use and experimentation. (I'm way past the honeymoon with Premiere.) So you'll get down-to-earth solutions to pesky problems—with a smile.

▶ **Who the Passion is For**

This book is for the full spectrum of Premiere users—from newcomers to experienced pros. Only three assumptions are made about your prior abilities:

• You're pretty comfortable with Macintosh basics, such as opening windows, clicking icons and moving around menus. Rest assured you do *not* have to be a power user to understand and work with Premiere.

• You have at least some basic experience with video (i.e. you know a close-up shot from a long shot). You don't have to be a video or animation wizard, though many of you are. And you don't need prior QuickTime movie experience, but the more you have, the faster you can zip through a few sections.

• You use—or are about to use—Premiere 2.0 or 3.0 for the Macintosh. This book integrally covers both versions. If you've already moved up to 3.0 (highly recommended), a simple **3.0** icon helps you to pick out new features and changes. If you plan to stick with 2.0 for a while, you can grow into both versions with this volume. Premiere LE users also will find the assistance they need.

▶ **The Guide to This Guidebook**

This book is organized by *process*. Chapters appear in the order you might use to complete a project. But since few people will read this book from beginning to end, the pages also are designed with other techniques in mind:

• *The Rear-End Approach.* You can successfully attack this book from the rear. Rest assured that much time and energy has gone into developing a *very* comprehensive Index. (When you *desperately* need to find an answer right away, this really becomes The *Crisis* Approach.)

• *The Intensive Approach.* You can tackle a single Premiere topic without having to hunt through several areas of the book. Each section focuses on a particular Premiere task and includes cross-references.

• *The Dip-Your-Toe-in-the-Water Approach.* If you like to ease into new things, the chapters gently start with the basics and then move into more advanced territory. You'll be surprised how easy the "hard" areas are with a little background preparation.

• *The Bathroom Companion Approach.* Prefer to browse around and learn about Premiere with your thumb? Everything is in digestible chunks (like this page). You can get just enough before you flush.

Whatever your learning style, here are the dozen chapters of this book in a nutshell:

1 Preparing for Takeoff
Here's help for your first clicks—how to set up and install Premiere and tune your Mac for maximum editing performance. If you're already up and running well, you can breeze through this chapter.

2 Placing Clips In Your Project
This chapter covers the opening acts of a Premiere project— assembling clips and working smoothly with the Project window. You'll see how to leap the importing hurdles of every source clip format.

3 Editing the Sequence, Part I
This first of two editing chapters introduces all of the controls and commands of Premiere's Clip window and Construction window environments. Mastering this is the first step to becoming an editing hotshot.

4 Editing the Sequence, Part II
This second editing chapter focuses more extensively on editing tools and techniques in the Construction window—the centerpiece of Premiere. It concludes with a handy digest of all editing actions.

5 Previewing & Printing Your Progress

To check your project's progress, turn to this chapter to discover the quickest and smoothest way you can preview your movie. You'll also see how Premiere can print storyboards and more on another media—paper.

6 Adding Visual Transitions

You'll find techniques for applying and tailoring transitions between clips plus a complete visual guide to Premiere's fifty-plus transitions to aid your selection. All sorts of visual acrobatics then follow.

7 Applying Digital Filters

Here's how to apply and customize Premiere's powerful filters. You'll also receive a complete visual guide to all of the filter varieties. Numerous tips and examples for each filter family appear along the way.

8 Flying With Motion Settings

Want to fly frames of other movies within a movie? Or accurately position an inset or split-image? Then turn to Premiere's motion settings. This chapter gives you all of the flight training you'll need.

9 Creating Titles & Graphics

Here we explore titles and graphics—an essential part of most movies. You'll see how to master Premiere's Title window, animate text and have lots of (practical) fun with titles and related effects.

10 Superimposing Clips

This reveals Premiere's superimposing powers, which include several keys and mattes for overlaying clips onto one image. You'll master transparency techniques and learn to create background clips in Premiere.

11 Optimizing Your Output

It's time to make the final movie. Here's how to optimize your QuickTime or videotape results. You'll also find tips about gluing movies into sequences, setting preferences and preparing for future project endeavors.

12 **Capturing Video & Sound**
Use these pages to grab clips cleanly with
Premiere (and perhaps take advantage of 3.0's nifty new
batch capture and waveform monitor features).

▶ **Addictive Appendices**

Appendices are sometimes treated as second-class citizens, but are often some of the most well-worn pages. This book includes two candidates for your fingerprints:

A. Choosing Compression Settings

Here are the essentials for properly setting a movie's QuickTime compression. You'll need to juggle those crucial compression variables in two places—when capturing clips and compiling your final movie.

B. The EDL Express

Are you editing video in Premiere *off-line* to create an edit decision list for broadcast-quality productions? These pages will show you what to watch out for in Premiere as well as several new 3.0 features that can help.

The Goodies Disk

This isn't an appendix but it sits nearby. You now proudly own a *Goodies Disk* full of plug-ins and other Premiere files that will extend your editing power. The goodies are *exclusively* available from this book (and in fact were developed specifically for this publication). There are over a dozen new transitions as well as files for the 3.0's new Displace transition and Convolution Kernel filter. You'll also find several practical plug-ins that will save you time during your projects. See the inside back cover and the disk's *Read Me* file for the juicy details.

▶ **Just a Few Icons**

The latest trend in computer books is to sprinkle around a bunch of icons to point out different kinds of tips and notes. This book is no exception, although my icon-craze is limited to the following:

The hand points to tips. Tips are integrated into each chapter—instead of in a separate chapter—so you can more easily find them where you need them.

These icons hone in on the major areas that are unique to the 2.0 or 3.0 version of Premiere. *Minor* differences are simply stated in the text rather than tagged with an icon. Everything else applies to both Premieres.

This icon signals a cross-reference to a page with related or more extensive information.

The disk notes items that are on or related to the book's *Goodies Disk*.

▶ And Just a Few Terms

Although the glossary tackles new terms, keep in mind a few terminology basics before beginning your travels:

• *Source clips* (or "clips" for short) are the raw materials—the movies, animations, graphics and sound files—that you edit in Premiere. Premiere doesn't actually touch the source clips. It works with *pointers* that represent each file.

☞ *"Linked clips" are simply clips with video and sound.*

☞ *If you send someone a project file, they need its source clips and Premiere to play the sequence. If you send a compiled movie, they can play it in any QuickTime-capable application.*

• A *project* is the Premiere environment that holds your editing decisions for a particular production. It's a separate file from your source clips and final movie.

• Last, a *compiled movie* (or *Premiere movie*) is a new QuickTime movie you build from your edits in a project.

▶ Getting In Touch

If you have a burning suggestion for future editions of this book, or a wild new tip, trick or technique from your own Premiere experiences, get in touch. Reach me through the fine people at Peachpit Press.

Michael Feerer, c/o Peachpit Press
2414 Sixth Street
Berkeley, CA 94710
(800) 283-9444 or (510) 548-4393 Fax: (510) 548-5991
CompuServe: 75430,1022   AppleLink: PEACHPIT
America Online: PEACHPRESS

▶ Enjoy!

As Apple likes to say, it's more fun to be a pilot (a Premiere author) than a passenger (a movie player). Premiere is the highest flying craft around on the Macintosh. So happy soaring!

▶ **And Now for the Acknowledgements**

Thanks first must go to Randy Ubillos, the creator of Adobe Premiere. He tirelessly answered my questions with enthusiasm during this venture and made the nifty *Goodies Disk* possible. Thanks also to Frank Schroeder for nicely handling the nitty-gritty of the *Goodies Disk* and inspiring much of its contents.

Five other individuals at Adobe were very helpful. Teri Chadbourne, Patricia Pane and Sonya Schaefer plugged me into Adobe with success. Tim Meyers, Premiere's product manager, was responsive despite his busy schedule. And David Rodenburn tackled tough early questions.

To test Premiere's full range of abilities required a few product loans. A big thanks to Carrie Reichenberger and Anne-Lise Stannard at RasterOps, Michelle Janin and Diana Iles at Cunningham Communications, Kathy Galvin and Mary Hill at SuperMac and Jill Ryan at Macromedia.

Production of the book was smoothed along by the friendly people at Seattle Imagesetting. Thank you Carole Quandt for nice, tight copyediting. I'm also indebted to Jonathan Gibson at Form and Function (makers of those handy *Wrapture Reels* CD-ROMs) who provided a bubbly clip for this book when my time was pinched.

Readers in the Northwest may recognize some of the movie subjets in this book. Several shots highlight Bert Bennett (and his students) at the Aikido Peace Education Center in Bellingham, Washington. Also featured is Rebecca Smedley of the Mount Baker Ballet, directed by Nancy Whyte. Thank you all for your time and energy.

Finally, here's a warm hug for the wonderful, fun bunch of characters at Peachpit Press. Ted Nace and Roslyn Bullas, especially, thank you for your unflagging support and encouragement. Here's appreciation in advance to Paula Baker, Trish Booth, John Grimes, Keasley Jones and Hannah Onstad who will push this book into the market. And thanks Cary Norsworthy for managing the book's press production.

Closest to the heart, thanks Sam and Betty for sitting and helping, Jeff and Marci for telephone support and all four of you for encouragement. And most of all, to Kim and Valerie, the other two passions in my life besides Premiere—here's love, kisses and more for sacrificing so much over the past year to make this dream come true.

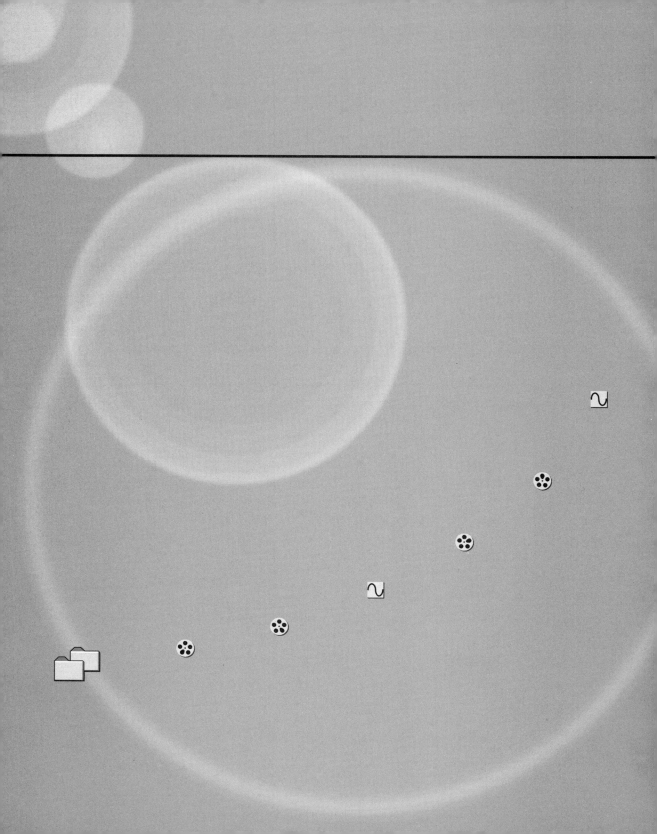

1

Preparing for Takeoff

Preparing to fly with Premiere calls for more than loading a few disks. You'll soon have to come to grips with several perplexing issues. What should I do with all of the extra files that come with Premiere? Should I add my Photoshop plug-ins to Premiere? Which system software settings will boost Premiere's performance? How much RAM will my projects need?

Those are just a few of many knots untangled ahead. This chapter will get Premiere and your Mac in top shape for editing. So even if you've installed Premiere without a hitch and your Mac seems to hum just fine, look over these pages. A proper setup will go a long way towards shooting problems before trouble starts.

First Clicks & Tricks

Remember the days when installing Macintosh software meant dragging a few files from a floppy disk onto your hard drive? So much for digital nostalgia. Premiere is a compressed, multi-disk (or CD-ROM) package that relies on an installation program.

Fortunately, the installation process is straightforward and takes only a few minutes. Adobe provides a *Getting Started* pamphlet that clearly takes you through the few steps. Rather than repeat that dry information here, let's concentrate on sorting out the new goods that Adobe's installer places on your hard drive.

▶ **Sorting Out the Goods**

2.0 ☞ *Premiere 2.0 users should avoid Apple's new Sound Manager 3.0 and Sound Control Panel. Premiere 2.0 has problems with them when handling 16-bit and stereo 8-bit sound files.*

The Premiere installer deposits everything in a new folder on your hard drive, even if you're upgrading from an earlier Premiere. Well, *almost* everything—depending on how you installed Premiere, a few items may have sneaked into your System Folder: the latest version of QuickTime, Adobe Type Manager, and (only from Premiere 3.0) Apple's new Sound Manager and Sound Control Panel. Ignore this System intrusion for the moment and focus on your Premiere folder.

Assuming you installed all parts of your Adobe package, your Premiere folder should look something like this:

3.0's folder is shown, but 2.0's looks the same. If you selectively installed files or have Premiere LE, fewer items may appear.

☞ *System 7 users: Consider making an alias of the Premiere icon for your Apple Menu Items folder. You'll be able to open a new project conveniently without having to dig into folders.*

Apple Menu Items

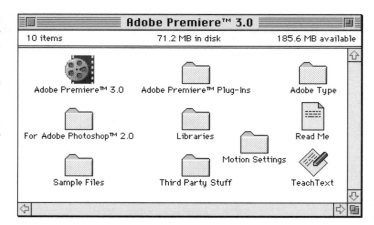

If you haven't used Premiere before, the folders may appear a bit mysterious. You're probably asking: "What is this stuff? What do I do with it?" Let's briefly peek at the inhabitants and find out more about setting them up.

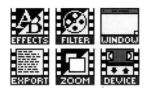

Adobe Premiere Plug-Ins

Premiere has a modular architecture—the program is a collection of files instead of a single file. The Plug-Ins folder holds everything that's not in the core application. Transitions, filters and many other components live in the folder as separate plug-in files. The great advantage of this modularity is you can add updated or new plug-ins as they become available.

In fact, you can fatten the Plug-Ins folder *now* to extend your editing power. Yes! It's as simple as ABC:

Checker Grid

A Sixteen extra plug-ins are already in arm's reach— on this book's *Goodies Disk.* Drag those fresh files into Premiere's Plug-Ins folder right away. Check the inside back cover of this book for details.

B When you look in Premiere's Plug-Ins folder, notice that Premiere borrows a few plug-in filters from Adobe Photoshop. (They give themselves away by wearing Photoshop's ubiquitous plug-in icon.) For some reason Adobe left a few behind. If you have Photoshop, you can add the following to Premiere's stockpile:

☞ *Lens Flare in Photoshop 2.5 isn't compatible with Premiere, but you can use 2.0's Lens Flare if you have it.*

From Photoshop 2.0
• Lens Flare
• Polar Coordinates
• Wind

From Photoshop 2.5
• Color Halftone
• Extrude
• Wind

Stay away from other plug-ins in Photoshop, though. They either aren't recognized by Premiere, work erratically, or duplicate what's already available in Premiere.

3.0 ☞ *Premiere 3.0's Deluxe Edition on CD-ROM includes several third-party filters.*

C Many third-party filters for Adobe Photoshop also happily work inside of Premiere. If you have HSC's *Kai's Power Tools*, Aldus's *Gallery Effects* or other similar packages, consider dropping a copy of their filters in Premiere's Plug-Ins folder. Not all will work well with movies, but you'll gain many worthwhile additions.

If you have Photoshop on your Mac, you may wonder if you can combine Premiere and Photoshop plug-ins into one mega-folder. Technically it's possible, but it can cause confusion. That's because each application will list some filters as available that do not really apply or operate well. For example, Premiere will list 2.5's *Lens Flare* filter even though it doesn't work in Premiere. So stay away from making a mega-folder unless you have an uncanny ability to keep whose-filter-is-whose straight.

Libraries

Libraries are storehouses for clips or other Premiere files that you may want to use in several projects. Adobe gives you a running start to your library collection by including a few handy files in this folder. One holds several full-screen solid-color *mattes*. The full version of Premiere also throws in a library of textured *backdrops*—marble, granite, crinkled paper and more—that you can customize in Premiere in many different ways. All serve effectively as backgrounds for superimposed clips.

Here's a sampling of the backdrop textures that ship with all versions of Premiere except LE.

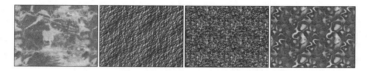

You don't need to do anything now with the libraries, but take a moment to look over their contents. Keep in mind that you can create new libraries of clips without eating up much hard disk space. Libraries are made up of small file *pointers* that obediently point Premiere to the original source clips. (Ruff! Atta boy!)

For more about Premiere's libraries, see page 34. For more about mattes and backdrops, see page 278.

Sample Files

This folder holds a sample Premiere project and various source clips for the project. Keep them around for a while. When other clips aren't readily at hand, you can use these materials to learn and experiment with Premiere.

▶ Beyond Premiere LE

The remaining folders that Premiere offers are in various full versions of the application. If you're a Premiere LE user, you can skip this section—or read and drool over the creative possibilities upgrading offers.

Motion Settings

Motion settings store reusable ways to fly (and zoom, spin or distort) a movie within another movie. Adobe provides several sample flight paths to get you started. As you'll see in Chapter 8, Premiere provides flexible controls to create and customize such acrobatics.

Tumbling a clip through another clip is easy with Premiere's motion settings.

Adobe Type

COPPERPLATE
Imago Book
Imago Medium
LITHOS LIGHT
LITHOS BOLD
Times New Roman
Times New Roman Bold

The Adobe Type folder includes seven Type 1 Postscript typefaces intended for movie titles. You can preview the fonts by double-clicking each file in the *Bitmaps* suitcase.

    To make use of these resources, move them into your System Folder. If you use System 7, be sure to drag the outline *and* bitmap font files into a *closed* System Folder. System 6 fans will have to resort to the clumsy *Font/DA Mover* to install the bitmap fonts.

For Adobe Photoshop

FilmStrip

Aaaiieee—another plug-in! This one's not for Premiere—it's for Adobe Photoshop. If you have Photoshop 2.0, drag the plug-in file at left into Photoshop's Plug-Ins folder. If you're using Photoshop 2.5, you don't have to do this—it already has the plug-in. The plug-in enables Photoshop to import a *filmstrip file*. That's a special file that holds individual movie frames from Premiere so you can paint, squiggle or distort the images with Photoshop's powerful tools.

For more about creating filmstrip files, see page 96.

Third Party Stuff

VISCA™   Selectra VuPort™

This last folder holds several third-party enhancements. For example, Sony's VISCA folder and the Selectra folder contain a control panel and plug-in, respectively, that enable Premiere to control frame-accurate VCRs. Depending on the Premiere version you have, other third-party files may also be available for that purpose.

Premiere 3.0 includes several *presets* from major QuickTime board vendors in this folder. Presets are a nifty new feature that can save you much time and headache. These third-party presets automatically configure Premiere's myriad of preview and output settings to take maximum advantage of a particular board's capabilities. We'll find out more about presets not too much further ahead.

DigitalFilm Presets File

📖 *For more about 3.0's presets, see page 24.*

Premiere 3.0 also throws in a Goodies folder with the third-party files. It contains a few last-minute plug-ins Adobe's engineers cooked up. Unfortunately, the files haven't endured the usual testing and Adobe provides no technical support for them. So use them at your own risk.

Goodies

If your setup can use a third-party item, move the appropriate file to its proper home (plug-ins to the Plug-Ins folder; control panels to the System Folder). Files for hardware you don't have can be trashed.

▶ What about Earlier Versions?

If you're upgrading from an earlier version of Premiere, you probably now have *two* Premiere folders on your hard drive. That's because Adobe's installation program doesn't delete any prior Premiere folders. Unlike some things in life, however, with Premiere there's little reason to keep the old with the new.

Projects created in an earlier (or even Limited Edition) Premiere will open automatically with a newer version and function identically. No subtle or gargantuan differences in movie results will be unleashed—with one exception: Premiere 2.0 projects with clips that have *motion setting delays* may open in 3.0 with the delays modified. That's because Premiere 3.0 uses a different basis for specifying motion delays. Fortunately, Premiere alerts you to this fact while opening such a file. With a few quick adjustments, you can mend the project.

👉 *Forget the reverse axiom: Projects from newer Premiere versions will not open successfully in older versions.*

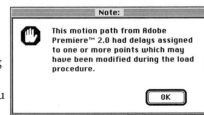

Note:

This motion path from Adobe Premiere™ 2.0 had delays assigned to one or more points which may have been modified during the load procedure.

OK

📖 *For more about this motion settings issue, see page 216.*

Before throwing your old Premiere folder in the trash, rescue *your* files that may be in the folder. Source clips, titles, Premiere projects, compiled movies and sequence files are the most obvious rescue candidates. If you're shifting from the full version of Premiere 2.0 to 3.0, don't forget *custom* files you may have created, such as:

Filmstrips for   Libraries   Motion   Backdrops   Mesh Warp
Photoshop   settings   filter settings

Also remember to retrieve any extra Photoshop or third-party filters that may be in your old Plug-ins folder—if only to avoid searching for them elsewhere.

After transferring these nuggets to your new Premiere folder, go ahead and drag the older folder into the Trash. This will eliminate any chance for confusion and free up a couple megabytes of disk space.

▶ Checking the Adorable ATM

The full Premiere package also includes Adobe Type Manager (ATM), which gives the gift of sharp, clean font characters at any size to your Mac's screen. ATM is essential for creating effective titles within Premiere.

Besides the obvious—turning ATM *on*—check the other two settings in the ATM Control Panel.

MinioMM

• Set *Font Cache* to at least 256K if you're using Adobe *Multiple Master* fonts, which perform extra text animation tricks in Premiere. Adobe even suggests as much as 512K, but try the lower figure first unless you've got RAM to burn. If the fonts erratically display on-screen as you manipulate them, come back and set the Font Cache higher. For users with only regular Type 1 fonts, 128K should be fine (although you can try surviving on 96K if your Mac's RAM is tight).

gjpqy

• Also select *Preserve Character shapes* in the box to prevent ATM from rudely clipping character descenders from the bottom of your Premiere titles.

▶ Eleventh-Hour Additions

Here are the last few items to double-check before taking off with Premiere. Your installation disks don't include everything that may be necessary to ignite the QuickTime engine in your Mac. So look over the short list below to see if you require a few last-minute additions.

32-bit QuickDraw

If you're using a Mac II, IIx or IIcx with System 6.07 or 6.08, make sure *32-bit QuickDraw* (version 1.2 or later) is in your System Folder. QuickTime will not run without it. If necessary, check your system software disks for a copy.

VDIG

VDIGs are the system software extensions that allow Premiere to control and communicate with video digitizers. Every QuickTime-compatible video capture board should come with one. If you own a pre-QuickTime model, check with the manufacturer or on-line services for the VDIG—they're usually available at little or no cost.

Sound Driver

If you're using the built-in sound digitizing function of a recent Macintosh, the sound driver is already in your system software. If you desire higher quality sound or have an older Mac, however, you'll need a sound driver extension for your capture device. This is true whether you're using a separate sound digitizer (such as Macromedia's *MacRecorder*) or a video digitizing board with sound capture abilities.

Once you have the eleventh-hour files you need, drag them into your System Folder (as usual, a *closed* System Folder if you're running System 7). Congratulate yourself and then ▪ **Restart** ▪. Premiere is now ready and rarin' to go. All that's left is to check a few other areas on your Mac to ensure it will operate at peak performance for your Premiere flights.

Tuning for High Performance

To extract all of the power your Mac can offer to Premiere, a tune-up may be necessary. You may need to tweak your System software to give Premiere more memory and reduce CPU interruptions, adjust your monitor's color depth, or clear out megs and megs of storage. Let's consider each area below.

▶ The Case for More RAM

Just as you can never have enough spare time or money, you can never have enough RAM in Premiere. There are three compelling reasons to outfit Premiere well beyond its four megabyte bare-bones minimum.

Peppier Editing Performance

As you edit, Premiere will be able to rely more on speedy RAM instead of a relatively pokey hard disk. Common tasks—such as scrolling the Construction window—will operate quicker, especially in long or complex projects. If your Mac isn't the fastest model on the block, more RAM also may be your best route to smoother previews.

Higher Quality Video Captures

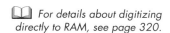

Premiere can capture video *directly to RAM* instead of to hard disk. Since RAM is much zippier, you can capture higher quality video clips—even with a relatively slow Mac. The captured video could sport a smoother frame rate or larger images, for example. The more RAM in Premiere, the longer the clip you can digitize this way.

📖 *For details about digitizing directly to RAM, see page 320.*

Larger Movies

To author anything larger than a business card, you have no choice—Premiere *requires* extra RAM. Otherwise, you'll be riddled with out-of-memory messages. To work with 320 x 240 pixel movie images, for example, Premiere needs *six* megabytes of RAM. For 640 x 480 movies (full-screen on standard monitors), boost Premiere to at least *eight* megabytes of RAM.

Now that you know the reasons for giving Premiere more RAM, don't frantically rush out and acquire some high-capacity SIMMs. Let's first consider some simpler steps for making the most of the RAM you already have.

▶ **Thanks for the Memory Settings**

Memory

If you're using System 7 or later, our first area to service is the *Memory* Control Panel. It's in the Control Panels folder within your System Folder. This innocent-looking critter holds several powerful settings that can boost (or reduce) Premiere's performance on your Mac. All you need to do is click where needed to match the example below. (Your control panel may look slightly different, depending on your hardware and System 7 flavor.)

Disk Cache
This sets aside RAM for rapid retrieval of frequently accessed data on your hard drive. Premiere really wants this to be minimal. Try 64K or 96K to leave more RAM for Premiere.

Virtual Memory
Turn virtual memory off. Treating part of your hard drive as extra RAM can sometimes be useful, but QuickTime (hence Premiere) doesn't work well with it. Your captured clips will have significantly slower frame rates. And editing in Premiere will be like pouring molasses. Turning virtual memory off also frees up over 350K of RAM for Premiere.

3.0 👉 *Premiere 3.0 will automatically warn you if virtual memory is turned on.*

```
┌──────────────────────────────────────────────┐
│ ▓▓         Memory                             │
├──────────────────────────────────────────────┤
│  ▢      Disk Cache      Cache Size    96K  ▲▼ │
│         Always On                             │
│ ·············································· │
│                      Select Hard Disk :       │
│         Virtual Memory   Macintosh HD      ▾  │
│  ◉        ○ On         Available on disk: 146M │
│           ◉ Off    Available built-in memory : 12M │
│ ·············································· │
│  32     32-Bit Addressing                     │
│           ◉ On                                │
│           ○ Off                               │
│ ·············································· │
│              Percent of available memory      │
│                to use for a RAM disk :        │
│  ▢      RAM Disk    ◖▒▒▒▒▒▒▒▒▒▒▒▒▒▒▒◗         │
│           ○ On      0%      50%      100%      │
│           ◉ Off     RAM Disk Size    OK       │
│ ·············································· │
│  v7.1                  ┌─────────────────┐    │
│                        │  Use Defaults   │    │
│                        └─────────────────┘    │
└──────────────────────────────────────────────┘
```

32-bit Addressing
If your Mac has more than eight megs of RAM, turn this on to allow Premiere access to that extra RAM juice. Note that Mac II, IIx and IIcx models need MODE32 software to take advantage of this feature. (Look for it on your System software disks.) System 7.1 users on those machines can use Apple's 32-bit System Enabler extension instead.

RAM Disk
Appearing on Quadras, PowerBooks and other select Macs, this feature turns part of your RAM into a super-fast hard disk—the inverse of virtual memory. Unless you have tons of RAM buried in your Mac, leave any RAM disk off (whether built-in or from third-party software) to devote more memory directly to Premiere.

If you're running System 6, select "Control Panel" under the Apple Menu to find the *RAM Cache* setting in the *General Controls* dialog box. Set it to 64K or 96K as suggested above for System 7.

▶ Farewell to File Sharing

Another System 7 feature, file sharing, can interrupt your Mac at the worst of QuickTimes. Someone on the network accessing a file on your machine can burp your Mac's CPU during time-sensitive capture or playback situations.

File sharing isn't very useful while authoring movies anyway because most networks are too slow for *primary* movie storage (*archiving* is a different story). And since only one user at a time can open and edit a source clip, Premiere thwarts collaborative movie editing on the net.

3.0 Premiere 3.0 begins to address the problem by automatically providing a dialog box for turning off AppleTalk prior to *capturing* clips. It also politely turns AppleTalk back on after the capture session.

But to avoid System burps while *editing* or *playing* movies with Premiere 3.0 (or you simply have Premiere 2.0), take this simple step: Open the *Sharing Setup* Control Panel and click Stop in the file sharing box. The bonus is you'll free up another 250K of RAM.

Sharing Setup

If file sharing is on in your Mac, click the Stop button in the Sharing Setup dialog box to reduce potential slowdowns for crucial movie work.

▶ Cleaning Out the System Attic

Now for the unspeakable: Consider sweeping away some frivolous extensions and control panels you may have collected. (Heaven forbid!) Although most have modest RAM appetites, collectively they can add up in a hurry—robbing Premiere of precious RAM resources. (Don't worry about extra fonts or sounds, they have no effect.)

To clean house, drag each discard out of its folder in the System Folder—or entirely out of the System Folder if you use System 6. Or use a utility such as *Extensions Manager*, written by Ricardo Batista (available on most on-line services). This nifty control panel allows you to select which system doodads will load at your Mac's start-up. You can even define a custom set of start-up items just for Premiere sessions. Maybe you can keep all of that fun stuff around in your attic after all!

▶ Time to Jam the RAM

Since we're through meddling with memory, *restart* your Mac so that all changes will take effect.

If your Mac has only eight megabytes of RAM, there's nothing further to do—Premiere's six megabyte default appetite for RAM will probably eat up everything your system software doesn't use. But if you're blessed with double-digit RAM, let's throw some of that into Premiere. You could eyeball how much RAM to assign, but look below for a more precise way to figure it out.

1 First quit any applications that are open on your Mac. Then see how much RAM Premiere can self-ishly hog. Choose *About This Macintosh* from the Apple menu. On System 6, it's called *About the Finder*.

The About This Macintosh box shows how your Mac divvies up available RAM. "Largest Unused Block" reveals how much memory is available to Premiere.

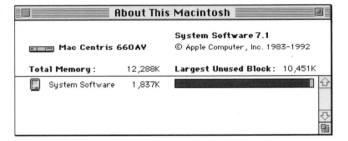

☞ With System 6, Premiere can't use more than 8 megabytes of RAM, unless you have Connectix's Maxima software.

2 Now subtract about 500K from the *Largest Unused Block* number. After all, QuickTime and the rest of your System software need some elbow room. (Squeeze them too tight and they'll randomly send you crashing.)

☞ Beyond a whopping 32 megabytes, Premiere's zip doesn't significantly improve—in case you're so RAM-bunctious.

3 Select the Premiere icon and choose *Get Info* from the File menu (Command I). At the bottom of the dialog box, change the *Current size* field (*Preferred size* in System 7.1) to the amount figured in Step 2. Then close the Get Info box. Now Premiere can sing on your Mac!

▶ Is Your Monitor Deep?

The *Monitors* Control Panel is the site of another step in our tune-up process. Depending on your monitor, the top half of the control panel will look something like this.

Your Monitors Control Panel may appear different, depending on your screen and video board.

Generally, set your monitor to its *highest* color level. That's a good rule of thumb for any QuickTime application, not

☞ *For playback of small-frame movies, users of 24-bit monitors can shift to 16-bit color without a speed penalty.*

just Premiere. At lesser color levels, your Mac has to *dither* images that have more color depth—requiring processing time that can slow display performance. So clips may digitize and play at an unnecessarily slow frame rate.

Note that the Monitors Control Panel will *not* affect the color depth of your *captured* clips. That's determined by your video capture board and the compression settings you choose for the movie (as you'll see in Chapter 12).

▶ Hard Disk Hang-Ups

Let's leap over one final hurdle—getting your Mac's hard disk in shape to capture clips. Despite the impressive file compression abilities of QuickTime, movies still have a voracious appetite for storage. Depending on your hardware setup and compression choices, captured movies may consume anywhere from *five to eighty megabytes of storage per minute.* Ouch!

The problem is that such large movie files are prone to *disk fragmentation*. Since your hard drive writes data wherever there's available disk space, enormous clips are more likely to be spread over several locations. Capture or playback will therefore have to be briefly interrupted whenever the drive head moves to another location. That can noticeably reduce the movie's frame rate—affecting the smoothness of the show.

☞ *Dedicating a fast, roomy hard drive or disk partition to movies can simplify your disk optimization upkeep.*

Fortunately, there's a simple antidote to the problem: Before working with Premiere (and regularly thereafter), *optimize* your hard disk. Products such as Symantec's *Norton Utilities* or Fifth Generation Systems' *Public Utilities* make the process relatively swift and painless. They'll bunch together all of the files on your hard drive. You'll then have a nice large pocket of storage space left for your new multi-megabyte masterpieces.

▶ Time to Fly

☞ *If you're new to Premiere, spend a few moments with Chapter 1 in Adobe's manual. It's a good overview of Premiere. Afterwards, return to this book to soar higher from there.*

Now that Premiere and your Mac are ready for high performance editing, let's assemble clips in a new project. You could use material in Premiere's *Sample Project* folder or other existing clips at hand. If you prefer capturing new video or sound before proceeding, consider detouring to *Capturing Video & Sound* (Chapter 12) before moving into the next chapter. Then load them up!

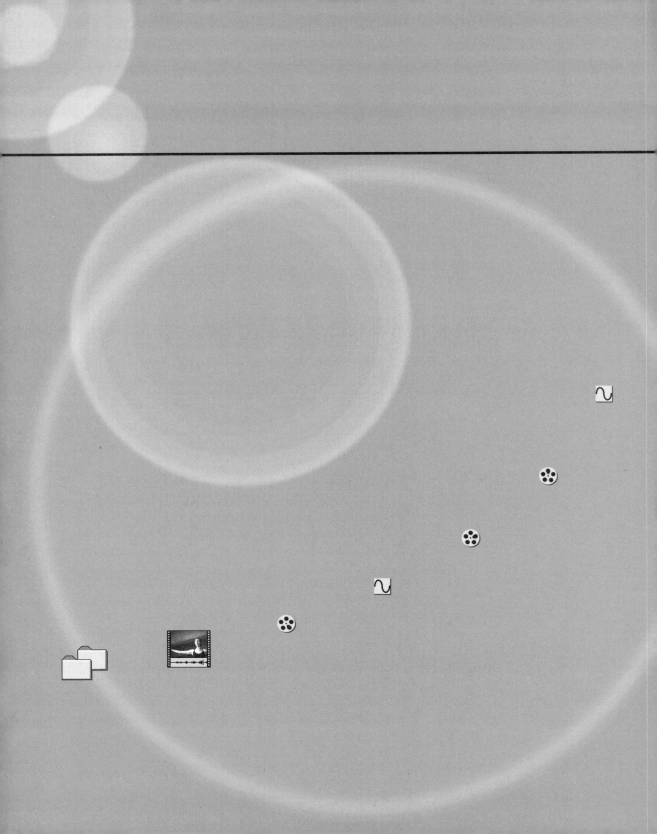

2

Placing Clips in Your Project

The more efficiently you can load source clips into a new Premiere project, the faster you can take off to the main event—editing. So use this second chapter to avoid baggage handling delays. Learn how to open and import source material quickly. Discover time-saving ways to manipulate the Project window. And see how to handle the toughest clip formats. Then take a deep breath and relax as we taxi to takeoff—you'll be on your way.

Opening Acts

Do you have source clips for your project ready to go on your hard drive? Do you have a clear idea of your production's intent and direction, or better yet a detailed storyboard or list of segments? If you can answer "yes" to these questions, it's time to start a new Premiere project and load it up with coveted clips.

▶ **Preset Destinations**

To begin a new project, double-click the Premiere icon on your Mac's desktop. Or if you're already in Premiere, select "Project" from the New submenu of the File menu (Command N). You'll have to close any project that's already open since Premiere allows only one open project at a time.

Before new windows appear, Premiere 3.0 presents a dialog box full of *presets*—a terrific new feature. (2.0 users can skip to the bottom of the next page unless you want to go berserk about not upgrading yet.) Each preset automatically configures your project for a different output goal.

Choose a preset to open a new 3.0 project. Adobe provides over a dozen varieties. Simply select whichever preset most closely fits your intended output. If you're unsure about which one to pick, click on a preset to see a brief description to the right. Still unsure? Select "Presentation - 160x120" as a beginning point.

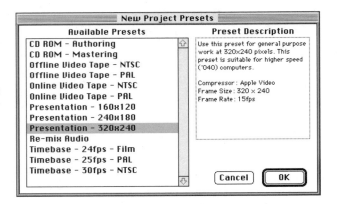

If you've used a style sheet in a word processor or a spreadsheet template, you'll quickly catch on to presets. Presets give you a running start on options in three crucial (and complex) dialog boxes in Premiere: Compression Options, Output Options and Preview Options. Presets also set a project's *time base* (more about that next page). Since those four items represent more than *thirty* settings, presets can greatly reduce your dialog box fiddling. They're a godsend for users who don't want to plunge into codecs, frame rates and other QuickTime minutiae.

Select a preset and click the Load button (or just double-click the preset). The new settings will appear in the Current Settings box. If the preset doesn't perfectly match your needs, click the buttons in the lower left corner to individually tweak the settings. Then click OK.

For more about a project's time base, see below; compression settings, page 328; output options, page 286; preview options, page 112.

Rest assured, however—if intentions change later, you can load a different preset into your project. You aren't locked into your initial selection. Switching presets will instantly adjust the thirty-plus settings at once. To do that, choose "Presets…" from 3.0's Make menu while your project is open. You'll see the dialog box below.

This dialog box also offers a further time-saver: You can create *new presets*. That's handy if you find yourself altering the settings of an existing preset often. Making a new preset takes only a few moments, but will repeatedly save you time in future projects. Who can resist that?

To create a new preset, first customize the current settings with the Time Base, Compression, Output Options and Preview Options buttons in the above dialog box. Then click the Save button. You'll get the dialog box at left to name and describe your creation. (If you enter an *existing* preset's name, Premiere *replaces* the preset— which is how you can customize existing ones.) After filling that in, click OK to add your preset to the list of available candidates in the main dialog box. To discard unwanted presets from the list, use the Delete button.

▶ **Get the Time Base Right**

The best time to resolve the time base is when you start a new project. The time base is the project's frame rate standard—how many frames form one second of your movie. It can be the NTSC standard of 30 frames per second (fps), 25 fps (Europe's PAL and SECAM norm) or 24 fps (film).

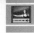

00:00:01:29

The time base affects time code frame numbers, the Construction window's time ruler and other small but important details of how Premiere represents clips.

Choosing the right time base up-front for a project is important. In Premiere 2.0, it's the only project setting that *cannot* change. Premiere 3.0 allows changes, but things can get sticky if you've already edited some clips. Changing the time base may alter your editing work—worse yet, you can't undo the change. Yeeuck!

If you're producing full-motion movies, take note of another important implication: The time base limits the *maximum* frame rate of your compiled movie. For example, let's say you compile a movie at 30 frames per second from 30 fps source clips. If the project's time base is 25 fps, the new movie will only have 25 fps despite compression settings that appear to be creating 30 fps. (And you thought your Mac never lies.)

The time base doesn't limit the captured frame rate of source clips—just the frame rate of compiled Premiere movies.

Are you making movies with slower frame speeds? Select a time base that's an *even multiple* of your final movie's frame rate for the cleanest results. For example, a 30 fps time base is ideal for a 10 or 15 fps movie.

3.0

Premiere 3.0 houses the time base in each preset (see the previous page). When opening a new project, just pick a preset with the desired time base standard. All presets that ship with Premiere use a 30 fps time base, except those with a *PAL* or *Film* label.

Re-mix Audio
Timebase - 24fps - Film
Timebase - 25fps - PAL
Timebase - 30fps - NTSC

2.0

Premiere 2.0 users must access a separate dialog box to set the time base. In the File menu, select "Time Base..." in the Preferences submenu to see the dialog box below.

Use the top pop-up menu to set a project's time base. Changes won't take effect until the next new project. So if you've just opened a project, fool Premiere by closing it and opening a new one to get the revised time base.

Time Base Settings

Time base for new Projects, Libraries and Sequences:
24 fps
25 fps
✓ 30 fps

Time base for clip windows: 30 fps ▼

Cancel   OK

▶ Window Arrangements

When a new Premiere project opens, you should see five windows: the *Project, Construction, Preview, Info* and *Transitions* window. Premiere 2.0 calls the latter window the *Special Effects* window.

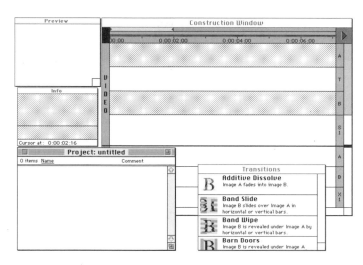

The arrangement and appearance of your Premiere windows may vary from this example, depending on the size of your monitor and (in Premiere 3.0) your preset choice.

3.0 ☞ *In this book, dozens of keyboard shortcuts are highlighted for each window. Premiere 3.0 provides an online reference to most of them. Select "Keyboard Shortcuts" in System 7's Help menu (or choose the same command in the Tools submenu of 3.0's File menu). If you have an extended keyboard, you can tap the Help key instead.*

3.0

☞ *In Premiere 3.0, Option-clicking a window's close box closes all Premiere windows.*

Any windows missing on your screen? Premiere's *Prefs* file has an elephant-like memory for such details. If you left a window closed in the previously open project, your new project will begin with it closed also.

Bring missing windows out of hiding by selecting them in the Windows menu. If your screen feels too crowded, though, consider keeping some windows closed (such as the Info and Transitions windows). Then use the Windows menu to call them up only when needed.

Incidentally, in Premiere 3.0 you can select the "Re-Arrange" command in the Windows menu to keep your multi-window arrangement orderly. It quickly returns any on-screen mess you gleefully created to a standard layout—saving you at least a few drags and clicks.

With your windows all set, your next step is to place source clips into the project (more specifically, the Project window). So let's check out the importing business.

▶ The Importing Business

☞ *Are you adding large-format clips? Consider creating miniatures of the clips to speed Premiere's editing performance. See page 43 for details.*

Importing is the fastest way to bring clips into your project. There are three ways to import clips—all sitting in the Import submenu near the top of the File menu.

Import File brings in one clip at a time. *Import Multiple* does the same task but repeats the process so you can select more

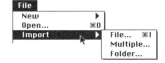

files. And *Import Folder* handles an entire folder at once—a time-saver if you've thrown source clips into a folder or two beforehand. Let's look at each method more closely.

Import File

Choose "File..." from the Import submenu (Command I) to see a standard dialog box for selecting files. To help you recognize your target, thumbnail-size previews are available. Movies and audio clips created with QuickTime 1.5 or later also have playback controls below the image.

 You can't import Illustrator files. Use the "Open..." command described on the next page.

Premiere 3.0's dialog box is shown (2.0's is the same but lacks Find buttons). To see previews, make sure the Show Preview check box is on. Click Create to make a preview, if necessary—it only adds a few K.

 In such dialog boxes, type the first character or two of a file name to select the file quickly.

After finding the clip you want, double-click it or click the Import button to push it into your project.

Import Multiple

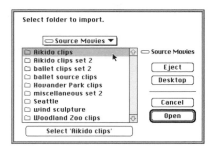

If you select "Multiple..." from the Import submenu, you'll get the same dialog box as above (except in 3.0 the Cancel button is labeled *Done*). The only difference occurs after you select a file and click Import. The dialog box sticks around so you can add more files. Click the Done button when you're finished. (In 2.0, click *Cancel*.)

Import Folder

If you choose "Folder..." from the Import submenu, you'll see a narrower dialog box that lacks previews.

To proceed, highlight a source clip folder and click the Select button. Premiere 3.0 features a wide Select button at the bottom (shown). In 2.0, the Select button is smaller and is squeezed above the Cancel button.

Importing a folder-full of source clips will be successful as long as you remember the following two caveats:

• Within a selected folder, Premiere will import individual clips, but not any clips that are buried in subfolders.

See page 40 for more about importing numbered files.

• In Premiere 2.0, avoid using "Import Folder…" for a numbered series of animation files. Doing so will import individual frames into Premiere, not a cohesive movie.

▶ Opening Clips

Opening clips is sometimes a better choice than importing. Perhaps you prefer to examine a clip's contents before adding it to your project. Maybe you want to mark or trim the clip beforehand, too (ambitious little devil, you).

After you select "Open…" in the File menu (Command O), Premiere provides the same file selection dialog box as "Import Files…" (except the Import button is labeled *Open*). Depending on the type of clip you select, one of three Clip windows then appears after your OK.

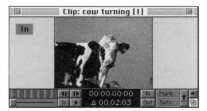

The Clip windows for movies (top) and sounds (lower left) have numerous controls to review, trim and mark the material. Premiere 3.0's version (shown) introduces several new touches to both windows. The simpler Clip window for still-images (lower right) is unchanged from 2.0.

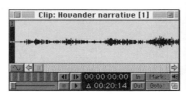

Next chapter we'll delve into the various Clip window controls. For now, simply understand how easy it is to add an open clip to your project: Drag it from the Clip window to the Project or Construction window. Or select "Add This Clip" from the Clip menu (Command J).

☞ *Dragging a clip directly into the Construction window saves a step: Premiere will add the clip to the Project window.*

Keep in mind that's not your last chance to peruse the clip in the Clip window. Call up the window anytime—double-click the clip in any Premiere window that holds its thumbnail. Or select "Open…" in the File menu again.

▶ Finding Buried Source Clips

3.0

Find: my lost source clip

Cancel   OK

☞ *If you're using a file dialog add-on utility that conflicts with the Find buttons, you can remove the buttons. See page 297.*

Sometimes it can be difficult to find the source clip you want, particularly if you have many different folders or volumes loaded with clips. To aid your search, Premiere 3.0 adds two Find buttons to the bottom of all file selection dialog boxes—such as the Import File, Import Multiple and Open dialog boxes we just visited.

To use these neat new search capabilities, click the Find button. In the dialog box that appears, type the name of the clip you seek (or whatever part of the name you know). Then click OK—the first matching clip or folder accessible to your Mac will highlight. Click the Find Again button to see other matches.

Keep in mind the Find function isn't case sensitive. However, it only turns up clips that are acceptable to Premiere, not all types of files. So your word processing and other mundane files are safe from Premiere's touch.

▶ Pointers about Pointers

Where is 'Closeup'?

☐ Sample Files ▼

☐ Circus audio
☐ Closeup
☐ Cross position
☐ Fall Forward
☐ Final Bow

3.0 ☞ *In Premiere 3.0, Control-click the Skip button to skip only temporary preview files.*

When you bring a clip into the Project window, you're actually working with a *pointer*. A pointer is an obedient dog—ooops, an obedient small file—that "points" Premiere to the source clip. Ouch! Quit biting my leg!

By working with pointers, you don't have to work laboriously with large files as you edit. Yet pointers will look and perform just like your original source files.

There are a few consequences you should be aware of in exchange for this convenience. A pointer depends on a source clip for its data. So you need to keep source clips accessible to your Mac while working on a project. In fact, they should stay in the same folder throughout your endeavor. Otherwise, Premiere will put the burden of finding them on *you* when you open a project. (Luckily, 3.0 users have the Find button duo to help.)

Of course, you can choose not to locate a missing file by clicking the Skip button (or skip all files by Option-clicking it). But files you skip may leave a nasty hole to fill in your project.

Skip

Also, if someone *changes* a source clip before your project is complete, the revisions will creep unannounced into your movie. You can use such automatic updating to advantage, though. For example, you can fine-tune a

☞ *Illustrator files are an exception to this updating rule.*

Photoshop graphic in Photoshop without having to re-import the clip into Premiere—as long as you use "Save…" and not "Save As…" in Photoshop.

▶ Movie Analysis

Do you need to know more about a particular QuickTime movie before adding it to your project? Perhaps you're unsure about a movie's quality or need to know its nitty-gritty details. Premiere 3.0 has a Movie Analysis tool just for this purpose. It gives you a movie's key performance specs, such as average frame rate and data rate, compression settings and audio quality (if there's a sound track).

☞ *If the movie's Clip window is already active (in front), press the Option key as you choose "Movie Analysis…" to save yourself the file selection step.*

From the File menu, select "Movie Analysis…" in the Tools submenu. You'll get the standard file selection box. After choosing a movie to diagnose (it can be in or out of your project), Premiere opens the analysis window.

Premiere 3.0's analysis volunteers important movie data that's hard to get from many other QuickTime applications.

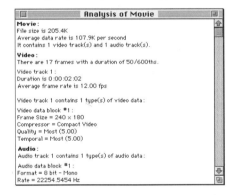

☞ *While this window is active, you can print its contents by selecting "Print Window…" in the File menu (Command P).*

Now let's turn our attention to the first destination for your project's source clips—the Project window.

▶ Project Window Personalities

The Project window has a split personality. It can present your stockpile of project clips in two icon views that mimic your Mac's desktop—but aren't very informative.

These Project window formats are known as "by Icon" and "by Small Icon."

☞ *To alphabetically sort clips in these views, choose "Clean Up by Name" in the Project menu.*

Premiere 3.0 (shown) adds to these views a small reel or sound wave icon next to the name of any clip that's also in the Construction window.

The Project window can also take more screen space to spill the beans about every clip. In fact, this is the default viewing format for the Project window in Premiere 3.0.

Besides a thumbnail image, the "by Name" format states the clip's name, type, frame size and duration. Audio clips indicate sound quality factors.

Clips start with a [1] in the right corner. Copies show [2], etc. Clips in use in the Construction window sport a small icon (a reel for visuals; waveform for audio).

3.0 ☞ *Using 3.0's ability to sort clips by a column of notes can help you to group or prioritize clips—a great aid to project management.*

13 items	Name	Comment	Label 1	Label 2
advancing to left [1] Movie Duration: 0:00:05:05 320 x 240 22KHz – 8 Bit – Mono			video	1.01
arms extended [1] Movie Duration: 0:00:00:16 320 x 240 22KHz – 8 Bit – Mono		Add Sharpen filter?	video	1.02
backgrnd music 1a [1] Movie Duration: 0:00:19:28 22KHz – 8 Bit – Stereo		Volumes fades near the end. This segment repeats.	audio	

Project: Mt. Baker Ballet 3

Premiere 2.0 (not shown) has one column for your comments and notes. Just click in a box and type. Cut, Copy, Paste and Clear commands are also available. Premiere 3.0's Project window when fully stretched (shown) adds two more columns. You can click on the column names at the window's top to sort clips alphabetically by that column.

3.0

Premiere 3.0 makes the Project window even more schizophrenic by providing a choice of four icon sizes for each of the three display formats. Fortunately, 3.0 hands you this extra flexibility in a friendly manner. First click the Project window if it's not already active (the topmost window). Then select "Project Window Options…" at the top of the Windows menu. You'll see the dialog box below—default selections are shown.

☞ *A Premiere 3.0 concept to remember: The first item in the Windows menu (Command 1) always holds display options for the active Premiere window.*

Selecting a smaller icon size than the default hides some clip data in the "by Name" (top) format.

Turn on "Snap clips to grid" to keep icon views of the Project window organized. Pressing the Tab key when the Project window is active toggles this on or off. Or like the Finder, you can press the Command key while moving icons to override the grid.

Using Sort buttons is the same as clicking column headers in the "by Name" view (see above).

☞ *The bottom of the box reveals two other nifty shortcuts.*

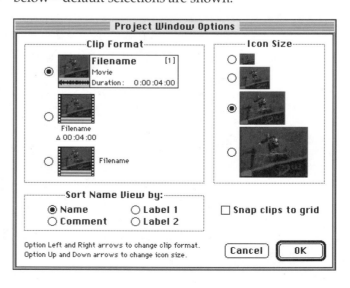

Project Window Options — Clip Format — Icon Size — Filename [1] Movie Duration: 0:00:04:00 — Sort Name View by: ⦿ Name ○ Label 1 ○ Comment ○ Label 2 — ☐ Snap clips to grid — Option Left and Right arrows to change clip format. Option Up and Down arrows to change icon size. — Cancel OK

In Premiere 2.0, select a Project window format by visiting the Window View submenu in the Project menu. Or use one of the three Command key shortcuts shown at right.

▶ Project Window Tips

Consider the following tips which can help you to take advantage of your Project window's full abilities.

The Info Window Assistant

Although either icon view of the Project window ("by Icon" or "by Small Icon") are not very informative, you can rely on the Info window to take up the slack. It will display a clip's vital statistics when you click the clip's thumbnail image in any Premiere window.

Quick Selections with the Keyboard

Premiere can be clairvoyant. In any active Project window, you can type the first letter or two of a file name to select it quickly. Use arrow keys to navigate alphabetically up or down your clip stockpile.

Wiping the Window Clean

To delete a clip from your project, select it in the Project window and tap the Delete key. If that clip is also sitting in the Construction window, you'll immediately see an alert box so Premiere can confirm you're aren't delirious. That's good protection for you—deleting a clip in the Project window cannot be undone.

In complex projects, you'll likely accumulate several unused clips in the Project window—clips that you didn't ultimately drag by their thumbnails into the Construction window. Those clips can clutter your Project window and bog down efforts to find other clips. Deleting such superfluous clips one-by-one would be tedious.

Fortunately, Premiere can quickly get rid of all unused clips in one simple step. With the Project window active, select "Removed Unused" in the Project menu. (In 2.0, that same command is buried in the Window View submenu of the Project menu.)

3.0 Searching for Elusive Clips

In case you pile up so many clips in the Project window that you cannot find the one you want, Premiere 3.0 adds a handy search command. With the Project window active, select "Go to/Search…" in the Project menu. Use the dialog box below to hunt down the clip.

No matter what view your Project window is in, you can search in any or all columns. For example, you may want to find clips that are labeled "intro" in the Comment column.

Click the Find button to locate one-by-one each matching clip in the Project window. Use the Find All button to highlight all matching project clips at once.

3.0 Renaming Clips with an Alias

Premiere 3.0 allows you to rename any clip in your project. For instance, if you've imported a clip more than once for use in different parts of your movie, you can now denote that in the clip's name. Or maybe you want to clarify a poorly-named source clip for easier reference.

☞ The new name only affects the clip's pointer in Premiere—the source clip's name in the Finder isn't affected.

To rename a clip, highlight it in the Project window (or any other Premiere window the clip appears in) and select "Name Alias…" in the Clip menu (Command {).

Keep in mind that only the first 16 characters or so will appear in the Project window's "by Name" view. Click None to return to the original name.

☞ Look in here anytime you need to know the original name.

```
┌─────────── Set Clip Name Alias ───────────┐
│                                            │
│ This clip is from the file: footwork 1     │
│                                            │
│  Enter new name alias: │small steps left│  │
│                                            │
│              ( None )  ( Cancel )  [ OK ]  │
└────────────────────────────────────────────┘
```

Like file aliases in the System 7 Finder, the new clip name will appear in italics throughout Premiere as your visual clue to its alias nature.

▶ Going to the Library

Library windows in Premiere look and act like extra Project windows. They both hold collections of clips. And they both have similar display options, keyboard shortcuts and search capabilities (in 3.0). So why bother with Library windows? Here are two good reasons:

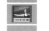

• Premiere allows only one Project window open at a time. But an unlimited number of Library windows can be open. You can therefore use libraries to store and categorize clips from several projects. Just open the appropriate library when you want to add one or more clips to a future project. You can also rely on libraries as a vehicle for transferring clips immediately from project-to-project.

• Unlike clips in the Finder, clips in a Library retain the edits you may have made, such as new In or Out points or added place markers. (Hang on. If you aren't familiar with those editing terms, we'll learn more about them in the next chapter.)

To open an *existing* library, select "Open..." in the File menu and choose the library name from the file list (or double-click the library's icon from your Mac's Finder). The full version of Premiere ships with two sample libraries—one with several textured backdrops and the other loaded with full-screen color mattes.

To create a *new* library, choose "Library" from the New submenu of the File menu (Command L). A new untitled Library window will then be at your service.

Color Matte Library

A Library window looks like a Project window (3.0's is shown). Select "Library Window Options..." in the Windows menu to adjust the display. See page 32 for display details.

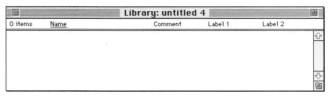

There are several ways to get clips into a library. You can drag (or copy and paste) a clip from almost any Premiere window—even another library. Or you can use an Import command in the File menu. Like the Project window, each item you add to a library is a *pointer*—not the actual source clip. So you'll need to keep the source files accessible to use the library later. Also, any changes to the source clips will transfer to your library without notice.

☞ *Save new libraries in the Library folder. They will be easy for you to find (and will not be confused with a project).*

Okay—that's all for Premiere's opening acts. If you're comfortable with the areas we've explored, save your project, pat yourself on the back and take a break. Then turn to the next section where we'll find out how to work smoothly with each type of source clip Premiere handles.

Tips about Source Clips

Adding QuickTime movies to a project is a piece of cake—just a few simple clicks. However, most Premiere endeavors also include other types of files. Still images and sound clips in various formats as well as numbered animation files may play important roles. Suddenly, there's much more to know about bringing such clips successfully into Premiere. This section devotes itself to guiding you through that knottier process.

▶ Qualified Clip Sources

Let's first view the big picture—the wide range of source material that Premiere graciously accommodates. Besides *QuickTime movies*, the following other type of files qualify as acceptable fodder for building a new movie:

Still-Images

Premiere opens its doors to **PICT files**, which virtually all Macintosh scanning and graphics applications support. PICTs also are your ticket to using screen images from other applications, such as charts or graphs in a presentation program. Adobe **Photoshop files** are equally agreeable, saved as PICTs or in Photoshop's native format. Adobe **Illustrator files** are welcome too (although not in Premiere LE), but their Postscript nature requires *rasterizing*—more about that a few pages ahead.

Animations

Animations saved as **QuickTime movies**, **PICS files** and **numbered PICT files** are satisfactory to Premiere. It even swallows **numbered Illustrator files** (but not in Premiere LE). Each numbered file represents one frame, which Premiere automatically glues into a single cohesive sequence. Besides full-blown animations, these formats put quick production of animated three-dimensional titles in reach from Adobe *Dimensions* or similar products.

PICS and numbered PICT files become 1 frame per second clips in Premiere. To change that frame rate, use the "Speed..." command (see page 88).

Audio Clips

Premiere can work with sounds saved as a **QuickTime movie**, whether they're attached to a video clip (in Premiere lingo, that's a *linked clip*) or an independent file. Premiere also comfortably handles **SoundEdit files**, the format made popular by Macromedia's *MacRecorder*.

Premiere (with QuickTime 1.5 or later) accepts MACE-compressed audio clips but cannot retain the file size savings when compiling a movie.

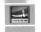
☞ *AIFF files created with SoundEdit 2.03 or earlier may fizzle in Premiere. Try converting the files to SoundEdit format before adding them to a project.*

Industry-wide **AIFF files** are fine, as are any chirps, beeps, groans or other rude noises you may have as **snd files**—the resources most commonly known as Macintosh system and Hypercard sounds.

Special Premiere Files

☞ *Premiere LE 2.1 or later can digest filmstrip files.*

Premiere (except LE) also accepts three files only it can propagate: **filmstrips**, **titles** and **backdrops**. Filmstrips are the vehicle for moving frames to and from Photoshop. Premiere's Title window creates title files. And backdrops are a special Premiere format for background patterns. We'll find out more about these files in Chapters 4 and 10.

3.0

Windows Files

☞ *For more about adding such files to your Mac-based project, see page 41.*

Yes, Premiere 3.0 is on speaking terms with *Premiere for Windows* (which is essentially a Premiere LE look-alike) and *Photoshop 2.5 for Windows*. Cross-platform teams rejoice! With a few simple steps, Premiere 3.0 accepts **QuickTime movies**, **Photoshop 2.5 files** and **filmstrip files** from its PC siblings. However, you can't move *projects* between Mac and Windows versions of Premiere.

Well, that's fourteen clip formats Premiere can digest. Now that we know the entire source clip population, let's uncover tips and tricks for each clip family.

▶ Cracking the Illustrator Egg

Illustrator images are the toughest files to crack open in Premiere. You need to keep several issues in mind while creating and converting the images. Follow this advice:

Know the Alpha Answer

☞ *For more about alpha channels, see page 269.*

Premiere automatically adds an *alpha channel* to Illustrator files when they're converted into Premiere-acceptable bitmaps. Alpha channels are very useful for superimposing clips. It's an extra, invisible layer that defines which part of the image will be transparent or opaque. Darker pixels in the alpha channel, for example, can turn pixels at the same location in the image more transparent. We'll explore alpha channels further in Chapter 10. For now, realize that all *filled* Illustrator objects—whether white, black, grey (a percentage of black), process color or pattern—create a *solid white* alpha channel mask.

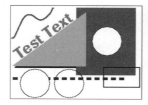

On the left is an image as seen in Illustrator. The right image is the alpha channel Premiere creates when opening the file. As you can see, all filled objects (even if light grey) become solid white in Premiere's alpha channel.

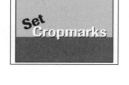

Crop Before You Drop

Before leaving Illustrator, use its "Set Cropmarks" command to limit the drawing's bounding area. Otherwise, Premiere may surround the image with a few white pixels (see left). Premiere can get rid of such superfluous pixels, especially if you use 3.0's Crop or Image Pan filter. But it's quicker and cleaner to avoid the problem from the start.

Save to 3.2 None

Premiere only recognizes certain Illustrator file varieties. In Illustrator, save your movie-bound documents in "None (Omit EPSF Header)" or "None (Include EPSF Header)" format. If you're using Illustrator 5.0, also set the Compatibility pop-up menu to "Illustrator 3.2."

Choose either "None" preview format at the bottom of Illustrator's Save dialog box.

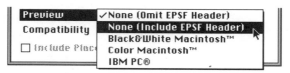

Open, Don't Import

Illustrator files can only enter Premiere if you choose "Open…" in the File menu (Command O), not any form of importing. After selecting a file to open, you'll face the dialog box below that controls Premiere's *rasterizer*.

The dialog box states the frame size of the selected Illustrator file. If necessary, enter different pixel values to scale the clip to your output size. Keep "Lock Aspect" checked if you do not want to distort the image.

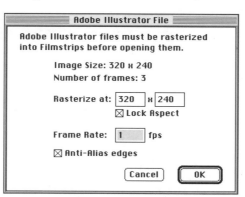

If you open a numbered sequence of Illustrator images, the Frame Rate box appears. Most often, enter the animation's original frame rate. You can then change the rate later with Premiere's "Speed…" command (see page 88).

Note that the rasterizer's "Anti-Alias edges" feature—which will rid the converted Illustrator image of jagged pixel edges—requires *lots* of RAM. Without enough RAM, in Premiere 2.0 it's usually a lit fuse that will bomb your Mac. (3.0 provides a more considerate out-of-memory alert box.) If you're short of memory, you can instead apply Premiere's AntiAlias filter to the clip later. It's not nearly as RAM-ravenous but produces similar results.

For more about the AntiAlias filter, see page 185.

With that caution in mind, click OK to have Premiere convert the Illustrator file to a bit-mapped image (in Premiere's filmstrip format). The results will appear in a Clip window just like any other opened clip. You can view the alpha channel by clicking the Alpha button at the bottom of the Clip window.

Illustrator Indigestion

Certain Illustrator files are hard for Premiere to digest. A dialog box may cryptically inform you that something wasn't rasterized. Gasp—your converted image has *missing pieces!* That's because the rasterizer can't handle certain Illustrator elements such as defined patterns, stroked text, and placed artwork.

Photoshop generally has the same problem with Illustrator files, so it doesn't offer a way around this problem.

Note:
This file contains elements which this rasterizer does not handle, such as: patterns, stroked text, text used as a mask or placed artwork.

OK

Therefore, stay away from these elements as you create Premiere-destined Illustrator artwork. Or rely on a sneaky trick: Use a screen capture utility to grab a full-size Illustrator image directly as a PICT file. You won't get an alpha channel this way, but if necessary you can go into Photoshop to create that missing channel.

Premiere LE users: this is how you can bring Illustrator files into Premiere without Photoshop.

If you lack Photoshop, you can also use this trick to create clips from file formats Premiere normally doesn't accept, such as TIFF or EPS images. All you need is the native application and a screen capture utility.

▶ Photoshop and PICT Tips

Unlike Illustrator images, Photoshop and PICT files do not pass through a visible conversion process that forces you to make decisions about the image. Opening or importing is automatic. But keep in mind the tips on the next page while *creating* the files:

One Size Doesn't Fit All

Photoshop's "Canvas Size…" command determines the size of the frame that opens in Premiere—not the "Image size…" command. PICTs from most other graphics applications, however, behave oppositely. They appear in Premiere with a frame equal to the image's size (or, more likely, the size of the image's bounding box).

Forget the Extra Bits

Movies are always 72 dpi regardless of the resolution of any source image.

From Premiere's perspective, a higher resolution than 72 dpi in the source image only sucks up extra disk space. And working at a deeper color depth than your final movie is also unnecessary (and worse yet, probably misleading). When Premiere compiles your movie, it strips out the extra color information.

Save the Alpha Beforehand

Unlike rasterized Illustrator images, a Photoshop-created alpha channel can retain greyscale values in Premiere. Partial transparencies therefore are possible. For more about alpha channels, see page 269.

Premiere does not automatically include an alpha channel in Photoshop clips. *Before* opening the image in Premiere, create and save the alpha channel with the file in Photoshop. Keep in mind that Premiere only recognizes the *first* alpha channel in a Photoshop file, even if the image includes additional alpha channels.

▶ We've Got Your Numbered File

Animations saved as PICS files or QuickTime movies are very convenient. Opening or importing them into your project's clip arsenal is automatic. But if you find yourself trying to coax a *numbered series* of PICT or Illustrator files into Premiere *as a single sequence*, you need to follow two rules to experience success:

The Name Game

Make sure numbered file names follow this format:

name.number

(i.e., myFile.008, myFile.009, myFile.010)

Consecutive numbers must have *the same number of digits*. The name is optional, but can include spaces. You may also add spaces immediately before or after the period. Whatever you do, stay consistent for predictable results.

Who's on First?

3.0 ☞ *In 3.0, you also can use "Import Folder..." to add numbered PICTs in a folder to your project. See page 28.*

The PICT sequence starts with whatever numbered file you select. As mentioned earlier, Premiere initially gives the sequence a frame rate of 1 fps. To change the frame rate later, use the "Speed..." command in the Clip menu (see page 88).

"Open..." or "Import File..." commands will successfully bring several numbered PICTs as a single file into your project. In the dialog box that appears, select the *first* numbered file you want.

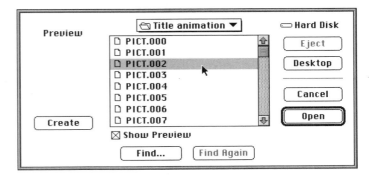

To grab numbered Illustrator files for your project, you can only use the "Open..." command. As with numbered PICTs, open the first file in the desired sequence. You'll then see the rasterizer dialog box (described a few pages earlier). Enter values in the box as necessary. After clicking OK and waiting for the rasterizing process, you'll end up with a filmstrip sequence.

▶ **Files from Windows**

To get a *PC-flavored* QuickTime movie, Photoshop 2.5 file or filmstrip file into Premiere 3.0 on your Macintosh, follow these three steps:

1 Convert the Windows file to a file format a Macintosh can read. Premiere can handle three file types that DOS-to-Macintosh conversion software may assign to the files: TEXT, ???? and BINA.

2 Make sure converted QuickTime movie files have a *.MOV* extension at the end of their name. That's necessary for Premiere to recognize the file. Likewise, Photoshop files must have a *.PSD* extension and filmstrip files must have *.FLM* tacked onto their name.

Win Spin.MOV

3 Use Premiere 3.0's "Open…" command to bring each file into your project. You'll see a dialog box that asks you to confirm the file type. Click the "Change & Open" button. The file will then appear in a Clip window. Finally, drag the Clip window image into the Project or Construction window. That's all, folks!

The file 'Win Spin.MOU' appears to be a QuickTime movie. Do you wish to change the file type and open it as a QuickTime movie?

Cancel   Change & Open

▶ Fat & Thin Clips

Movies and still-image clips come in all sizes and proportions. Premiere 3.0 can accept clips from 60 x 45 pixels to as large as 4000 x 4000 pixels (in theory at least; does anyone have a 55-inch square image?). That's up from 2000 x 2000 pixels in Premiere 2.0—still plenty.

Ideally, your source clips should match the final size of your Premiere production. Here's why: When compiling a project, Premiere scales clips to a single frame size (based on a setting in the Output Options dialog box).

If your source clips vary in size but have *the same aspect ratio* as your output target, there's no problem (although sticking to the same size previews faster). Premiere will scale the clips without distortion. Oddball clips with different aspect ratios than the norm, however, will distort unless you take one of the following three actions:

3.0 ☞ *If your clip has the same aspect ratio as the intended output but is different in size, try applying 3.0's Resize filter. It scales image slightly better than QuickTime can. See page 199.*

Fix It Beforehand

You can re-proportion clips *before* they're brought into your project, either in their native application or with a versatile graphics package like Photoshop. This is often the best solution, particularly for still-images.

Respect the Aspect Ratio

The alternative approach is to adjust the clip *after* bringing it into Premiere. One way is to select the clip (in any window it appears in) and turn on "Maintain Aspect Ratio" in the Clip menu. A black background will then fill part of the frame to correct the clip's aspect ratio.

Premiere normally squeezes or stretches clips with a different aspect ratio than your compiled movie (left image). Turning on "Maintain Aspect Ratio" eliminates the distortion, but frames the image in black (right).

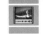

3.0 In Premiere 3.0, you can save yourself from having to turn on "Maintain Aspect Ratio" for each disproportionate still-image clip. In the File menu, select "Still Image…" in the Preferences submenu. Then turn on the "Lock Aspect Ratio" check box in the dialog box that appears. While you're there, notice you can adjust the default *duration* of still-image clips (Premiere 2.0 also offers this latter capability in its Still Image dialog box).

Crop the Clip

3.0 If you can crop a non-conformist source clip to the intended aspect ratio, Premiere 3.0's Crop or Image Pan filters may be a third option. This method will avoid distortion *and* any black boxes in your movie frame.

Premiere 3.0's Image Pan filter can precisely crop this vertical clip to the usual 4:3 aspect ratio.

📖 *See page 198 for more about the Image Pan filter.*

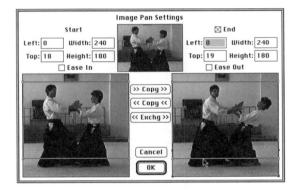

📖 *See page 150 for the Zoom transition technique; page 220 for Motion Settings details.*

Premiere 2.0—which is sans Image Pan and Crop filters—can also crop clips with a slightly more complicated approach. You can "freeze" a Zoom transition to a fixed percentage. All except Premiere LE users can use Zoom controls in the Motion Settings dialog box also.

▶ Working with Miniatures

3.0 👉 *If you have a device control setup, Premiere 3.0's new batch capturing abilities offers a second alternative with similar benefits. See page 314.*

Will you be working with large frame-size movies (i.e. quarter-screen or bigger) or with movies compressed with a slow playback codec such as *Photo* or *None*? Consider creating *miniatures* for editing purposes. Miniatures are a fresh, small frame-size copy of your source clips.

Editing and previewing your project will be faster with miniatures because they contain less data for Premiere to juggle. Even with a high-end Mac and hardware compression, miniatures can save hours in complex projects. When you're ready to compile the final movie, Premiere can quickly retrieve the original clips.

Miniatures are not all peaches and cream, though. Bear two things in mind: First, you can only make them from a *folder* of clips. If you've scattered source clips over several folders in the Finder, some convenience will be lost. Second, miniatures are full-fledged QuickTime movies. Premiere therefore needs time to build them. Premiere 2.0 will hold your Mac hostage until compiling is complete. Premiere 3.0 running on System 7, however, will allow you to switch to the Finder or another application. Compiling will resume when you return to Premiere.

If miniatures seem like a good idea for your project, here's how to create them from a folder of source clips.

☞ You must convert and save Illustrator files as a Premiere clip before they can be miniaturized. See page 38.

3.0

1 From the File menu, select "Miniatures…" from the Tools submenu. (In Premiere 2.0, it's in the New submenu.) That will reveal the same dialog box as when importing a folder of clips. Choose the folder with the original source clips and then click the Select button. You'll see the dialog box below.

Name and place your new folder of miniatures here. If necessary, click the Output Options or Compression buttons to change the movie compiling settings. (In Premiere 2.0, the two buttons are handled by one Options button.)

2 In this dialog box, name the new folder of miniatures that you'll create (or live with the *.mini* Premiere tacks on to the original folder's name). Also select an appropriate Save destination.

3 Now click the button(s) at the bottom of the box to adjust the miniature's settings. The goal is to create a set of *rough* clips *quickly*, not your final movie. So go with small, low-quality images and basic sound. Refer to the next page as a model. (3.0's boxes are shown, but 2.0 has similar options in its Project Output Options dialog box.)

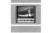

Miniatures can be as tiny as 60 x 45 pixels. To keep nose smudges off your screen, however, 120 x 90 or 160 x 120 pixels is usually more reasonable. If you have a hardware compression board and are working with full-frame images, 320 x 240 may be best. Be sure to set the sound quality relatively low, too.

Unless you have hardware compression, use Apple's fast Video compressor so your Mac isn't tied up too long while making miniatures. Drag the image quality slider to the left to maximize compression.

☞ *Do some of your source movies or still-images include alpha channels? If yes, put them in a different folder and make a separate miniatures pass with a compressor that supports a color depth of "Millions of colors+" which will retain the alpha channel information.*

Make Miniatures Output Options

Output: [All Clips ▼] as [Original Type ▼]

☒ Video
Size: [120] h [90] v ☒ 4:3 Aspect
Type: [Full Size Frame ▼]

☒ Audio
Rate: [5 kHz ▼]
Format: [8 Bit - Mono ▼]
Blocks: [1 sec ▼]

☐ Beep when finished
☐ Open finished movie

[Cancel] [OK]

Compression Settings

Compressor
[Video ▼]
[Color]

Place a clip on the Clipboard to view here

Quality
|————●——————————|
Least Low Normal High Most

Motion
Frames per second: [10] ▼
☒ Key frame every [10] frames
☐ Limit data rate to [ ] K/Second

[Cancel] [OK]

Set the frame rate as low as you can tolerate. Full-motion projects may need at least 15 fps for sufficiently tight editing.

To further reduce clip file sizes, turn on key frames and set it to one key frame per second.

4 When you're done tweaking the settings, click OK in the Save dialog box you started in. Premiere will then create a new folder full of miniatures that will have the same name as your original clips.

5 Rapidly bring the material into your project by selecting "Folder…" from the Import submenu of the File menu. Now you can edit with those scaled-down clips. When you're ready to compile the final movie, select "Re-Find Files…" in the Project menu to automatically replace the miniatures with the original source clips. Good-bye, miniatures! You served us well.

📖 *For more about the Re-Find Files command, see page 284.*

▶ **Into the Air**   Time to take a deep breath and relax. Enjoy the view as you rise into the skies with Premiere. With this chapter behind you, let's climb to cruising altitude and have lots of fun editing your movie sequences.

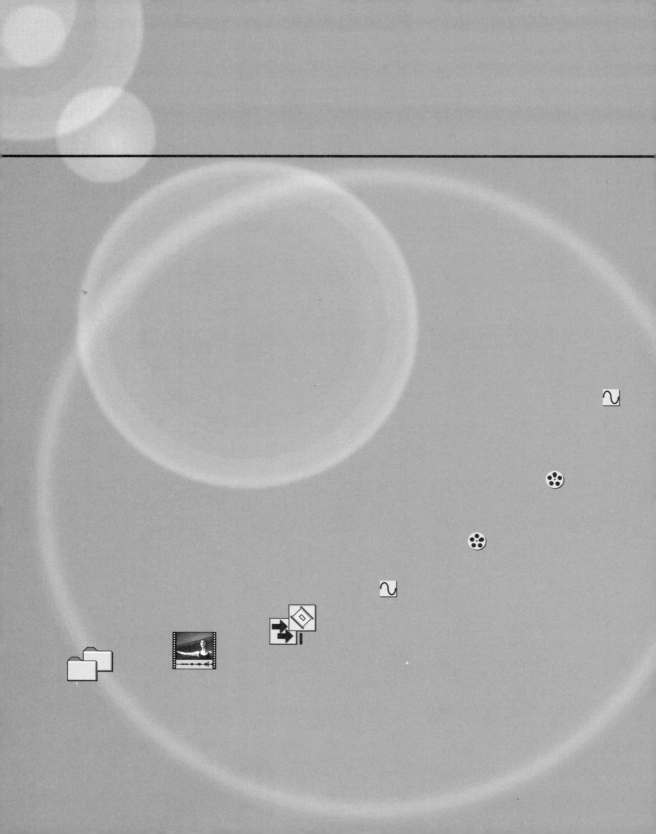

3

Editing the
Sequence, Part I

With clips loaded into your project, you're ready to enter
the heart and soul of Premiere—editing. The Construction window and Clip window work in tandem as your
editing environment, each offering strengths the other
lacks. You'll frequently switch back and forth between
the two as you fine-tune and massage your clips.

This chapter gives you a close look at each window's
operation. You'll see how to adjust the window controls
and take some basic editing steps. Then you'll be ready
for next chapter's romp into editing tools and techniques.

Clip Window Close-Up

The Clip window is your main tool to view and edit a *single* clip with precision. You can examine a movie at different speeds, frame-by-frame or even backwards if desired. You can trim a clip by changing its starting and ending points. And you can mark frames to help you precisely align material in the Construction window.

Most of these tasks are possible in the Construction window, but the Clip window is more nimble and offers more control. You'll depend on the Clip window continually, so use this section to harness its power.

▶ Clip Window Openings

First let's recap how to call up a Clip window.

☞ *Open just the audio of a linked clip by double-clicking the waveform in the clip's thumbnail.*

• If the clip *isn't* in your project yet, select "Open…" in Premiere's File menu (Command O) and choose the desired clip in the file selection dialog box. Premiere 3.0's nifty "Find…" button can hone in quickly on your target.

• If the clip *is* in your project, double-click it in the Project or Construction window. Or select the clip and choose "Open Clip" under the Clip menu (Command /). You can also use these techniques wherever else the clip appears in Premiere, such as in a Library or Sequence window.

• Finally, if the clip was captured in Premiere, you can always double-click it directly on your Mac's desktop.

Which Clip window variety you get depends on whether you open a movie (or other visual sequence, such as a PICS file), a sound file or a still-image.

Clip windows for movies and sounds have a similar flock of buttons and other gizmos. The still-image Clip window (far right) holds just a few controls. New 3.0 items are highlighted.

3.0 ☞ *Do you have more than one monitor? In 3.0, use "QuickTime Screen…" from the Preferences submenu of the File menu to consistently open Clip windows on a separate monitor.*

New to 3.0

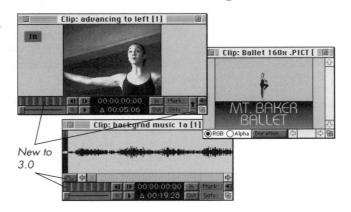

The key to increasing your Clip window agility is to try all of the controls and see how they work. Since the controls for movie and audio Clip windows are so similar, let's get acquainted with those devices together. We'll start with the powerful array of playback controls.

▶ Playback Controls

There are so many ways to play a movie or audio clip in the Clip window, you'll rarely use them all. Including Premiere's keyboard modifications and shortcuts for playback, there's simply too much for most users to remember. Look over the playback possibilities below to settle on a few favorites and get relief from feature-itis.

Jog/Shuttle   Frame Forward/   Sound
(3.0)   Backward   Volume

Slider Bar   Stop/Play

Slider Bar

This works like the slider bar in a standard QuickTime movie window. The bar's length represents the entire source clip and the slider crawls to the right as the clip plays. To travel to any point in the segment, click in the bar or drag the slider. If you're working with an audio clip, you'll hear sound as you drag.

Many users rely on the slider bar to jump quickly to the beginning or end of a clip. Keep in mind you can also reach those extremes from the keyboard: Tap the Up Arrow key (or the Home key on extended keyboards) to go instantly to the first frame; tap the Down Arrow key (or End key) for the last frame.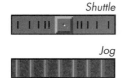

Jog/Shuttle Control

Premiere 3.0 provides two controls in one: a jog wheel (turned on its end) and a shuttle. Both are inspired by their real-world counterparts on high-end editing decks.

Premiere 2.0 offers just the shuttle, but even that alone is helpful for many clip maneuvers. Drag the shuttle to the right to go forward, left to play in reverse. Both ways play with sound. The farther you drag from center, the

Shuttle

Jog

☞ *In either Premiere version, you can hold down the F key to fast-forward movies (but not audio clips) or the R key to "rewind." Both are about ten times normal speed.*

faster the clip's speed. When you release the button, the clip stops and the button snaps back on-center.

Premiere 3.0's alternative—the jog wheel—is a better choice for frame-by-frame movement. Every few pixels left or right that you drag the "tractor treads" moves the clip forward or back a frame (wwiitthh ssoouunndd). How fast you drag determines the playback speed. You can even drag beyond the control, off the window's edge and across your screen!

To toggle between the two controls in 3.0, Option-click whichever one is visible (on the shuttle, Option-click right on the button). You can also set which control the windows will initially show in your project. With the window active, select "Clip Window Options…" in the Windows menu (Command 1) to see the dialog box below.

In the top pop-up menu of this 3.0 dialog box, select the control you initially want to use in the Clip window. (We'll cover other options in this dialog box a few pages ahead.)

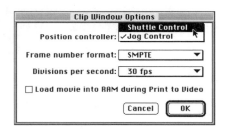

To set your preference for future projects, choose your favorite control in a similar pop-up menu within Premiere 3.0's *General Preferences*. Access that dialog box from the Preferences submenu of the File menu.

Frame Forward/Back

☞ *Right and left arrow keys can substitute for these buttons.*

Click the right or left button to step one frame forward or back. Hold either down with your mouse to scrub frames (with sound in 3.0). Here are two variations:

• Press the Shift key and a frame button to step faster—five frames at a time.

• Press Command-Shift and a frame button to move one *QuickTime* frame forward or back. In less than full-motion clips, this will save you a few clicks when trying to reach the previous or next image. In a 10 fps source clip, for example, every *third* frame (assuming the project's time base is 30 fps) is a new QuickTime frame.

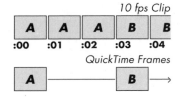

Play/Stop

These most basic playback buttons—with a keyboard boost—can do more than just play or stop the show.

• *Command-Play* runs a movie backwards with sound (this doesn't work on sound clips). That's fun to see in a spare moment, if not always practical.

• *Option-Play* drives a clip solely between its In and Out points. And *Control-Play* repeatedly loops playback between those frames. These two are much more useful. Playing between the In and Out points can help you to settle on the best place to trim a clip.

Keep in mind that tapping the spacebar is the same as clicking the Play or Stop button in every play possibility above. If you're running System 7.1, however, Command-spacebar and Option-spacebar are not available as shortcuts because System 7.1 uses them to switch international keyboards. Oh well, that's "the price of progress."

Sound Volume

Turn to the far right side of the Clip window for this last playback control. If the speaker in this sound volume button is grey, you have a soundless clip—end of story. A clip with sound, however, opens at full volume. Click the button to toggle to half-volume or silence. If full volume is too faint (or half-volume too ear-shattering), a trip to the *Sound* Control Panel in your Mac's System Folder may improve the volume.

Now that you know how to deftly play movies and sounds in the Clip window, let's see how the window's control bar can track your playback mileage.

▶ The Clip Odometer

Current Position

Clip's Duration

The middle of the Clip window for movies and sounds holds a versatile frame counter. The top figure is your *current position* within the clip in SMPTE time code format (hours: minutes: seconds: frames). The bottom figure with the *delta* is the *duration* of the clip from its first frame (In point) to its last frame (Out point). If you set the In point to 00:00:04:05 in the example at left, for instance, the clip's duration would shorten to 00:01:00—one second.

The Clip window always opens at the In point, which for new clips is the first frame. If the frame counter doesn't show the first frame as 00:00:00:00, Premiere didn't fail in its math—the clip merely is embedded with time code. In that case, your current position within the clip—the top SMPTE figure—will always reflect the time code values of the clip's *source tape*, as shown below.

☞ *Although audio is continuous data, QuickTime synchronizes it to a frame rate. Premiere can therefore accurately refer to a frame location even in an audio clip.*

This time code-embedded clip is at its true first frame (since the slider bar is all the way left). Instead of 00:00:00:00 as the current position, Premiere shows the time code of the original source tape.

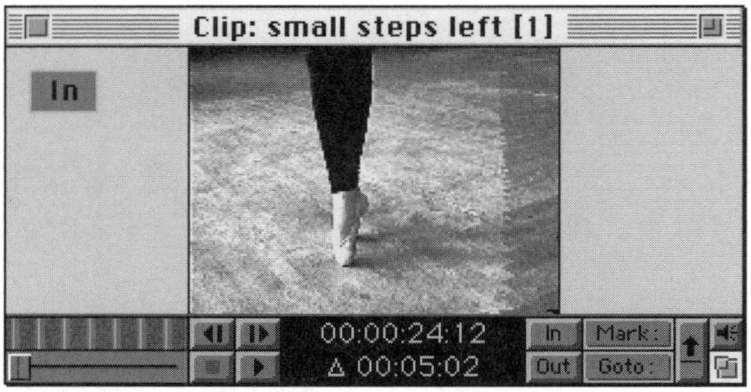

Let's clear up another potentially confusing SMPTE situation. For clips that start at 00:00:00:00, you may notice the clip's duration is *always one frame more* than the end of the clip. Is there a secret frame that requires a special QuickCode? No—you *are* seeing the last frame. The difference is just in the figures. Duration measures to the *end* of the last frame. The last frame's time code, however, is the frame's *beginning*. So much for juicy secrets.

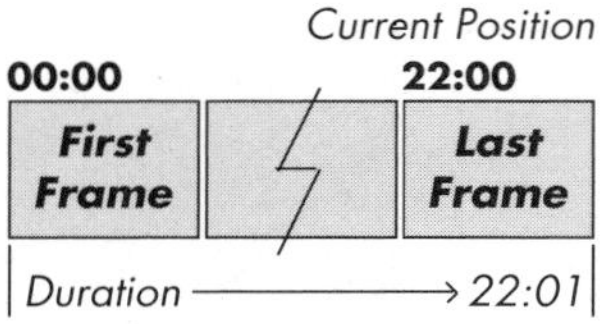

Current Position

00:00		22:00
First Frame		**Last Frame**

| Duration ──────────→ 22:01 |

With that enigma behind us, realize that the frame counter can do more than *show* your clip position. If you know where you want to go to in SMPTE time code, it can instantly take you there. Tap the Tab key to select the top figure, type a new SMPTE value and hit the Return key. If you prefer an insertion point before typing, click the figure once (in 2.0) or twice (3.0). Or *quickly* double-click between the colons to select just a portion. Copy and Paste are available in the File menu, too.

3.0 ☞ *To move ahead or back by a precise distance in 3.0, add a plus or minus sign in front of an entered time code. To jump two seconds and ten frames ahead, for instance, type "+2:10."*

3.0

Premiere 3.0 adds the ability to switch both SMPTE figures to a frame count format (as shown at left). Option-clicking the top figure toggles between the two formats. If you prefer to always start with the frame count approach, select "Clip Window Options…" in the Windows menu (Command 1) to set how future Clip windows will open.

Besides switching to a frame count in Premiere 3.0, you can also have the Clip window display drop-frame time code (29.97 frames per second) if the clip was captured in that format. That more precisely matches the NTSC rate.

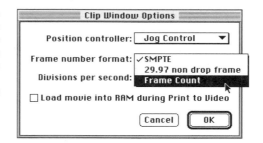

▷ **The Ins and Outs of Clips**

☞ *To go to the current In or Out point, tap the I or O key.*

Moving to the right third of the Clip window control bar, we encounter the In and Out twins. Use these buttons to trim a clip—in other words, to set a new starting or ending frame for the clip. Initially, the In and Out points are a clip's first and last frame, but change either one at will to use only a portion of a clip in your project. Since you're working with the clip's *pointer*, the entire source clip remains available if you change your mind.

To set a new In or Out point in a movie, use any Clip window control to display the desired frame. Then click the In or Out button (or tap the Shift-I or Shift-O keys). After that decisive action, the frame or waveform point will wear an appropriate In or Out icon.

After setting a new In point, a movie's Clip window shows the In icon at that frame. The clip will open there the next time you access the Clip window.

In an audio Clip window, the In and Out icons are small flags along the waveform.

For more about breaking a linked clip, see page 84.

Premiere instantly updates the duration in the Clip window's frame counter and in the Project window. If the clip also sits in the Construction window, the clip will widen or narrow along its Construction window track.

Note that changing the In or Out point of a *linked* clip—a clip with video and sound—affects both components. To alter the duration of just the audio or video, you must permanently *break* the clip's link.

Also, although setting a new In or Out point alters a clip's duration, you're only changing what *portion* of the clip will play—not the clip's speed. To make a clip play at a faster or slower rate, use the "Speed…" command in the Clip menu. That's how you can squeeze (speed up) or extend (slow down) a movie or sound clip to fit into a fixed duration—just like Play-Doh.

For more about the Speed command, see page 88.

▶ More In and Out Tips

Keep in mind a few more caveats while trimming a movie or audio clip from the Clip window.

Freezing a Frame

The longest possible clip Premiere can handle is one-hour, the briefest is one frame. If you want a single frame, though, consider a different approach than setting a movie's In and Out points one frame apart: Display the frame you want in the Clip window and then issue the "Frame as PICT…" command in the Export submenu of the File menu. That will create a still-image clip of the frame. You can then save and use that in your project like any other still-image clip.

For more about the "Frame as PICT…" command, see page 94.

The advantage is that you can easily adjust a PICT's duration. Changing the duration of a single-frame *movie*, however, requires the less intuitive "Speed…" command in the Clip menu. In either case, two uses for such clips are (a) to create *freeze-frame effects*, and (b) to extend too-short movies through transitions, as shown below.

Here a PICT of an earlier movie's last frame is added to extend the visuals through the transition. That allows most of the movie's action (which was shot or captured too short) to play before the Cross Dissolve transition begins to obscure it.

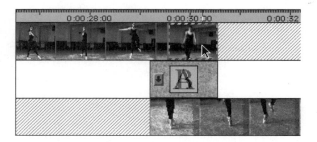

Cross-Window Conventions

For clips that are already in the Construction window, sometimes you can't extend an In or Out point that was trimmed earlier in the Clip window. That's because other clips are in the way in the Construction window track. Beep! Beep! Premiere follows two rules to ensure your clips don't crash together from your Clip window actions.

• No matter what In or Out point you set from the Clip window, Premiere doesn't change the *In point's location* in the Construction window. Only the Out point shifts.

• You can only lengthen a clip's duration from the Clip window if there's room on the Construction window track for the clip's Out point to slide later (right) without intruding on the *next* clip.

The Out point of the left clip cannot be set later in the Clip window because the Peace title is in the way in the same track.

3.0 **SMPTE Out**

Premiere 3.0 offers another convenient way to set a clip's Out point—the "Duration…" command in the Clip menu. In fact, you can apply this command to any selected clip in most other Premiere windows.

In the dialog box that appears, enter the duration in SMPTE time code. If your value exceeds the original source clip's duration, the Out point will stretch only as far as the original source clip (or available space in the Construction window track) allows. In either case, Premiere won't alter the clip's In point.

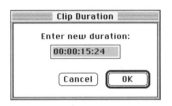

☞ *You can use colons, semi-colons or periods as number separators for the time code.*

3.0 **The Cleanest Audio Ins**

In Premiere 3.0, you can position an audio clip's In point within 1/600th of a second accuracy. When well-synchronized sound is crucial to your project, this feature can be an ear-saver. You'll need to take the following steps:

1 While displaying the audio clip in the Clip window, select "Clip Window Options…" from the Windows menu. In the dialog box that appears, choose a high value in the Divisions per second pop-up menu. Then click OK.

The Divisions per second pop-up menu reveals two high-resolution choices. Its default is your project's time base.

☞ *Audio may not play smoothly while the window is in high resolution. The problem is fixed in Step 3 (see next page).*

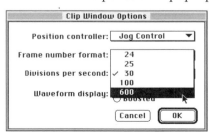

2 Back at the audio Clip window, use the window's controls to move to the In point you want. Frame Forward/Backward buttons (or the Right and Left Arrow keys) move one division in either direction. Notice how time code frame numbers are in three-digit form, too.

3 Click the In button (or tap Shift-I) to set a higher resolution In point. Although you can't see the difference in the Construction window, Premiere will use the higher resolution In point when you align the clip.

▷ **Place Markers for Clips**

Place markers allow you to denote important points in a sequence so you can build your movie with precision. Perhaps you want to mark exactly where a transition should start or where another clip should fade in. Maybe you want to compare potential In or Out points. Or maybe you want to add markers while an audio clip plays so you can synchronize video cuts to the beat. Place markers fulfill all of these roles because you can easily align clips to them in the Construction window.

Place markers set in the Clip window appear as small blue tags within the clip in the Construction window.

Premiere gives you ten *numbered* place markers per clip, from 0 to 9. Nearly a thousand *unnumbered* place markers are also available per clip in Premiere 3.0. (For audio clips, that means you can go wild with marking a *fast* beat without the fear of running out of markers.)

3.0

☞ *You can also set markers in the Construction window's time ruler. See page 67.*

To set a numbered place marker, display the desired frame (or select a point on the sound waveform) in the Clip window. You can also *play* the clip and wait for a particular frame to appear. Then hold down the Mark button and select a number from the pop-up list. After you select a marker, its number will appear over the frame's image. In the pop-up menu, the number will sport a bullet to show it's been assigned.

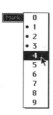

☞ *You can also embed a numbered place marker in a clip directly from the Construction window. Select the clip, position the cursor at the desired time point, and hit Shift-number.*

Instead of using the pop-up menu to set a numbered marker, you can hold down the Shift key and type a number from 0 to 9. The keyboard is also the way to set Premiere 3.0's unnumbered place markers. Just tap the = or * key at the appropriate frame.

Rid a movie of a place marker by pressing C on the keyboard while the marked frame is visible (or the mark point on the sound waveform is selected). In Premiere 3.0, you can also press X to eliminate a marker—that's easier for some of us wackos to remember. If you delete a numbered marker, the other marker numbers stay the same.

To travel instantly to any numbered marker, you can use the Clip window's Go To button. Pressing the button unfolds a convenient pull-down menu with each marker number. Select one with a bullet—the others will just beep.

If you prefer to punch the keyboard, press a number key (0–9) while the Clip window is active to go to that numbered marker. In Premiere 3.0, from any frame you can tap the Command-Left Arrow keys to move to the previous marker (previous by location, not by number). Command-Right Arrow keys move to the next marker.

`3.0`

Whew! With all of these alternatives, you'll never lack a way to get to an important frame.

▶ Collapsing the Clip Window

 `3.0`

To expand the Clip window, click the button again. The button isn't available for audio clips.

☞ *Type "L" when the Clip window is active to inflate or deflate its display.*

You already have a Preview window to view images. Why take up more screen real estate with the Clip window image? That's the rationale behind this sexy new button found in the movie Clip windows of 3.0. Click the Collapse button to reduce the window to its control bar.

When collapsed, the images play in the Preview window (at the size of that window). This is *very* handy if you have several movie Clip windows open at once. It's also an efficient way to preview clips at full-screen size on a separate monitor (just drag the Preview window there *once* and set it to full-screen size).

To tell Premiere whether to *always* open Clip windows in a collapsed or expanded state, select "General Preferences…" in the Preferences submenu of the File menu. Among many items in the dialog box is an "Open QuickTime clips 'collapsed'" check box.

Hold down the Shift key and drag to size the Clip window between the snap points.

While focusing on the Clip window's size, remember the Resize button. As you drag the button, the image will jump to double or half size. For example, a 160 x 120 pixel clip will snap up to 320 x 240 (and 640 x 480 if the monitor is sufficiently large) or down to 80 x 60 and 40 x 30.

Before switching to a new frame size, however, keep in mind that a movie always plays smoothest at the original frame size of the source clip. Larger images only magnify pixels, not the resolution.

For audio clips, the Resize button will simply stretch the window horizontally. Click the window's Zoom box to toggle between the widest size that will fit on your screen and the Clip window's prior width. It's usually much easier to find sound points and set place markers along a wider waveform.

▶ Audio Appearances

3.0

In Premiere 3.0, you can adjust your view of an audio Clip window in a few other ways besides the Resize button and Zoom box mentioned above. The first one to consider is the new Waveform button located to the left of the Clip window's scroll bar.

The Waveform button toggles between expanded, normal, condensed and extra condensed audio views. The expanded view shows more detail, but condensed presents a longer duration of sound.

When an audio Clip window is active, selecting "Clip Window Options…" in the Window menu (Command 1) will reveal two additional waveform display options.

The bottom half of this dialog box is exclusive to sound clips. All of those options only affect the visual display of audio clips, not their performance.

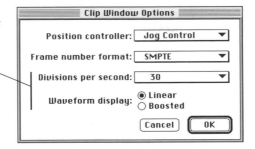

We visited the Divisions per second pop-up menu a few page back. That allows you to set an audio clip's In point with as fine as 1/600th of a second precision.

Select "Boosted" in the dialog box if you want to see more detail in the lower amplitude audio areas. Remember, this doesn't affect the sound—only it's display.

Here's the same audio waveform in the Clip window; linear (left) versus boosted (right).

▶ The Window for Still-Images

So far, we've focused all of our attention on Clip windows for movie and audio clips. Chances are your project also includes an assortment of still-images. So let's not forget the still-image version of the Clip window. It has two simple controls that yearn for a clicking.

If the still-mage clip includes an alpha channel, click the radio-style button at the bottom to see it.

📖 *For more about alpha channels, see page 269.*

The Duration button calls up a simple dialog box to modify the duration of the clip. The default for new still-image clips is 1 second, but you can change that by selecting "Still Image…" ("Still Image Duration…" in Premiere 2.0) from the Preferences submenu of the File menu.

That's all for the Clip windows. Hooray! Now that you're a whiz with all aspects of that window, lets focus on its editing companion—the Construction window.

Construction Window Close-Up

Premiere's centerpiece—the Construction window—is where you assemble and manipulate clips to form a new movie. Use this section to get comfortable with all of the window's controls and some essential editing maneuvers. Then you'll be ready to edit clips individually or collectively in dozens of ways. There's a lot to cover in this powerful window, so let's take a grand tour first.

▶ **The Construction Site Tour**

The Construction window is simply a multiple-track time-line. Each row in the window is a track. You build a new movie by arranging and editing clips in the tracks, which will play from left to right. The width of each clip in the window determines how long it may play.

(2.0) Let's visit the Premiere 2.0 version of the Construction window first to see the window's major elements.

Work Area Bar
The yellow bar defines the project "work area" which enables you to preview a portion of the project.

Time Ruler
The time ruler indicates when each clip begins and ends in SMPTE time code format.

In Premiere 2.0, the Construction window opens with seven tracks.

Video Tracks
Tracks A and B carry movie and still-image clips. The FX track is for visual transitions between the A and B clips. The SUPER track superimposes material on top of the A and B clips. Each clip in the SUPER track has a "rubber-band" fade control that can alter the clip's opacity.

Audio Tracks
Audio tracks hold audio clips, which also have faders for adjusting their volume over time. Premiere effortlessly mixes the sounds together wherever audio clips overlap.

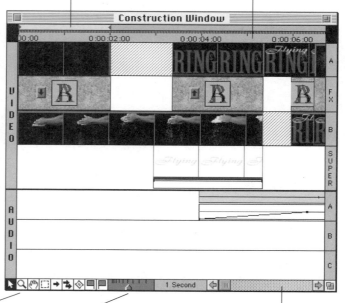

Tool Palette
An array of editing tools can select, dissect, move and trim your clips (see next page).

Time Unit Slider
The time unit slider adjusts the scale of the window's time-line. The default is 1 second per thumbnail, but from 1 frame to 2 minutes per thumbnail is possible.

Scroll Bar
Use the scroll bar to shift to other time-line regions.

The next chapter extensively explores every editing tool of the window. For now, here's a quick glimpse at the basic purpose of each Premiere 2.0 tool.

Click on an icon to select a tool. In the Construction window, the cursor will reflect your choice.

Selection Tool
To select a clip, transition or place marker

Zoom Tool
To view the window at different time scales (like the time unit slider)

Block-Select Tool
To select a segment of clips across all tracks

Razor Tool
To slice a clip into clippettes

Hand Tool
To scroll the window

Track Tool
To select clips in one track

Multi-Track Tool
To select both tracks of a linked clip

In/Out Point Tools
To shorten or lengthen a clip's duration

3.0

Now let's see how Premiere 3.0 further enhances the Construction window. If you don't have Premiere 3.0, you can skip ahead to *Assembling Clips*.

Preview Files Bar
The bar shows where time-saving preview files exist (more about this in Chapter 5).

Preview Button
This on-screen button triggers a preview of the project work area. It's the same as selecting "Preview" in the Project menu or tapping the Return or Enter key.

More Tracks!
Seven tracks initially appear in the Construction window. As many as 99 video tracks (gulp!) are now available, labeled A, B and S1 to S97. And 99 audio tracks also are possible: tracks A, B and X1 to X97. That should be enough tracks to handle almost any editing endeavor.

Note that the FX track is renamed the T track (for transitions) but otherwise functions identically.

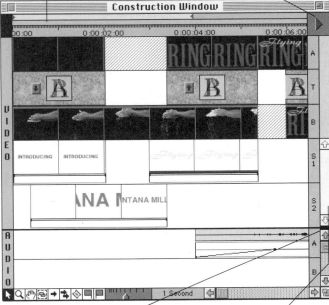

Window Divider Bar
Drag the window divider to determine how many extra S and X tracks are visible.

Vertical Scroll Bars
Use the new vertical scroll bars to see extra tracks if your screen isn't big enough to show all at once.

Some of Premiere 3.0's editing tools are significantly more meaty than their 2.0 equivalents. As mentioned earlier, we'll learn more about each tool in the next chapter. Look below for a sneak preview of the major changes.

Zoom Tool
You can now drag this tool to define a zoom area

Multi-Track Tool
This includes several new ways to select multiple tracks, not just linked clips

3.0's tool palette looks much like 2.0's, despite the extra power.

Marquee Tool
Formerly the Block-Select tool, this can now create powerful "virtual clips"

Razor Tool
You can now slice all clips at once along a time point

Are you drooling over the thought that Premiere 3.0's Construction window can have up to 99 video tracks and 99 audio tracks? Then let's see how to create them.

▶ Adding & Deleting Tracks

3.0

When a new project first opens in Premiere 3.0, three video tracks (A, B and S1) and three audio tracks (A, B, and X1) are available. You can add extra tracks to that initial allocation by using the "Add/Delete Tracks…" command in the Project menu (Command 3). In the dialog box that appears, enter the quantity you want.

You can separately specify video and audio track quantities. Three tracks each is the minimum.

☞ *Stick with the same number of video and audio tracks unless you have a compelling reason not to. It's less confusing when working with linked clips.*

Extra video tracks always are Superimpose (S) tracks. Extra audio tracks are labeled from X2 to X97.

If you find out later you do not need some or all of the extra Construction window tracks, you can return to this dialog box to lower the quantities. Premiere removes tracks with the highest numbers first (i.e. S10, then S9, S8 and so on). If a track you want to eliminate holds a clip, however, a dire warning appears to allow you to cancel the operation. Consider Premiere's warning carefully because you cannot undo a track's deletion.

If the Construction window isn't tall enough to display additional tracks, stretch the window vertically with its Resize button in the lower right corner. Fiddling with the window's vertical scroll bars and the window divider bar can help, too.

☞ *To see more tracks at once, also consider reducing the clip's icon size in the window. See page 68 for details.*

▶ Assembling Clips

With the tour's overview fresh in your mind, let's see how to feed clips to those tracks that are begging to be filled. Assembling clips in the window is typically a two-step process. The general idea is to first arrange clips in their rough location, then later position clips more precisely.

The simplest arrangement is to butt video clips up to each other in one track, producing a movie that would *cut* from clip to clip. To create smoother transitions, however, *overlap* video clips in the A and B tracks. Then place one of Premiere's splendid transitions between them in the T track (FX track in 2.0)—the subject of Chapter 6.

Overlapping clips in the A and B video tracks allows you to use Premiere's transitions between the clips. If you only want a cut, however, you can butt clips together in the same track.

To bring a clip into the Construction window environment, place the cursor over the desired clip in the Project or Clip window (Library or Sequence windows work fine, too). The cursor turns into a hand, as shown at left. Then hold down the mouse button and drag the clip onto a track in the Construction window.

As you drag, part of the track highlights to indicate where the clip may land. Release the mouse button and the clip appears—as a series of thumbnail images.

Premiere is smart enough to keep you on the right track. It knows you can't drag an audio clip onto a visual track, for example. Only appropriate tracks will highlight.

The width of a clip's thumbnail strip in the track equals the clip's duration. If desired, you can adjust the time scale of the window to see a wider swath of clips. Just click or drag the pointer in the time-unit slider at the window's bottom. For example, changing from a one-second to two-second scale will shrink clips to half as wide—but you'll see twice as much of the time-line.

Several time units are available, from as brief as 1 frame per thumbnail to as long as 2 minutes each. 1 second is the default.

The top window has a one-second time scale. Switched to a two-second time scale, the same window (bottom image) shows twice as much time-line and half as wide clips. In either case, the clips play the same—you're just altering their display.

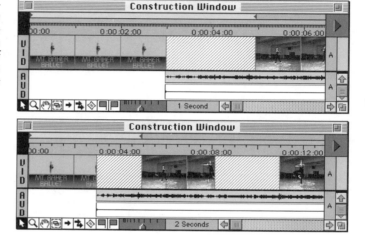

After working with the Construction window for awhile, you'll get a better feeling for which time scale works best for each editing situation.

Back at the Project window (in 2.0, only in the "by Name" view) and in the Info window, a color icon appears to indicate that the clip is in use in the Construction window. You see a small color reel for visuals; a waveform for audio, or both icons for linked clips.

Of course, you don't have to tediously drag clips one at a time into the Construction window. Following the convention of most Macintosh applications, you can hold down the Shift key as you click to select more than one item. "Select All" in the Edit menu is also available to grab an entire collection of clips.

In any icon view of the Project window, you can also drag a selection marquee (the ants go marching one by one...) around desired clips.

Keep in mind, though, that you'll have to drag them into a track. That's right—*a* track. Multiple clips lay down *in a single track in the order they appear in the Project window*—no matter what order you selected them. In Premiere 2.0, they'll end up in alphabetical order, since that's the only way the Project window can appear. Since you can sort Premiere 3.0's Project window in different ways, you have a little more flexibility there.

To delete a clip, select it in either the Project or Construction window and tap the Delete key (or choose "Clear" from the Edit menu). If you try to delete a clip from the Project window that also is in the Construction window, Premiere wisely will give you a dialog box to confirm your action since it cannot be undone. If you delete a clip from the Construction window, it will remain in the Project window in case you need it later.

Here's one more tip about assembling clips: Are you using the same clip repeatedly in your project, but giving each copy a different In or Out point? Premiere 3.0 has a time-saver that allows you to set the ins and outs of *all* clip copies from *one* Clip window.

Set the In and Out point for a clip in the Clip window and then Option-drag it into the Construction window. That drags a *copy* of the clip, so the visible Clip window can manipulate the *next* clip copy. Adjust to your heart's content and then Option-drag again. Repeat the cycle as often as needed. Think of it as Option-drag racing.

If too many unused clips are piling up in your Project window, issue the "Remove Unused" command from the Project menu to get rid of them. See page 33.

▶ **Linked Clip Connections**

Bringing linked clips—clips with both audio and video content—into the Construction window is a bit different than single-track clips. Let's figure out their unique behavior before going further.

If you drag a linked clip into the Construction window, both portions of the clip drop into the respective tracks that share the same letter or number.

When you drag a linked clip, both tracks will highlight as they accept the clip.

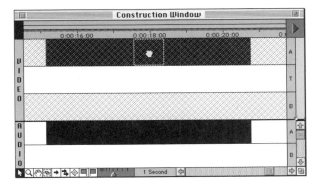

3.0 Since in Premiere 3.0 you can create a different quantity of video and audio tracks, you'll have to drag a linked clip into an S track that has a similarly numbered X track (or vise versa). For instance, dragging a linked clip into video track S8 places the clip's audio in track X8. If an X8 track doesn't exist for the audio, Premiere will not allow the video portion of the linked clip to land in the S8 track.

Once both parts of a linked clip are in the Construction window, though, you can shift its audio or video to a different track in good ol' 3.0 and retain the clip's link. Just hold down the Shift-Option keys as you use the Selection tool to drag part of the linked clip elsewhere.

Sometimes you may really want only the audio or video of a linked clip. In either Premiere, hold down the Shift-Option keys (there's that key combo again) as you click and drag only one part of the clip's Project window icon into the Construction window.

If you can't always remember that key combination, use another method: Drag both parts of the linked clip into the Construction window. Then select and delete the portion you do not want. This method works since the video and audio of a linked clip delete independently.

For more about linked clips, see page 84.

▶ Precision Clip Maneuvers

☞ *You always have Cut, Copy, Paste and Undo (yeah!) available in the Edit menu to move clips one at a time, too.*

Once clips are in the Construction window, you can easily change their order by dragging them around. Drag them left or right in the track or into another acceptable track—wherever a wide enough space exists. You can also move several clips at once to make room for a new clip. Such are the wonders of nonlinear digital editing.

As you drag a clip in the Construction window, a glance at the time ruler will reveal the clip's position.

Whenever you drag a clip in the Construction window, vertical guides arise to assist the clip's positioning and alignment.

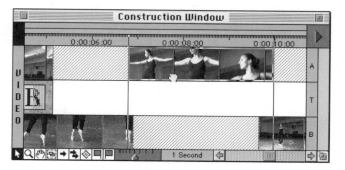

With the window set to a large time scale, however, you may want more precise positioning than your eyeballs can provide. In that case, look in the Info window. (If the window isn't visible, select it in the Windows menu.) SMPTE figures for the clip continually update to help you line up the clip to a specific time. As you skate around, the cursor's SMPTE location also stays current.

Lastly, here are two keyboard tips for precision clip moves: A tap of the Left or Right Arrow key will shift a selected clip one frame right or left—no matter what time scale the Construction window is in. Shift-Arrow key combinations slide clips five frames ahead or back.

▶ Place Markers, Part II

We've seen how to add place markers to *clips* using the Clip window. (See page 56 if you missed it.) They appear as small blue tags in a clip's thumbnail strip. Besides embedding markers in a clip, you can add up to ten more in the Construction window's *time ruler*. This can help you to align a clip to *any* point—not just where another clip exists. You can also use time ruler markers to quickly travel to a particular region of the Construction window. (With no clips selected, type the marker's number.)

Place markers in the time ruler can serve as additional alignment points. A vertical alignment guide appears as you drag. When you drag a clip by its marker, the arrow cursor turns blue.

☞ *For a clip or marker to snap to alignment with another marker, make sure "Snap to edges" is on (see page 69).*

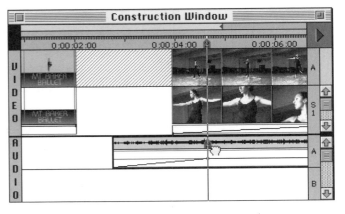

To mount a place marker in the time ruler, first make sure no clips are selected. Then move the cursor so its *hairline indicator* in the time ruler is at the desired point. (The cursor itself doesn't have to be in the ruler.) Now with the Shift key down, type a number from 0 to 9. A green marker will appear at that point in the time ruler.

You can also add place markers to the time ruler *while previewing a movie*. (There are several ways to preview which we'll cover in Chapter 5. For now, press the Return key if you don't know other methods.) Use the procedure just described while the preview plays—hold down the Shift key and type a number from 0 to 9. The marker will then appear at the time point of the displayed frame.

The accuracy of marker placement during a preview depends on your Mac's speed and the preview's frame rate.

To delete a place marker in the time ruler, place the cursor's hairline on the marker and press the C key (or the X key in 3.0). Premiere will not renumber the other markers. If you just want to hide or temporarily deactivate all markers, turn off "Show Markers," as shown below.

▶ Window Display Options

3.0

Premiere 3.0 consolidates several Construction window display options into one command. With the Construction window active, select "Construction Window Options…" at the top of the Windows menu (Command 1). Let's look over the large dialog box that appears.

Besides the default thumbnail format, you can view clips in two less-graphic but swifter views. Filename-only displays fastest, but the head-tail thumbnail option is noticeably speedier too.

Smaller icon sizes can be handy if you have several extra tracks you want to see at once.

To unclutter your screen, turn off any unneeded tracks.

Look here for two nifty keyboard shortcuts—they're the same ones that work for the Project window.

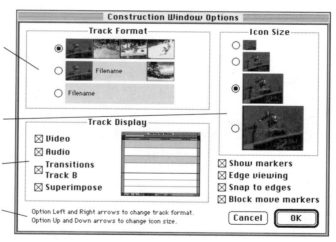

Four check box options in the lower right corner of the dialog box also are very potent:

Show markers

Most often you'll want "Show markers" on to see place markers in the Construction window so you can align clips easily. Turn this off if there's too much clutter or you're desperate for a slightly speedier display.

Edge viewing

As you drag a clip's edge to lengthen or shorten it in the Construction window, "Edge viewing" plays the affected frames in the Preview window. That enables you to see the frames you've trimmed. Keep this option on unless the playback slows your dragging too much.

 Press the ` key to toggle this on or off whenever the Construction window is active.

Snap to edges

Aligning clips in the Construction window is literally a snap with "Snap to Edge." Any clip you drag within a few pixels of the edge of another clip or place marker will snap to that point. Most users will want this on most of the time—especially while initially placing clips.

 Toggle this on or off anytime the Construction window is active by tapping the Tab key.

Block move markers

Turning this on allows place markers in the Construction window's time ruler to move *with* clips when you use the Track or Multi-Track tool. This preserves the markers' relationship to the clips for alignment purposes. Turn this on or off depending on your editing task.

For more about the Track tool and Multi-Track tool, see page 79.

(2.0) Instead of a dialog box, Premiere 2.0 Construction window display options are set from the Construction View submenu in the Project menu.

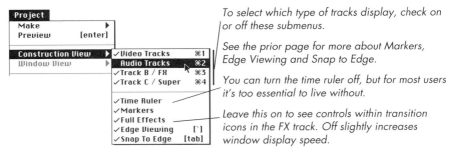

To select which type of tracks display, check on or off these submenus.

See the prior page for more about Markers, Edge Viewing and Snap to Edge.

You can turn the time ruler off, but for most users it's too essential to live without.

Leave this on to see controls within transition icons in the FX track. Off slightly increases window display speed.

Before moving on, realize that in either Premiere version there's one other way to simplify the Construction window so it displays faster. You can show audio clips as a simple grey bar instead of as a waveform. You'll especially notice the display speed difference when the window's time scale is small, such as eight frames or less.

The top example shows the usual audio waveform in the Construction window. Below is the speedier grey bar display.

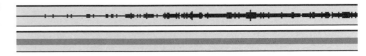

To change the style of audio clip display, select "Audio…" from the Preferences submenu of the File menu. When the Construction window's time scale exceeds the value in the pop-up menu, the grey-audio bar will appear. A range of choices from 1 frame to 1 minute are available—as well as "Always" or "Never."

▶ Time-Line Travel

What's the use of having powerful editing tools if you cannot move around the Construction window with ease? Yes, there's the standard Macintosh horizontal scroll bar at the bottom of the window. But using the scroll bar to shift to a new time interval can be a hit-or-miss operation. Fortunately, Premiere provides several other ways to time-travel through your project. Let's look at each one.

Choose "Go to/Search…"

The first alternative is to choose "Go to/Search…" ("Go to Location…" in 2.0) from the Project menu. Or type Command-G. Premiere 2.0 offers a small dialog box to enter the SMPTE time code for your destination. Premiere **3.0** 3.0, however, significantly enhances this command and turns it into a *very* appealing navigation tool. Its version of this dialog box has a nifty miniature view of your Construction window—complete with little color bars that visually represent your arrangement of clips.

The bracket above the miniature image indicates the time-ruler range that is currently displayed in the Construction window.

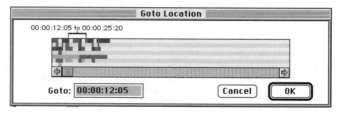

Click in or above the miniature image or slide the time indicator bracket to the interval you desire. Or type in SMPTE time code in the text box below. Then click OK.

☞ *You do not have to enter colons or other separators for the time code.*

Zoom Out and In

Another navigational method for large projects is to zoom out for the "big picture" of the Construction window and then zoom in. A convenient way to do that is to whip the time unit bar rightward (perhaps to 1 or 2 minutes,

depending on the length of your project). Then select the Zoom tool at the bottom of the window and click as many times as desired to zoom into the area you want to see. Each click of the tool zooms in by a scale of two.

From a large time scale, you can easily go to a specific region with the Zoom tool.

3.0 ☞ *In 3.0, you also can drag the Zoom tool to define a zoom-in area—saving you many clicks. See page 76.*

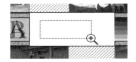

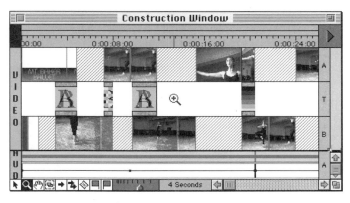

Type a Marker

Let's repeat a tip from a few pages ago. If you have staked place markers in the Construction window's time ruler, you can immediately jump to each one by pressing the appropriate number on your keyboard. This method only works, however, if the Construction window is active and no clips are selected. Otherwise, you'll just hear a beep.

Find the Darn Clip

Not sure where a clip is in the Construction window? Rather than scrolling around and getting frustrated, highlight the clip in the Project window and choose "Find Clip…" from the Clip menu (Command =).

3.0 ☞ *In Premiere 3.0, if you use "Find Clip…" with a virtual clip, the clip's source segment will become selected.*

You can also work this process in reverse to find a clip in the Project window. Highlight the clip in the Construction or Clip window and issue the "Find Clip" command. The clip will highlight in the Project window.

▶ On to Tools and Techniques

By now you should be pretty comfortable with the Clip and Construction window environments. If not, spend more time with them on your Mac before reading further. Then get ready for some editing action. Next chapter explores all of the editing tools and techniques Premiere offers to whip your rough composition into shape.

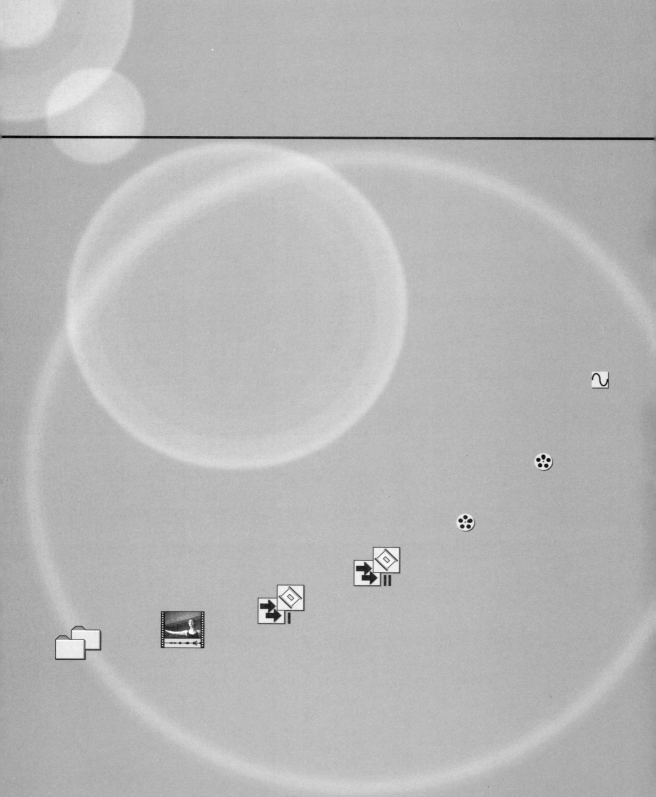

4

Editing the Sequence, Part II

Premiere's non-linear nature allows you to arrange, change and experiment *endlessly* before finalizing your movie. So use these pages to master the Construction window's palette of editing tools. And help yourself to a smorgasbord of editing tricks and techniques in the chapter's second half. Then there will be no limit to what you can accomplish--and still be on-time and on-budget.

The Editing Toolkit

After roughly assembling your clips in the Construction window, the editing toolkit at the bottom of the window becomes indispensable. Premiere provides a powerful array of widgets, some of which are available only from the keyboard. This section examines each tool in detail, covering Premiere 2.0 and 3.0's enhancements together. Along the way, we'll explore dozens of editing techniques.

📖 *Prefer learning about Premiere's editing by technique rather than by tool? Check the summary at the end of this chapter (page 100)*

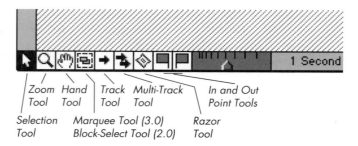

One note before we begin: Besides clicking tool icons in the palette, you can select tools from the keyboard while the Construction window is active. Tap the key that's the first letter of a tool's name. Now if only you could remember each tool's name *and* the one exception to the rule (3.0's Marquee tool). Oh well. In this section, the key appears near each tool's icon as a reminder.

On with the show! Let's learn how each tool can help you create your movie masterpiece.

▶ Selection Tool

S

👉 *While using another tool, hold down the Command key to temporarily return to this tool.*

This is the default tool. Use its black arrow cursor to select and move a *single* clip or transition.

When the cursor touches a clip's place marker, the arrow turns blue. You can then click and drag to align the clip in the track by the place marker.

When you place the cursor near the left or right edge of a clip, it changes to a "stretch pointer." Then it's ready to perform one of the most common editing operations in Premiere: trimming a clip. Click and drag either clip edge to shorten or lengthen the clip's duration (thereby changing the clip's In or Out frame).

Dragging a clip's edge in a track trims the clip. It's the same as setting a new In or Out point in the Clip window.

This is most convenient if you already have a good idea of the clip's In or Out point target or you just want to do some rough editing. If you aren't sure where to trim the clip or need extra precision, however, the Clip window is often a better venue than the stretch pointer.

For precise stretch pointer work in the Construction window, you'll need to set the time scale sufficiently small—two seconds or less. Otherwise, each pixel will represent more than one frame. Also keep an eye on the Info window as you drag to see time code values for the clip's duration and starting and ending points. And consider turning on "Edge viewing" (Command `) so you can watch the affected frame in the Preview window as you drag the clip's edge.

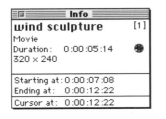

Before leaving the Selection tool, keep in mind three more pearls of trimming wisdom.

• When lengthening a clip, you cannot exceed the *source clip's original length*. The only way around that is to use the "Speed…" command in the Clip menu to *slow down* a clip and extend its duration. This Premiere principle was mentioned earlier, but is worth going over again.

📖 *For more about the Speed command, see page 88.*

• Moving or trimming a *linked* clip with the Selection tool affects *both* parts of the clip. If another clip is in the way in just *one* portion of a linked clip as you move or extend the material, you can't proceed. The solution is to break the clip's link—either temporarily or permanently.

📖 *For more about breaking linked clips, see page 84.*

3.0

• Premiere 3.0 users: If you know the intended duration of *a* selected clip in SMPTE time code, try choosing "Duration…" in the Clip menu. Use the dialog box that appears to precisely change the clip's Out point, eliminating the need to manually trim. (Premiere 2.0 also has this feature, but only for still-image clips from the Clip window. 3.0's is for *any* selected clip in any window.)

▶ Zoom Tools

Z

☞ *While using another tool, press Option-spacebar to get the Zoom-Out tool; Command-spacebar for the Zoom-In tool.*

Option-clicking a clip zooms out to the next larger time unit.

Zoom tools work like the time unit slider at the bottom of the Construction window—except you can aim them at a specific portion of your project. They don't suffer from the slider's knack for drifting you into another portion of the time-line, forcing a scroll back to where you started.

Click the Zoom-In tool (the default) on a track to zoom *in* where you click—at the next smaller time unit. Option-click to zoom *out* to the next larger time unit.

When you reach the smallest or largest time unit (1 frame or 2 minutes, respectively), the magnifying glass loses its plus or minus symbol and can go no further.

`3.0` In Premiere 3.0, you also can draw a marquee with the Zoom-In tool. The Construction window then fills with the selected view (automatically adjusting the time scale if necessary). This trick can save you many zoom-in clicks.

After you draw a marquee with the Zoom-In tool in Premiere 3.0 (center of the top image), the Construction window's time scale adjusts to show just that portion of the window (bottom image).

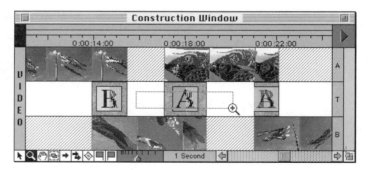

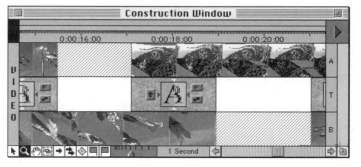

▶ Hand Tool

H

 While using another tool, you can temporarily get a hand by holding down the spacebar.

Drag the Hand tool left or right to scroll the Construction window forward or backward along the time-line. It's the same as using the horizontal scroll bar at the bottom of the Construction window.

That's all about this tool—you've reached the briefest subsection of the book. If only every tool was this easy....

▶ Block-Select Tool

(2.0) B

Premiere 2.0's Block-Select tool grabs material across all tracks of the Construction window. Note that it also affects tracks that currently may not be visible.

If you're using Premiere 3.0, you can skip to the next page. The Marquee tool has superseded this tool.

In Premiere 2.0, the Block-Select tool selects an equal segment *across all tracks*—even if all tracks are not visible in the Construction window.

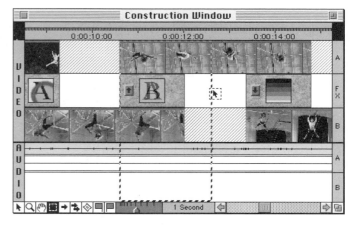

The first step to using this tool is to drag it to select a block of clips, as shown above. Then cut or copy the block selection to another track location.

• To *cut* the selection, click the selected block and drag it to another location.

• To *copy* the selection, click the selected block and hold down the Option key as you drag elsewhere.

 *If the block includes just a portion of any linked clip, links will be lost.*

The block's new location must be (a) at least as wide as the block, and (b) empty in *all* tracks. (If necessary, drag other clips to clear out sufficient space beforehand.) You'll know when you've reached a valid area when Premiere highlights all tracks as you drag. In their new location, the block of clips will live as a collection of independent clips.

▶ Marquee Tool

 B

👉 *Double-click this icon to use it repeatedly without having to re-select the tool.*

The Premiere 3.0 version of the Block-Select tool (hence the "B" keyboard shortcut) is significantly enhanced. Like its ancestor, this tool selects an equal segment of clips *across all tracks*. After such a selection, however, the editing possibilities are much more interesting. You have three alternatives. Let's look at the hottest one first.

Virtual Clips

By clicking in the selected block and dragging it elsewhere, you *copy* the selected block and create a *virtual clip*. A virtual clip is like *a new source clip* that has been compiled from the selected block of clips.

Dragging a selected block of clips (left image) creates a virtual clip in 3.0. After you release the mouse button, the virtual clip appears as a single linked clip (right image).

👉 *To create a video- or audio-only virtual clip, press Option-Shift keys (the cursor changes to below) as you drag the block to a new destination.*

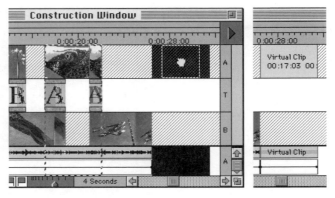

👉 *To select the block of clips a virtual clip came from, double-click the virtual clip or click it once and choose "Find Clip" from the Clip menu.*

Finding a new home for a virtual clip is much easier than a block of independent clips. You no longer need an empty swath across *all* tracks to fit a block of clips. This factor alone can greatly simplify your clip arrangement.

Virtual clips act like regular clips. You can move, drag, shorten or extend them like other clips in the Construction window. Later in this chapter (page 90) we'll witness several unique effects that virtual clips can create.

Let's not overlook the other two options for the Marquee tool—even if they are less glamorous. Instead of creating a single new virtual clip, both of the following techniques retain the selected block of clips as *independent* clips (like Premiere 2.0's Block-Select tool).

Block Cutting

👉 *With block cutting and copying, if the selection includes a portion of a linked clip, the new block of clips will lose the link.*

To *cut* and move the selected block of clips, *Control*-click as you drag the selected block to another location. This is equivalent to the Block-Select tool's default in 2.0.

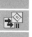
Block Copying

To *copy* the selected block of clips, *Option*-click and drag the block selection. This is unchanged from Premiere 2.0.

▶ Track Tool

T

This tool selects the clip you click—and all other material forward (to the right) in the track. In one stroke, you can then move the selected material as a group within that track. If you want to add a clip before other clips in a track, for example, this tool saves you from having to individually drag several clips to make room.

The Track tool selects all clips right of your click in one track.

☞ *Hold down the Shift key and click to select additional clips in the same track or other tracks.*

3.0

📖 *For more about the "Maintain virtual clip source areas" option, see page 298.*

If your selection includes linked clips, Premiere temporarily releases the links as you slide the selection along the track. Links are restored afterwards. In 3.0, if the selection includes virtual clips, the tool may also select additional tracks if "Maintain virtual clip source areas" is turned on in 3.0's General Preferences dialog box.

▶ Multi-Track Tool

M

In Premiere 2.0, this tool operates like the Track tool, except when you click a linked clip. In that case, the tool selects all clips to the right of your click in *both* tracks occupied by the linked clip. You can then slide the selected clips to a new location in the same tracks.

(2.0)

While using another tool in Premiere 2.0, press the Option key to temporarily switch to this tool.

In Premiere 2.0, click this tool on a linked clip to select material in both tracks.

☞ *Hold down the Shift key and click to add or remove clips from your selection.*

☞ *To select all clips, choose "Select All" in the Edit menu (Command A) while the Construction window is active.*

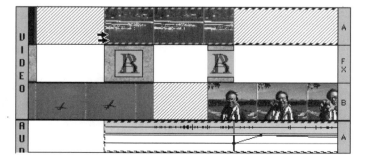

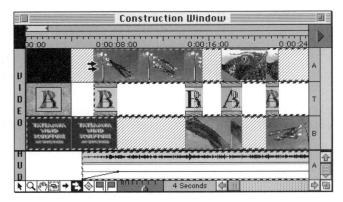

3.0
In Premiere 3.0, the Multi-Track tool's function changes significantly. It now selects clips in *all* tracks of the Construction window to the right of where you click.

In 3.0, the Multi-Track tool selects material in all tracks. Notice the tool also grabbed two clips which started earlier—since they extend past the clicked point.

☞ *Option-click this tool on a linked clip to select material only in the linked clip's tracks. More tracks may select if "Maintain virtual clip source areas" is on in the General Preferences dialog box. See page 298.*

☞ *You can use vertical scroll bars in 3.0 to access other tracks without losing your selection.*

Add or subtract clips in a track by pressing the Shift key and clicking again. You also can do that by switching to the Track tool—3.0 won't lose your prior selection.

One last note: To consistently *exclude* tracks when using the Multi-Track tool, *lock* the tracks. For example, you may want to insert a block of video material but not touch an audio track or a reference track. While a track is locked, the clips are immune from selection. As we'll soon see, locking prevents Razor tool slices, too.

To lock (or unlock) a track, Option-click the track's label on the right side of the Construction window. Or visit "Lock/Unlock Tracks..." in the Project menu. Locked tracks wear a yellow/orange cross-hatch pattern.

▶ **Razor Tool**

R

☞ *Double-click the icon to slice repeatedly without re-selecting the tool.*

The razor's location shows as a hairline in the time ruler. The Info window can also clue you in to the SMPTE edge.

This sharp tool allows you to slice a clip into two or more separate clips. (Actually, they're copies of the same clip with different In and Out points.) You'll rely on this often, such as when you want to filter only part of a clip. Or perhaps you wish to delete frames in a clip's middle, such as a siren in an otherwise subtle background audio clip.

To slice a clip, click the razor icon on top of the clip.

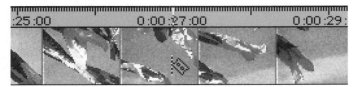

☞ *Slicing a linked clip slices audio and video portions.*

☞ *In Premiere 3.0, turn on "Snap to edge" (Tab key) to razor in alignment with place markers or edges of other clips.*

☞ *You can lock tracks to exclude them from the razor's slice. See the previous page.*

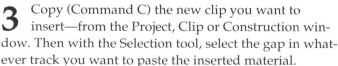

Option-click the Razor tool to slice all clips at the desired time point (left image). Then use the Multi-Track tool to shift later clips to the right to make room for inserting the new material (right image).

After you slice a clip, the Project window updates itself to reflect the new clippettes in its inventory. Like a real razor, use this tool with care because you cannot stitch a sliced clip back together. However, you can change the In and Out points of any piece (such as by dragging the clip's edge) to restore the earlier clip.

In Premiere 3.0, hold down the Option key with the Razor tool to slice clips in *all* tracks of the Construction window at once. Together with the Multi-track tool, this is how you can clear a gap for new material—an *insert edit* in Premiere. Let's walk through that process step-by-step.

1 Option-click the Razor tool at the place you want to slice across all tracks of the Construction window.

2 Select the Multi-Track tool and click a clip just to the right of the split to grab all rightward clips. Then drag those clips further right to create a gap for the insert.

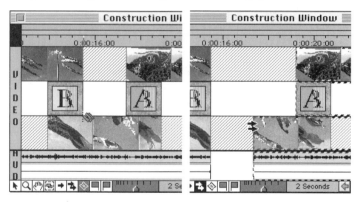

3 Copy (Command C) the new clip you want to insert—from the Project, Clip or Construction window. Then with the Selection tool, select the gap in whatever track you want to paste the inserted material.

4 If the gap is the correct width for the inserted material—or you want to fit the insert into the available space—a simple task remains: Paste the clip (Command V). You're done. Otherwise, choose "Paste Special…" from the Edit menu (Command H). In the dialog box that appears, select the "Shift All Tracks" option in the Content pop-up menu. Then click the Paste button to complete an insert edit.

(2.0) ☞ *To insert edit in 2.0, you can use the same four-step process with one exception: You'll have to razor and move clips in each track individually.*

With this Paste Special command in Premiere 3.0, all clips right of the gap in the Construction window will shift so the gap perfectly matches the length of the inserted (pasted) clip.

📖 *For more about Paste Special options, see page 87.*

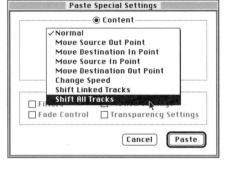

Premiere 3.0 has one other nifty place where the Razor tool can slice across all clips. Users doing *cuts-only editing* will especially benefit. Consider the following situation.

You're not sure exactly where you want to slice across all clips. To get a better idea, you want to preview a small portion of the project to find the decisive moment for your cut. Here's what you can do:

Set the yellow work area bar in the Construction window over the region you want to preview. Then select "Snapshot" from the Make menu (Command \). After Premiere takes a few moments to build the preview to disk, you'll have a wonderful *Work Area Snapshot*—a preview that plays in a close-cousin of the Clip window.

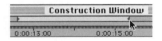

Lo and behold, in the Work Area Snapshot there's a big fat Razor button sitting in place of the usual In and Out buttons in a Clip window.

Play and shuttle around the preview area as much as desired. A vertical line in the Construction window will show the current frame position. You can even use the Mark button to stake place markers of potential cut points in the Construction window.

Use the Work Area Snapshot's playback controls and markers to figure out the best point for your razor cut across all tracks.

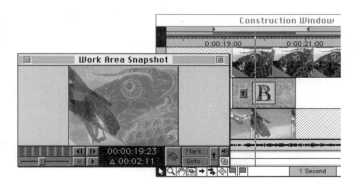

For more about Work Area Snapshots, see page 109.

When you have the frame you want, punch the Snapshot window's Razor button. All clips will be sliced just *before* the displayed frame. To exclude a track or two from the razor's sharp cut, lock those tracks with the Option-click technique described on page 80.

▶ In/Out Point Tools

I/O

☞ Double-click either icon to trim repeatedly without re-selecting the tool.

You don't have to drag a clip's edge to trim the clip. Just click with these tools where you want the new In or Out point to be.

You can always *drag* the edge of a clip or transition in the Construction window to trim it. But sometimes using the In and Out Point tools is handier, especially if you're extensively trimming a long clip.

Select the In Point (left flag) or Out Point (right flag) tool. Then click on a clip at the desired time point—checking the time ruler or Info window if necessary for precision. The clip will instantly adjust its length.

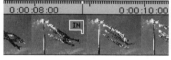 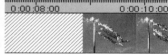

When using either tool, you can hold down the Shift key to temporarily switch to the opposite tool. When using other tools, you can temporarily switch to the Out Point tool by holding down the Control key. Likewise, Control-Shift temporarily switches to the In Point tool. (Is that enough tool switches for you?)

Keep in mind you also can use these tools to set the length of the yellow work area bar at the top of the Construction window. That may save you a few clicks when setting up a preview.

The tool becomes a red triangle (circled) in the work area bar. Click to adjust the bar's length.

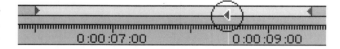

▶ Ripple Tool

This is the first of three additional editing tools that are available only as keyboard modifications of the Selection tool. That doesn't mean they're second-rate. In fact, they're powerful widgets for Construction window work.

Use the Ripple tool to adjust a clip's duration while rippling the change through the remainder of the track. In other words, *all* clips in the track to the right of the adjusted clip will shift the same distance that you drag. The duration of those forward clips (and the length of any gaps within that material) will not change.

Shortening the title clip with the Ripple tool (top image) shifts later clips to the left in the same track (bottom image).

☞ *If any affected clips are linked clips, the linked material in other tracks will likewise shift.*

Access this tool by choosing the Selection tool and holding down the Command and Option keys. The cursor will then turn into the Ripple icon near any clip's edge.

▶ Rolling Edit Tool

This tool adjusts the durations of *two adjacent clips* while keeping their *combined* duration intact. When you trim one clip shorter, for example, the next clip in the track will correspondingly increase its duration. When you stretch one clip longer, the next clip will shorten equally.

To inspire such clip teamwork, choose the Selection tool, position the selection cursor on the joint between two clips and hold down the Command and Shift keys.

The Rolling Edit tool shortens the title clip (top image), extending the adjacent clip to fill the gap (middle image). No other clips are affected. If the adjacent clip cannot stretch far enough, a gap will remain (bottom image).

▶ Link Override Tool

The linked override tool independently moves the audio or video portion of a *linked clip* without affecting the other portion. You can move the audio or video to a different track or slide it left or right in the same track. The audio-video link returns after using the tool—so think of this as *temporarily* breaking the linked clip's link.

 For more about linked clips, see page 65.

☞ *You also can cut and paste one part of a linked clip to move it without breaking the link.*

In this example, the Link Override tool is shifting the linked clip's video rightward so the sound will start slightly ahead.

Access this tool by choosing the Selection tool and then pressing the Shift and Option keys. The arrow cursor will turn white. Then drag one portion of the linked clip.

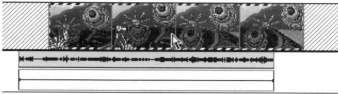

3.0

☞ *To start out with a broken linked clip, Option-Shift-drag each icon portion from the Project window. See page 66.*

To cut to the next linked clip's video before the audio is complete—an edit known as an "L cut" or "split edit"—first break the links of each clip. Premiere 3.0 then considerably adds an unnumbered marker at the clips' mid-point, which you can use to keep each portion in synch.

In Premiere 3.0, you also can *permanently* break a linked clip into audio and video pieces. You'll end up with separate audio and video clips which you can edit and move independently. Sometimes that's the only way to achieve what you want. To break a link, first select the linked clip, then choose "Break Link" from the Edit menu.

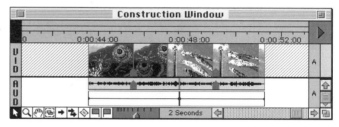

Besides breaking links, Premiere 3.0 can forge new links—a "soft" link. Soft links keep *any* audio and video clip in synch—even if the clips were captured separately or have different durations. If you prefer to capture video separately from sound (to maximize your captured frame rate), use a soft link to lasso those pardners back together. Best yet, unlike a regular linked clip, you can trim a soft link clip's audio and video *independently* if you hold down the Option-Shift keys. Split-editing nirvana!

3.0 ☞ *To quickly change a linked clip to a soft linked clip (to gain the ability to trim its audio and video independently), press the Option key while selecting "Break Link" in the Edit menu.*

☞ *You can't soft link an already linked clip—nice try.*

Here's how to secure a soft link: Click a video (or audio) clip, and then Shift-click an audio (or video) clip counterpart. You'll see the cute chain-link icon at left before your second click. In a flash, the audio-video clips will marry. To get rid of a soft link, use the same break link techniques described above.

Well, we've covered editing tools in the Construction window and many techniques. But a few editing nooks still remain. Take a break and then come back for more.

More Editing Techniques

Just when you think you've got all of the bases covered, Premiere offers more. A few additional editing areas warrant your attention (including some nifty new items in Premiere 3.0). So push ahead for a few more pages. And be sure to check the reference chart at the end of this chapter that summarizes every technique we've covered.

▶ Powerful Paste Commands

Want to squeeze a long clip into a brief track space in the Construction window? What about spread a short clip into a wide track destination? Or how about change the destination's width to match the pasted clip? Premiere's collection of powerful paste commands in the Edit menu can do all of these tasks and more. Let's see how each command works so you'll know which paste to apply in any sticky track situation.

☞ For simplicity, "clips" in this section refers to clips or transitions. "Destination" means an empty track space in the Construction window or a selected clip you want to replace.

Keep in mind that the following paste commands will become available only after you (a) copy a clip, and (b) select a destination in a track for your paste.

Paste (Command V)

The regular "Paste" command throws a clip *unaltered* into a *longer* Construction window destination. However, if the destination is *shorter* than the pasted clip, the clip's Out point will move earlier so the clip can fit. Paste is therefore all you need to squeeze a clip into a smaller selected area in the Construction window.

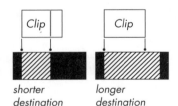

shorter destination   longer destination

Paste to Fit (Command U)

"Paste to Fit" is the same as Paste when the destination is shorter than your clip. When you want a clip to stretch into a *longer* destination, however, it goes two steps further. Premiere first will extend the Out point as far as needed to fit. If that alone can't fill the destination (since the Out point can only stretch to the source clip's last frame), Premiere will then try to slide the In point earlier.

If the fully extended clip isn't long enough, "Paste to Fit" will leave part of the destination blank to the right.

Paste Special (Command H)

This is the most controllable paste approach. By choosing options in the dialog box that appears, you determine how the pasted clip and selected destination interact.

Turn on Content to paste a clip's content into the selected destination—as specified by the pop-up menu (see below).

Turn on Settings to transfer some or all of a source clip's effects settings—not any content— to another clip.

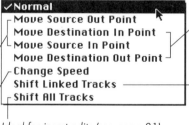

A small animation in the dialog box nicely illustrates the Content option you select. It even shows miniature versions of your actual clips and chosen destination area.

All eight Content alternatives are summarized below (including a few facts the animations don't reveal).

The default works exactly like the regular Paste command.

This will adjust the pasted clip's Out point (or In point) to fit the destination. If the clip can't stretch far enough into a longer space, you'll get a gap.

This is an automatic version of the Speed command in the Clip menu (Command I). It will adjust the pasted clip's speed—not the In or Out point—to precisely fit the clip into the destination space.

✓ **Normal**
Move Source Out Point
Move Destination In Point
Move Source In Point
Move Destination Out Point
Change Speed
Shift Linked Tracks
Shift All Tracks

Ideal for insert edits (see page 81), this option will shift later clips in all tracks equally so the destination's duration matches the pasted clip. It preserves linked clip relationships.

This will adjust the destination to fit the pasted clip by moving the In point of the next clip (or the Out point of the previous clip).

This will shift later clips to make room only in track(s) that will be occupied by the pasted clip. If linked clips are shifted, their portions in other tracks will shift too. (They may end up overlapping other clips in the same track! Separate the overlapping clips or move one to another track to fix that.)

2.0 Users Note: *The last two options in Premiere 2.0 are "Shift Track" and "Shift All Tracks." Shift Track will slide later clips only in the destination track—not linked portions in other tracks. Shift All Tracks is identical to Premiere 3.0's "Shift Linked Tracks" described above.*

Paste Special Again (Command R)

This command repeats the "Paste Special…" action you set up. Use it as a shortcut to apply the same filters to several clips, for example, or to repeatedly paste a clip.

In Premiere 3.0, if you first use "Paste Special…" to apply *settings* to a clip, you can then select several clips (with the Track or Multi-Track tool) and apply "Paste Special Again" to *all selected clips at once*. Pasting the same effects into many clips can now be done in a flash. Hot!

▶ Speeding Clips

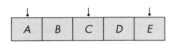

☞ *The Speed command is the only way a clip can exceed its original duration.*

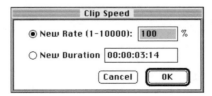

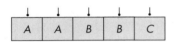

3.0

The default percentage is 100%—normal speed. You can have a clip play up to 100 times slower (1%) or faster (10,000%), as long as the clip doesn't exceed one hour.

The "Speed…" command in the Clip menu provides fast or slow-motion control for movie and audio clips. Besides creating special effects (or goofy clips to impress friends), you can slow or accelerate a clip to match a particular duration. That's fundamentally different than moving a clip's In or Out point to fit a duration. Speed, unlike trimming, affects the clip's motion and sound character.

To change speed, Premiere selectively chooses frames from the clip to fit the new duration *and* the frame rate of your output. Doubling the speed (200%) of a 15 frames per second (fps) clip in a 15 fps movie, for example, uses *every other frame* of the source clip. In a 30 fps movie, *all frames* of the clip will be present—in half the duration.

One more example: If you set the speed so a clip runs half as fast (50%), Premiere will play the same frame *twice* to extend the duration. Each second, you'll see (at most) only 15 different frames of a 30 fps clip.

To shift a clip into high or low gear, select the clip in any window it appears and issue the "Speed…" command from the Clip menu (Command I). In the dialog box that arises, adjust the clip's speed up or down by a percentage. In 3.0, you also can enter a SMPTE duration.

Numbered PICT files brought into Premiere as a sequence initially are 1 fps. To speed them to 30 fps, enter 3000%; for 24 fps use 2400%. You get the idea.

Note that if you use an odd-ball value for the speed change, such as 113%, the clip's motion may become somewhat uneven, depending on the original frame rate of the clip. That's because Premiere has to choose existing frames from the clip—it can't extrapolate a new frame image for an in-between percentage.

If you don't know the necessary percentage or SMPTE duration but you can select the desired destination in the Construction window, use "Paste Special…" and the "Change Speed" option described on the previous page.

Whenever the clip's speed is not 100%, the Project window (in the by Name view) and the Info window note that fact, as shown in the example at left.

▶ **S Track Inserts**

3.0

So far in our editing explorations, we've ignored those delicious S Tracks of Premiere 3.0. The primary role of those tracks is to selectively superimpose material over the A and B video tracks (the topic of Chapter 10). But S tracks also offer a convenient way to edit insert shots in multiple-camera shoots. Let's briefly detour and see how.

The goal is to cut back and forth between cameras—while keeping the action in synch. Here are the steps:

1 Place the "master" shot in an S track, such as S1. Align clips that will form each insert shot in higher number S tracks (i.e., S2, S3), making sure that the action of all clips is synchronized.

In this example, simultaneous shots from a second and third camera are synchronized in tracks S2 and S3 with the master shot in S1.

☞ *You may need to use 3.0's "Add/Delete Tracks..." command to add sufficient S tracks. See page 62.*

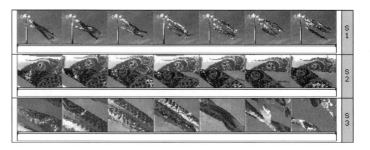

2 Use the Razor tool to trim the insert material to define each insert shot. Then delete the unwanted portions of each insert clip. You should end up with something like the tracks below.

The insert shots are trimmed with the Razor tool and unwanted material is deleted. Without multiple S tracks, editing material from several cameras at once would be more difficult.

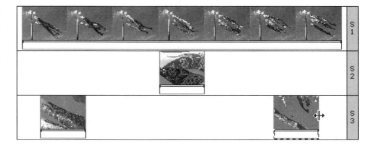

3 Now preview the segment. If you need to fine-tune your edits, simply drag the edge of any insert clip to change its In or Out point. As long as you don't drag to reposition an insert clip, everything will stay in synch no matter how much you fiddle around. Simple!

▶ Venturing into Virtual Clips

See page 78 for how to create virtual clips.

For wild barber-shop mirror effects with virtual clips, see page 157.

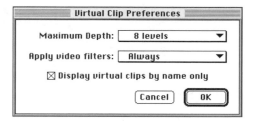

Use the top pop-up menu of this dialog box to set a higher virtual clip depth limit if necessary. Otherwise, there's little reason to fiddle with the setting.

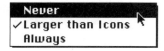

Earlier in this chapter you saw how to use the Marquee tool to create virtual clips from a block of existing clips— a very powerful new feature of Premiere 3.0. Now let's venture into virtual clips further.

Virtual clips look and act like single clips, even though they can represent multiple clips on multiple tracks. That's why they're so useful. You can use them as new source clips without taking extra time (usually *lots* of extra time) to compile material from your project.

What's amazing is that you can create virtual clips that have other virtual clips within them. Premiere 3.0 allows up to 64 generations of virtual clips, so there are very few constraints to your creativity.

For example, you can build new transitions that combine several existing transitions. You can have multiple clips or titles in motion within the same scene. And you can superimpose clips back onto themselves. *Multiply* almost any creative element in Premiere and you've got an idea of the virtual clip potential. You'll see such examples throughout later pages of this book.

Although you can have up to 64 levels of virtual clips within virtual clips, eight (the default) is plenty for most projects. If you ever encounter a yellow cross-hatch pattern in a preview, though, Premiere is telling you that you've exceeded eight levels. In that case, visit "Virtual Clips…" in the Preferences submenu of the File menu.

While you're at this preferences dialog box, consider the two other virtual clip settings in the box.

Apply video filters

Filters *in the original clips* that form a virtual clip can be handled in three ways. "Larger than Icons" (the default) tells Premiere to show the filters only when you preview or make a movie—at least if that's done at a larger size than thumbnail images. "Never" and "Always" are more absolute—affecting filters in all virtual appearances—including virtual clip thumbnails (see below).

Display virtual clips...

Virtual clips display much faster in the default text view (even if the rest of the Construction window is in a thumbnail display format). Only the label "Virtual Clip" and the start and end point of the clip's origin appear.

You can have thumbnail images by unchecking this box. But the images may be annoying slow to generate, especially if there are virtual clips inside virtual clips. So most users should opt to keep this check box on.

Here are a few more virtual clip tips:

Get in the habit of setting aside an area in the Construction window as a virtual clip "pasteboard," either before your movie starts (best) or beyond your movie's reach.

• This was mentioned earlier but is worth repeating: Double-clicking a virtual clip (or clicking it and choosing "Find Clip" in the Clip menu) selects the source area for the clip. When you need to check out something about a virtual clip's origin, that action swiftly takes you there.

• Once you're happy with a virtual clip, consider selecting the clip and choosing "Replace with Source" in the Clip menu. The command will replace the virtual clip with a newly compiled source clip of the same material. Premiere no longer will have to build the virtual clip's image on the fly. Therefore, previews that involve the virtual clip (such as when applying filters and other special effects) will display more rapidly.

One last virtual note: The "Maintain virtual clip source areas" General Preferences setting affects how the Track and Multi-Track tools work when virtual clips are selected. See page 298.

▶ Disabling Clips

3.0

With multiple tracks, virtual clips and flexible editing tools, Premiere 3.0 invites experimentation. Fortunately, you don't have to always sweep the Construction window clean of your extracurricular efforts. You can *disable* extra clips in the window—even within your work area. Disabled clips will not play during a preview or compile as part of your final movie.

The disabling mechanism is simple. Just select a clip in the Construction window and uncheck "Enabled" from the top of the Clip menu (Command > [Shift-period]). The disabled clip will thereafter wear a cross-hatch pattern. Turn on "Enabled" to re-activate the clip.

▶ Tuning In to Audio Editing

Although Premiere is a very capable sound editor, that fact tends to get lost among the video hoopla. Top-notch sound is as essential as visuals for an effective production, so let's spend some time in the audio tracks.

Premiere 2.0 provides three tracks for sound editing. Each track can handle any type of sound equally well— whether it's dialog, narration, background ambience, music or sound effects. Wherever clips overlap in the tracks, Premiere will mix the sound together.

Three tracks are sufficient for many projects. If you need more than three for a Premiere 2.0 project, you'll have to mix part of the audio into a single sound clip beforehand, either in another Premiere project or with a dedicated sound editor such as Macromedia's *SoundEdit Pro*. Of course, you can also go the traditional route and use a hardware mixer prior to digitizing the sound.

3.0

Premiere 3.0 offers up to 99 audio tracks, so mixing audio beforehand is unnecessary. With Apple's Sound Manager 3.0 (which ships with Premiere) and a capable sound board, your Mac can record *and* output 16-bit sound. Suddenly Premiere can tackle *very* sophisticated audio projects. Commercials, music re-mixing and a variety of other high-end audio ventures are in reach.

☞ *For more about adding audio tracks in Premiere 3.0, see page 62.*

In either Premiere, editing audio clips in the Construction window is similar to editing video clips. The same tools and techniques are available. However, audio clips have a fade control—a "rubber band" line in the bottom half of each clip's icon that adjusts the clip's sound volume. Initially, the fade line is set to mid-volume—in other words, no decibel gain or loss from the original recorded clip. But you can drag any part of the fade line up or down at will to change the sound volume. Here's how:

1 Place the Selection tool cursor over the fade line where you want to change the sound's volume. The cursor will turn into a pointing hand. Then click on the fade line to create a handle—a black dot. Think of the handle as a hinge point for the fade line.

Clicking on the fade line produces a handle.

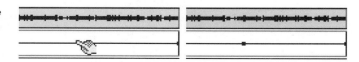

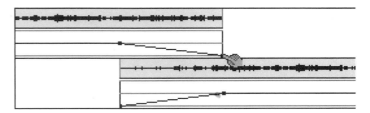

22KHz – 8 Bit – Mono
Fade Level: 70%

Cursor at: 0:00:54:20

One of the most common sound edits is fading out one sound clip as the next sound clip fades in— a cross-fade. Premiere accommodates this easily.

2 Drag the handle up or down. Higher is louder, lower is quieter. Refer to the bottom of the Info window for the fade percentage as you drag. A line that angles upward gradually increases sound volume; a downward sloped line decreases sound volume.

3 Create as many other handles as you want to shape the clip's sound volume. To delete a handle, just drag it off the fade area.

That's the fader basics. Here are a few keyboard tricks and related tips for your audio editing repertoire.

Shift a Segment

To shift the sound volume quickly *between* two handles, hold down the Shift key as you drag the fade line up or down. That's faster than dragging handles one-by-one.

Using the Shift key, you can quickly drop the volume in a background sound clip as a narrative clip begins.

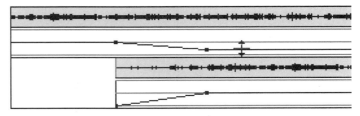

3.0

👉 Turn on "Snap to edges" (Tab key) to have scissor cuts align to place markers or edges of other clips.

Scissor Cuts

Holding down the Command and Control keys while in the fader area produces miniature scissors which can "cut" the fade line rubber band. The line doesn't actually break. You simply get two adjacent handles which you can drag as desired for sudden sound volume changes.

Clicking the scissors creates two adjacent handles that you can drag to any sound volume level.

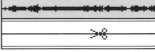
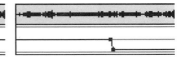

Gain Without Pain

Premiere 3.0 can adjust the gain of an *entire* sound clip in one step. That means you can now more easily balance the loudness levels of different clips. For example, maybe your background music clip is too loud for narration to be clearly understood. With this trick, you can drop the sound level of the entire background music clip *and* preserve the fades you created in that clip.

To adjust the gain, select the audio clip in the Construction window and choose "Gain..." from the Clip menu. Enter from 1 to 200% in the small dialog box that appears. After clicking OK, the fader line will not visually change. But its grey horizontal mid-point line will reflect the new percentage you entered.

The Big Bang

A movie that starts off with a bang—such as a sharp percussive note—can sometimes be cut off during the initial moments of QuickTime playback. So plan to leave about a half-second of silence in your movie to avoid the problem, perhaps during a fade from black.

Hidden Distortions

Increase the sound volume with care. At much higher volumes, even well-recorded sound can "clip" and produce distortion. Although you may not hear that distortion through your Mac's little speaker, it may be evident in separate speakers. The optimal time to increase the sound volume is always when you *record* the original clip, not during editing.

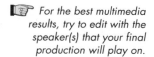 *For the best multimedia results, try to edit with the speaker(s) that your final production will play on.*

▶ Exporting Clips and Snips

Despite its depth and power, Premiere doesn't have all the editing answers for some projects. That's why being able to export your material into other applications can be crucial. Since not every application can accept QuickTime movies, Premiere provides four export options:

PICT Files

Save a single frame of a sequence as a PICT file—like a snapshot. Then modify the image in any Macintosh graphics application and bring it back to Premiere.

All you have to do is display the frame you want in the Clip window. Next, choose "Frame as PICT..." in the Export submenu of the File menu. Name and save the file with the Save dialog box that appears. The frame will then appear in its own Clip window. Now go into a graphics application and polish the PICT as desired.

Filmstrip Files

This format allows you to send individual movie frames to Photoshop and back. See the next page for the details.

Numbered PICT Files

Occasionally, you may need to export multiple frames to somewhere other than Photoshop, such as an animation or 3-D application. If the program cannot handle QuickTime movies, Premiere can compile a segment as a series of PICT files rather than a movie. Each frame will become a sequentially numbered separate PICT file.

The key to this process lies in two settings. First drag the yellow work area bar over the project area you want to export. Next, issue the "Make Movie..." command (in 3.0's Make menu or 2.0's Project menu). Click the Output Options button at the bottom of the Save dialog box that appears. Then adjust the following two settings:

To export frames as numbered PICT files, set the output to "Work Area as Numbered PICT files." Also set the correct video frame size. Ignore audio settings.

3.0's dialog box is shown, but the settings apply to 2.0 too.

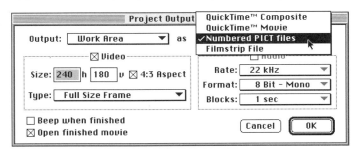

📖 *For more about compression settings, see Appendix A (page 328).*

Note that Premiere compresses exported PICT files, so compression settings matter, too. To avoid any image degradation from compression, use the None compressor at a color depth that's as high as your source clips.

AIFF Audio Files

If you need to tune or distort an audio clip in some way Premiere can't handle, send the clip to a dedicated sound editor (such as Macromedia's *SoundEdit Pro*). Then bring the enhanced audio back into Premiere. Almost all sound applications can read AIFF files (Audio Interchange File Format), so AIFF is the export format of choice.

First display the audio clip in a Clip window and adjust In and Out points as desired. Then select "AIFF Audio File…" in the Export submenu of the File menu to see the dialog box below.

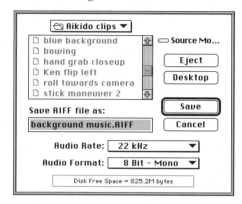

AIFF exporting doesn't retain faders, place markers or other Premiere-specific editing elements—just In and Out points.

Premiere automatically appends ".AIFF" to the original file's name. Change the name if desired, set the audio rate and format for the exported clip, and then click Save.

For more about the audio rate and format, see page 289.

"Disk Free Space" data at the box's bottom appears only in Premiere 3.0.

After clicking the Save button, the new audio clip will appear in a Clip window to confirm its existence. Now you can go into a dedicated sound editor and enhance it.

▶ Filmstrips to Photoshop

Adobe's Photoshop is an extraordinary tool for working with individual images. Before Premiere, Photoshop was the image-editing standard for videophiles on the Mac. Although Premiere has taken over (and extended) this role, there are still good reasons to call on Photoshop.

To send Premiere segments into Photoshop, create a *filmstrip file*—a special file format that bridges the dynamic Premiere and static Photoshop environments. You can then modify each frame with Photoshop's powerful tools and return the file to Premiere. In the film industry, such frame-by-frame editing is known as *rotoscoping*.

If the clip has time code and a reel name embedded, the filmstrip file will retain that data.

Yes, frame-by-frame editing in Photoshop is tedious. But it's endurable if you *really* want to add animation to a video scene—whether at a Roger Rabbit level or just a few squiggly snakes, thunderbolts, reflective highlights, logos, cloned objects or who knows what else. It's also a reasonable way to make minor pixel corrections, such as simplifying a busy background or erasing a blemish.

If you're driven by one of these motivations, let's see how to export all or part of *a single clip* as a filmstrip file.

1 In the Clip window, set In and Out points for the frames you want to modify in Photoshop. Filmstrip files are uncompressed, so they'll take plenty of hard disk space unless you limit yourself to a handful of frames.

☞ *If you're using miniatures in your project, open the full-size source clip in the Clip window— not the miniature version.*

Be sure to set the desired frame rate for the filmstrip with the pop-up menu before clicking Save.

"Disk Free Space" data at the bottom of the dialog box appears only in Premiere 3.0.

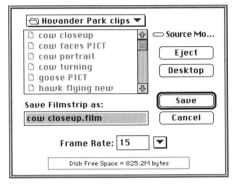

2 From the File menu, choose "Filmstrip File..." in the Export sub-menu. A Save dialog box tailored to filmstrips then appears (see at left). After naming and placing the file, click Save.

To send Photoshop *a segment from the Construction window* (which therefore can include several clips, effects, etc.), the process differs in the two versions of Premiere. In Premiere 2.0, the major steps are:

1 Extend the yellow work area bar over the segment you want to send to Photoshop.

2 Select "Movie..." in the Make submenu of the Project menu. In the Save dialog box that appears, click the "Output..." button to see the dialog box below.

Set output to "Work Area as QuickTime Composite."

Match the video size and frame rate to your intended movie.

You can ignore or turn off the Audio check box since it's irrelevant for a filmstrip.

To preserve image quality, set the compression method to None. Use the color depth of your source clip. And set the image quality slider to its highest level.

3 Click OK and then OK again in the Save dialog box that reappears to begin compiling the segment. When Premiere is done with the compiling, open the new clip in a Clip window if necessary.

4 Export the movie as a filmstrip by choosing "Filmstrip File…" from the Export submenu (see Step 2 at the top of the previous page).

3.0 Premiere 3.0 can create a filmstrip file of any Construction window segment without requiring you to spend extra time compiling beforehand. Hooray! No more compiling coffee breaks! Follow the steps below:

1 Set the yellow work area bar over the segment you want to send to Photoshop.

2 Select "Movie…" from the Make menu (Command K). In the Save dialog box that appears, click the "Output Options…" button to see the dialog box below.

Output Options...

Set Output to "Work Area as Filmstrip File."

Match the video size and frame rate to your intended movie.

Turn off or ignore the Audio check box since it's irrelevant for a filmstrip.

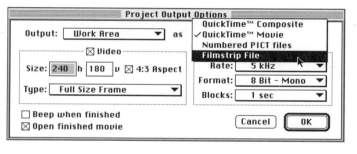

3 Click the "Compression…" button in the Save box that reappears. In the dialog box that arises, set the frame rate to determine how many filmstrip frames per second will go into the filmstrip file. Then click OK. You can ignore all other movie compression settings since a filmstrip file is uncompressed.

4 Once again back at the Save dialog box, name the file (perhaps giving it a *.film* appendage instead of *.movie* so you recognize the file as a filmstrip). Select a save destination for the file, then click OK. Premiere will then rapidly create the filmstrip file.

▶ Filmstrip Editing Nitty-Gritty

Photoshop 2.5 is ready to accept Premiere's filmstrip files out of the box. If you're relying on Photoshop 2.0, however, you'll need to drag the Filmstrip plug-in module into your Photoshop Plug-Ins folder. (Look for it in the "For Adobe Photoshop" folder that comes with Premiere.)

FilmStrip

In Photoshop 2.5, trigger "Open…" under the File menu to select the filmstrip file you want. In Photoshop 2.0, use the "Acquire…" menu under the File menu. In either case, if you added a *.film* suffix to the exported film strip file's name earlier, the file should be easy to pick out.

In Photoshop, the filmstrip file looks like, well… a filmstrip. Each frame appears consecutively from top to bottom, with time code and a frame number. The quantity of frames depends on the frame rate you chose and the duration of the segment you converted.

From this point, you can use almost any Photoshop method to modify the frames. The more frames you alter in a similar manner, the longer the effect will appear back in Premiere. Squiggle 30 frames, for example, to produce one second of worms in a full-motion movie. Keep a few caveats in mind as you play God in this way:

• Although Photoshop can work with multiple alpha channels (Channel 4 on up), stick to Channel 4 for any alpha channel modifications intended for Premiere.

• Stay away from "Image Size…" and "Canvas Size…" commands and other methods of cropping or resizing the filmstrip. Otherwise, the file may become corrupted.

• You *can* modify or draw on the grey lines between each frame. That has no effect on the filmstrip file.

• Take advantage of Photoshop 2.5's three ways to align a cut or copied selection from one frame to the next:

a. To *cut* a selection and move it to the same spot in another frame, press the Shift key and tap the Up or Down Arrow key.

b. To *copy* instead of cut the selection to the same position in another frame, press Option-Shift with the Up or Down Arrow key.

c. To move only a selection border to the same place in another frame, press Command-Option-Shift and tap the Up or Down Arrow key.

• If you have an extended keyboard, you can "play" your filmstrip in Photoshop 2.5—at least crudely enough to get an idea of your results. First resize the Photoshop window so only slightly more than one filmstrip frame shows. Then hold down the Shift key and tap the Page Up or Page Down key to display the frames in sequence.

☞ *Give the modified filmstrip file a different name than the original filmstrip to reduce the potential for confusion.*

When you're done jazzing up the frames, trigger the "Save…" or "Save As…" commands in Photoshop 2.5, selecting "Filmstrip" as the format in the pop-up menu at the bottom of the Save dialog box. In Photoshop 2.0, select "Filmstrip" in the Export submenu of the File menu.

When you return to Premiere, import or open the filmstrip file like any other source clip.

▶ The Editing Techniques Summary

The next three pages summarize just about every Premiere editing technique possible in the Construction window. It's organized by the following categories:

• Selecting Clips

• Trimming Clips

• Splitting/Joining Clips

• Aligning Clips

• Other Techniques (a grab bag of other handy edits)

Use the summary to avoid pulling out your hair when trying to recall how to do a particular editing task. There are so many techniques in Premiere that anyone can go bald quickly without such help.

Techniques that only work for one version of Premiere are prefaced with a **2.0** or **3.0.** Most have no number—you can do them in either Premiere. Each description also includes a page reference for more detailed help.

Now that you're becoming a Premiere editing hotshot, stay tuned for next chapter. We'll find out how to preview (and print) your Construction window efforts in the smoothest, quickest manner possible.

Selecting Clips

• **Select a clip or a portion of a linked clip**	Click with Selection tool (page 74).
• **Select later clips (right) ...in one track**	Click with Track tool. Shift-click to add or subtract clips (page 79).
...with linked material	**2.0:** Click with Multi-Track tool (page 79). **3.0:** Option-click with Multi-Track tool (page 80). In either Premiere, Shift-click to add or subtract clips.
...in all tracks	**2.0:** Shift-click with Track or Multi-Track tool (page 79). **3.0:** Click with Multi-Track tool (page 80). In either Premiere, Shift-click to add or subtract clips.
• **Select all clips**	With the Construction window active, choose "Select All" in the File menu (page 79). Shift-click to subtract clips.
• **Select an equal segment of clips across all tracks**	**2.0:** Click-drag with Block-Select tool (page 77). Then click and drag to *cut* the selection. To *copy* the selection, Option-click and drag. **3.0:** Click-drag with Marquee tool (page 78). To create a *virtual clip*, click and drag the selection. To select only video or audio tracks for a virtual clip, press Option-Shift keys then drag. To *cut* the selection as independent clips, Control-click and drag. To *copy* the selection as independent clips, Option-click and drag.
• **Select frames in the middle of a clip**	Slice the clip with the Razor tool to define frames, then select (page 80). Or copy and paste the clip, then trim (described below).
• **Select a frame**	Display frame in Clip window, then select "Export Frame as PICT..." in File menu (page 94). Drag the new still-image clip into your project.
• **Select a *copy* of a clip from the Clip window**	**3.0:** Option-drag from the Clip window into the Construction window (page 65).
• **Exclude a track from selection**	**3.0:** Lock the track before using either the Track tool or Multi-Track tool (page 80).

Trimming Clips

• **Trim a clip (set a new In or Out point) ...in the Clip window**	Click the In or Out buttons or tap Shift-I or Shift-O (page 53). To play a clip from its In to Out point, press Option-spacebar (or Control-spacebar to loop). **3.0:** To trim an audio clip's In point with 1/600th second accuracy, select "Clip Window Options..."(page 55).
...in the Construction window	Drag the clip's edge with the Selection tool (page 74). To see trimmed frames in Preview window, turn on Edge viewing (Command '). Or click with the In or Out Point tools (page 83).

Trimming Clips (cont.)

• **Trim a clip's Out point**	From the still-image Clip window, click the Duration button (page 59). **3.0:** Select any clip; then choose "Duration..." in Clip menu (p. 75).
• **Trim a linked clip portion**	Break the link (described at bottom of this page), then trim (page 84). To trim its audio and video independently (a split-edit), you can also create a "soft link" (see next page).
• **Trim a clip *and* shift later clips equally in the track**	Press Option-Command and drag the clip's edge with Selection tool (page 83). This is known as a "ripple edit."
• **Trim *two* clips (combined duration constant)**	Press Command-Shift and drag a clip's edge with the Selection tool (page 84). This is known as a "rolling edit."
• **Trim a movie to a single frame**	Display frame in the Clip window, then select "Export Frame as PICT..." in File menu (page 94). Drag the new still-image clip into your project.
• **Edit inserts in multi-camera shoots**	**3.0:** Synchronize clips from each camera in consecutive S tracks, then trim with the Razor tool to define insert shots (page 89).

Splitting/Joining Clips

• **Split a clip or linked clip**	Click with Razor tool (page 80).
• **Split one portion of a linked clip**	Break the clip's link (described below) then use the Razor tool. **3.0:** Lock the track you don't want, then use the Razor tool (page 80).
• **Split across all tracks (the first step of an insert edit)**	Razor each track individually. Block-select from the cut point to the end of the project, then drag. **3.0:** Option-click with the Razor tool (page 81). Or create a Work Area Snapshot preview, then use its Razor button (page 82). To exclude one or more tracks from a razor's cut, lock the tracks beforehand (page 80).
• **Create a virtual clip**	**3.0:** Click-drag with the Marquee tool to select source clip area. Then drag the selection to new destination (page 78). To select only video or audio tracks for a virtual clip, press Option-Shift then drag. To exclude one or more tracks, lock the track before selecting (page 80).
• **Shift portions of a linked clip (temporary break)**	Press Shift-Option keys as you drag one portion of the linked clip with the Selection tool (page 84). Or cut and paste portion to new location.
• **Break a linked clip**	Put only one portion of a linked clip into the Construction window by Option-Shift-dragging one part of the clip's icon in the Project window (page 66). Or drag the entire linked clip into the Construction window. Then select and delete one portion. **3.0:** Select the clip in the Construction window, then choose "Break Link" in the Clip menu.

• **Create a "soft link" between two clips**	**3.0:** Click a video (or audio) clip, then Shift-click an audio (or video) clip counterpart (page 85). To soft link a regular linked clip, choose "Break Link" in the Clip menu with the Option key held down.

Aligning Clips

• **Add place markers to a clip**	Display the desired frame in the Clip window, then use the Mark pull-down menu or tap Shift-(number key) to add a numbered marker. Tap the = or * key to add an unnumbered marker (page 56).
• **Add numbered place markers in the time ruler**	In the Construction window, place the cursor at the desired time point, then Press Shift-(number key). See page 67. **3.0:** Create a Work Area Snapshot preview, display the desired frame in the Snapshot window, then use the Mark pull-down menu or tap Shift-(number key) to add a numbered marker (page 82).
• **Snap clips and place markers to alignment**	Turn on "Snap to edges" (tap the Tab key if it's off). See page 69. **3.0:** "Snap to edges" also can align Razor tool cuts and fade-line scissors cuts (page 81and 93).
• **Move a clip left or right in its track**	Drag with Selection tool (page 74). Or select the clip, then tap the Left or Right arrow key to move one frame at a time. Hold down the Shift key to shift five frames at a time (page 67).

Other Techniques

• **Paste a selected clip**	Paste a clip into a selected destination in the Construction window. Paste, Paste to Fit and Paste Special are available (page 86).
• **Delete selected clip(s)**	Following any selection except a block-selection, tap the Delete key or select Clear (Command B) in the Edit menu (page 65).
• **Change a clip's speed**	Select the clip, then choose "Speed..." in the Clip menu (Command -I). See page 88. To change a clip's speed to fit a selected destination, use Paste Special with the "Change Speed" option (page 87).
• **Disable a clip**	**3.0:** Select the clip, then uncheck "Enabled" at the top of the Clip menu (Command >). The clip will no longer appear in previews or compiled movies. Turn on "Enabled" to re-activate the clip (page 91).
• **Add or delete tracks**	**3.0:** Select "Add/Delete Tracks..." in the Project menu. (page 62). To see more tracks at once, consider reducing the icon size (page 68).
• **Adjust an audio clip's sound volume**	Drag the "rubber band" fade line in the audio clip (page 92). **3.0 :** To adjust the entire clip's audio gain, select the clip and choose "Gain..." in the Clip menu (page 94).
• **Find a clip in the Construction window**	Select the clip in the Project window and choose "Find Clip..." from the Clip menu (Command =). See page 71.

5

Previewing & Printing Your Progress

Now that you're cruising smoothly in the Construction window, it's time to check your current position to see whether you're on course. Previews are handy for that purpose because Premiere builds them more swiftly than full-blown QuickTime movies. With less interruption, your creative juices can continue to flow.

Use the first two sections to choose wisely from Premiere's array of preview methods and options. As you edit and embellish your project, the best preview choice will vary—so it pays to be familiar with all approaches. When you need to show your editing progress *on paper*, peek into the third section. Those pages solve the mysteries of printing storyboards and clips in Premiere.

Preview Methods

Premiere provides three preview methods, each with different strengths and weaknesses. An easy way to remember the three is to rap off-tune to yourself: "scrub, tap or scratch." Scrub stands for *scrubbing the time ruler*—the most convenient but least powerful preview. Tap represents *tapping the Enter key*, which triggers the "Preview" command in the Project menu. That's a good technique for simple segments—or complex compositions on very fast or RAM-heavy Macs. Scratch means *build a scratch movie*. Scratch movies take longer to create but yield more accurate results—and they play in the very controllable Clip window.

Choosing the right preview depends on several factors. On the technical side is your Mac's processing speed and the amount of RAM assigned to Premiere. On the human side are your editing priorities: how much time you can spare to wait and the preview quality you desire. Let's invest a few pages in getting to know each method so you will be ready for any preview situation.

☞ *Premiere 3.0's previews are vastly improved—a key reason 2.0 users should consider upgrading. Previews can now run at the highest frame rate your Mac supports. And unchanged areas don't have to be re-compiled later, saving time.*

▶ Scrub the Time Ruler

Scrubbing the time ruler is a convenient way to check a single frame or small portion of your composition, such as where a transition begins. All you need is your mouse. Just place the cursor in the Construction window's time ruler—over any part of your project. The cursor will change to a downward arrow. Then hold down the mouse button and drag the cursor right or left (forwards or backwards) over the segment you want to see.

Scrubbed segments play in the Preview window. An arrow and vertical line show your scrubbing position. To see a single frame, hold down the mouse button at one spot in the ruler.

☞ *With sufficient RAM, scrubbing repeatedly over the same segment plays smoother since Premiere loads the segment into RAM during the first pass.*

Unfortunately, scrubbing is saddled with limitations. Since the playback rate of this preview depends on your cursor-dragging speed, you don't get much sense of pacing. And playback on slower Macs is very choppy, especially over clips with effects. After all, Premiere has to build and display each frame on the fly.

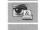

You'll soon realize one other scrub limitation: no audio. Scrubbing in Premiere 2.0 does not play sound at all. In Premiere 3.0, however, you can at least scrub audio *alone* (without visuals). Simply hold down the Option key as you drag the cursor through the time ruler.

3.0

With the Option key held down in Premiere 3.0, the scrubbing cursor sports a musical note and plays only audio tracks.

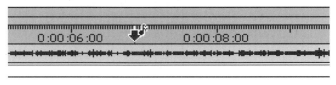

The quality of sound you'll hear won't get people dancing in the streets, but you should get a reasonable idea of audio clip placement.

A few pages ahead you'll see how Premiere's Preview Options can improve a scrub preview's performance.

▶ Below the Yellow Bar

For all other preview methods, Premiere checks the yellow *work area bar* at the top of the Construction window. The area under the bar is the portion of your project Premiere will preview. To review the first two seconds, for example, set the work area bar like below.

Shorten or extend the work area by dragging the red triangles at either end. For more precision, keep an eye on the Info window.

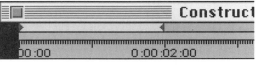

Note: 3.0's bar is shown, but 2.0's operates the same.

Since you'll manipulate the work area bar often, it pays to know the bar's tricks.

When using the In or Out Point tool, press the Shift key to switch to the other tool.

• You can click the In or Out Point tools anywhere in the bar's territory to set the start or end of the work area. For drastic adjustments, this can be quicker than dragging the red triangles to change the bar's length.

• Slide the entire bar at its existing width by dragging its middle with the arrow cursor (which turns into a hand).

Dragging from the middle keeps the bar's length constant.

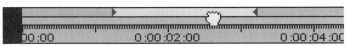

• Double-click in the bar's territory to stretch the bar instantly over the full width of the visible window area.

• In Premiere 3.0, Option-click in the bar's territory to set the work area over a *continuous* region of clips. That will cover your entire movie unless a gap exists in your arrangement. So this is a good way to test for gaps.

Now let's turn to the remaining preview methods—all of which rely on your yellow work area bar maneuvers.

▶ Tap the Preview Command

This second preview approach is nearly as convenient as scrubbing, but offers steadier playback. Video and sound will play together and the pacing will not depend on your cursor-dragging dexterity. Best yet, this preview can run at a high frame rate on slower Macs *if* there's sufficient RAM—a topic we'll cover a few pages ahead.

Tap previews require two steps: First extend the yellow work area bar over the area you want to preview. Then tap the Enter or Return key (or select "Preview" in the Project menu). In Premiere 3.0, you also can trigger this preview by clicking the large play button that sits in the upper corner of the Construction window.

Keep in mind that in Premiere 3.0 you also can select "Print to Video…" in the Export submenu of the File menu (Command M). It works the same as the Preview command except the show plays in the center of a black screen. No extra compiling time is required. You also can use this method to record your preview to videotape.

For more about the "Print to Video…" command, see page 293.

No matter how you launch the tap preview, you'll likely see a progress box at first while Premiere processes the data. Premiere 3.0 can build and save temporary preview files to hard disk (if "Effects to disk" mode is on; more about that esoteric setting ahead—page 116). If the preview segment remains unchanged, Premiere 3.0 doesn't have to re-compile it for later previews or your final movie—saving you time. Hallelujah!

Adobe Premiere™ Preview Files

For more about temporary files, see page 118.

When compiling is complete, the Preview window comes to life and plays. You can interrupt playback at any time by typing Command-period (.).

Like scrub previews, the Preview Options dialog box controls a tap preview's performance. Let's tackle the third preview technique, making a scratch movie, before digging into that dialog box.

▶ Two Places to Scratch

A temporary, or *scratch* movie, is a fully compiled QuickTime movie. It therefore accurately previews complicated Construction window arrangements that would choke the other two preview methods. Since scratch movies play in the Clip window, not the Preview window, you can play the preview repeatedly to your heart's content with plenty of control.

The confusing part to many users is there are *two* commands that can launch a scratch movie, each of which runs the preview based on different settings.

Make Movie

📖 *For more about the Make Movie process, see page 284.*

One approach is to use *Make Movie*—the same command for building a *final* QuickTime movie. This method makes most sense when you want to preview a segment at or near final playback quality.

Make Work Area ("Make Snapshot" in 3.0)

Triggering this command is usually the preferred scratch movie approach because it takes advantage of the *Preview Options* dialog box. Options in that box can add considerable zip to a preview's compiling and playback. Premiere 3.0 offers a second advantage: the preview will play in a *Work Area Snapshot* window. That close cousin to the Clip window includes enhanced editing tools.

To build a scratch movie this way, follow these steps.

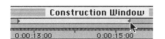

1 Position the yellow work area bar over the desired segment (see page 107 for tips how).

2 In Premiere 3.0, select "Snapshot…" from the Make menu. In Premiere 2.0, select "Work Area…" from the Make submenu in the Project menu. Or in either one, type Command-\.

3.0 👉 *Premiere 3.0 allows you to disable specific clips to leave them out of a preview. See page 91 for details.*

A progress box will then keep you informed as Premiere

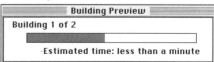

processes the movie data to hard disk before playback. How long the box will persist depends on how much data there is to compile. Premiere 3.0 courteously estimates the required time (roughly, at best). When the segment is fully digested, the Clip window will appear.

3 Use the Clip window's rich variety of playback controls to examine the preview. As mentioned earlier, in Premiere 3.0 you receive a *Work Area Snapshot* window which has several extra features.

The additional features of 3.0's Work Area Snapshot make it the best choice for most scratch preview situations.

A close look reveals a fat Razor button in the place of the Clip window's In and Out buttons. As described on page 82, the button cuts clips across all tracks.

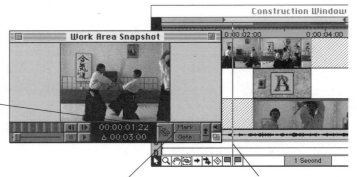

Use the Mark button to add numbered place markers to the Construction window's time ruler. This can help with aligning clips or marking potential trim points.

The current frame appears as a vertical guideline in the Construction window.

4 If desired in Premiere 2.0, you can save the Clip window for later reference (use the "Save..." command in the File menu).

In Premiere 3.0, you can't save a Work Area Snapshot directly (instead use the Make Movie command to save the same segment). But you get a more valuable benefit: Premiere will store the temporary files it produced for the preview in a folder for *later* use. If those portions of your project are unchanged the next time you preview the segment (or when you build your final movie), Premiere won't have to re-compile the material—saving you time down the road. This is another key reason to choose "Snapshot..." instead of "Movie..." in the Make menu when you need to see a scratch movie preview.

Adobe Premiere™ Preview Files

For more about temporary files, see page 118.

▶ **Previews in Review**

Well, we've boned up on the essentials regarding Premiere's four preview techniques. Which one is for you? To help you choose at a glance the most appropriate preview method for your editing situation, look over the summary chart on the next page. It's a blow-by-blow comparison of the major pros and cons.

Preview Method	Pros	Cons
Scrub the Time Ruler **Best Use:** *Quick review of a frame or brief segment.*	• *Most convenient—minimal delay.*	• *Choppy playback on slower Macs.* • *Can't evaluate pacing.* • *Premiere 2.0 cannot play sound. Premiere 3.0 plays video or sound, not both.* • *Requires mouse dragging dexterity.*
Tap the Preview Command *(Enter or Return Key)* **Best Use:** *Previewing small-frame movies without effects on any Mac. Previewing video with sound on fast or RAM-heavy Macs.*	• *On fast Macs, smooth playback and minimal delay are possible from disk.* • *On slower Macs, smooth playback is possible with sufficient RAM.* • *In Premiere 3.0, if "Effects to Disk" mode is selected in the Preview Options dialog box, temporary preview files are produced that can be re-used later.* • *Premiere 3.0 can "Print to Video" the preview on-screen or onto videotape.*	• *Plays in Preview window, so there's not as much playback control as a scratch movie.* • *Requires proper setting of Preview Options to be effective.* • *RAM-based playback is initially delayed as frames are cached.*
Scratch Movie *using "Make Work Area" in 2.0 or "Make Snapshot" in 3.0* **Best Use:** *When preview accuracy and Clip window control are important.*	• *Plays in the Clip window with full playback control.* • *3.0's enhanced Clip window—the "Work Area Snapshot"—includes a razor button, vertical guide and can add place markers to the Construction window.* • *Premiere 3.0 can re-use the temporary preview files, saving compiling time.*	• *Wait to compile the movie.* • *Always plays from disk, which can be choppy on slower Macs.*
Scratch Movie *using "Make Movie"* **Best Use:** *Testing and saving previews at or near final playback quality.*	• *Plays in Clip window with full playback control.* • *Can save the preview for later reference.* • *Based on the Project Output Options dialog box—the same process as creating a final movie.*	• *Wait to compile the movie.* • *Always plays from disk, which can be choppy on slower Macs.* • *Doesn't create preview files which can reduce compiling time later in 3.0.*

Preview Options

Now that you've mastered the preview methods, let's dig into the powerful options that can fine-tune a preview's performance. The focus of our attention will be on the *Preview Options* dialog box—the control center for all previews except Make Movie scratch movies. Chances are that by tweaking a setting or two, previews will appear sooner and play smoother on your Mac. If you're interested in that, keep reading.

Premiere 3.0 users should keep in mind that the *preset* you chose for a project initially sets the preview options. If you discover better options for your project needs, consider creating a new preset with those settings.

📖 *For more about creating presets, see page 25.*

▶ **Fundamental Preview Options**

Premiere 2.0 and 3.0 share several preview options. But they each spice up their option collections with a few unique controls. Let's first look at the shared options—the fundamentals—before considering the other settings.

To get to the Preview Options dialog box, select "Preview Options…" in the Make menu (in the Project menu in Premiere 2.0). Or type Command-[. Another way there is to double-click the Preview window.

3.0 *Premiere 3.0's Preview Options dialog box initially opens with a basic set of options. Additional settings are available by clicking the "More Options…" button at the bottom of the box.*

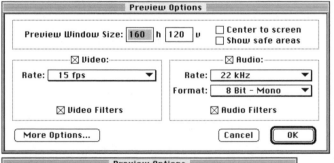

2.0 *Premiere 2.0's Preview Options dialog box has many of the same options, plus a few that were not retained in 3.0.*

Lots of options—help! Consider the following strategy which will make the individual choices much easier: *Reduce preview data to what you need to see and hear*. It's a simple but powerful idea that makes sense for most preview situations. The greater the image size, frame rate, quality and effects in a preview, the more data Premiere has to process. By meagerly keeping the settings to what you *really* need to evaluate each stage of your editing, there will be less data. Less data can mean:

☞ *Using miniatures can greatly help previewing if you're working with large-size source clips (see page 43).*

• less wait for Premiere to process the file before the preview begins

• a better chance of fitting into available RAM, which can smooth previews issued from the Preview command

• a faster frame rate (up to the maximum rate you set) from disk-based previews, such as scratch movies

• less hard disk space required to store the time-saving temporary files that Premiere 3.0 creates for later use

Even if you have a blazingly fast Mac setup that can handle full-frame, full-motion video, consider previewing at a lesser level. You will still gain the advantages of faster compiling and less hard disk space required for your project's temporary files.

With this strategy in hand, let's quickly tackle each preview option that Premiere 2.0 and 3.0 share.

Video/Audio On/Off

⊠ **Audio:**   ⊠ **Video:**

To preview *only* visuals *or* sound in a work area that includes both, turn the appropriate check box off. There's no sense compiling data you don't need in Premiere.

Preview Window Size

160 h 120 v

Set the window to the smallest size you can tolerate, especially for early editing and previewing. If you have a slower Mac, try 160 x 120 pixels (or 120 x 90 if your nose isn't too big). With faster Macs or hardware compression, you can stretch the window larger—but ask yourself if you truly need to preview bigger than quarter-screen size.

Keep in mind three other window size caveats:

☒ **4:3 Aspect**

• After you enter one dimension, the correct other dimension appears automatically. It's based on the aspect ratio set in *another* dialog box—the Project Output Options dialog box. (Smile while gritting your teeth.) For a different aspect ratio, briefly detour to there. (Select "Output Options…" in 3.0's Make menu or 2.0's Project menu.)

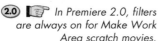 *In Premiere 3.0, you can use the "Process at" preview option to free yourself from this limitation (see page 117).*

• If your source clips are already small or you're using miniatures, *set the Preview window to their size*—not a slightly different dimension. The extra time Premiere needs to scale each frame will outweigh any speed gain.

• Instead of typing, you can drag the lower right corner of the Preview window to a new size. With the Option key down, the window will snap to standard QuickTime sizes. In Premiere 3.0, you can Option-click the window to quickly do that. Momentarily enlarging the window can help you examine an effect more closely, for example.

Frame Rate

There's no point in having Premiere compile more frames per second for a preview than either (a) your final production's frame rate, or (b) the frame rate your Mac can play. Extra frames will just extend your compiling wait.

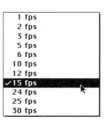

Video/Audio Filters

Until you're ready to review filter decisions, try turning these check boxes off. Of course, if you haven't applied any filters, these options won't matter.

 *In Premiere 2.0, filters are always on for Make Work Area scratch movies.*

Sound Quality

Selecting a higher audio quality level than your source clips will not create cleaner sound. It will only slow compiling (and playback unless your preview only has audio clips). So be sure to check the following factors.

• Sampling rate—Premiere gives you the standard kilohertz (kHz) choices. See if you can live with 11 kHz or less for most previews unless you're only editing audio.

• Format—Consider stereo only if your source clips are stereo, your Mac has stereo output and two speakers are connected. Otherwise, you won't hear a difference.

• Resolution—In Premiere 3.0, you also can choose 8-bit or 16-bit sound resolution. Stick with 8-bits unless your audio source clips are 16-bit, you have a sound board and you need to hear the extra quality during previews.

Premiere 3.0 has two more settings, neither of which alters a preview's performance. They only affect the Preview window's *appearance* on-screen.

Turn on the "Center to screen" check box on to snap the Preview window to the middle of your screen. You can also use it to center full-screen previews on a second monitor.

Activate this option to see borders showing NTSC safe areas for titles and animations—only while scrubbing the time ruler.

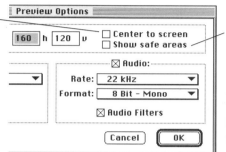

That's all for the basics. If you're using Premiere 3.0 and are ready to explore more advanced options, read on. If you're working with Premiere 2.0, you can skip ahead to the *2.0's Other Options* section on page 119.

▶ 3.0's Advanced Options

Premiere 3.0 has a few "advanced" options that control how previews are processed. For standard Mac setups, you probably don't need to fiddle with the settings. If your machinery leans towards the high-end, however, look over these pages to see how previews can take full advantage of your Mac's muscle.

Clicking the "More Options..." button expands the Preview Options dialog box and reveals more controls.

More Options...

Preview Options

Preview Window Size: **160** h **120** v   ☐ Center to screen
☒ Show safe areas

☒ Video:
Rate: **15 fps**
Mode: **Effects to disk**
Type: **Full Size Frame**
☒ Process at: **160** h **120** v
☒ Video Filters

☒ Audio:
Rate: **22 kHz**
Format: **8 Bit - Mono**
Build   Play
● Disk   ○ Disk
○ RAM   ● RAM
☒ Audio Filters

Fewer Options...   Cancel   OK

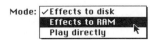

Mode

The mode only affects previews *launched with the Preview command*—not scratch previews or scrubs. It tells Premiere how to handle effects (any filters, transitions, superimposed clips or motions settings) in your preview segment. The idea here is to have Premiere process effects in the fastest part of your Mac setup. Choose from:

• *Effects to RAM*

This choice instructs Premiere to load the preview's video content into RAM and then process the effects on the fly as the preview plays. It's a speedy approach if you've given Premiere gobs of RAM or your previews are sufficiently brief and small. But since some effects may not process fast enough, you may see inaccurate results.

• *Effects to Disk*

This is the better choice for almost any Mac that doesn't have much extra RAM available for Premiere. In fact, all presets that ship with Premiere 3.0 use this as their default. Before playback, Premiere processes and saves each effects segment to hard disk as a temporary movie file in a folder (just like a *Work Area Snapshot*). As mentioned earlier in this chapter, these temporary files can save compiling time for later previews and your final movie.

Adobe Premiere™ Preview Files

📖 *See page 118 for more about 3.0's temporary files.*

• *Play Directly*

The last mode tells Premiere *not* to do anything before previewing. Instead, the preview is entirely processed as it plays. To achieve a high frame rate with this generally requires hardware compression and plenty of RAM—or cuts-only projects which have no effects. The advantage of this choice is you won't have to wait for processing to occur before playback begins.

Type

Most users can leave this option alone at its full-frame default. However, one scenario may call for a different setting: If you're using the "Print to Video…" command to record a preview to tape *and* your video board outputs in a different fashion than full-frame (check its documentation if you aren't sure), match the board's output here for better preview performance.

👉 *If there are virtual clips in your movie, 1/2 Horizontal or 1/2 Vertical may distort transitions or motion effects.*

Process at

Premiere 3.0 builds previews at the Preview window's size unless you enter a different size here. With a regular Mac and the Effects to Disk preview mode, entering your *source clips'* size will lead to the zippiest results. If you're blessed with a fast Mac, though, consider entering your *final movie's* dimensions (which may be different than your source clips). That may initially require extra compiling time, but you'll gain two key benefits:

• Many Premiere filters are *size-sensitive* (an issue explored further in Chapter 7). When Premiere previews a filter in a smaller window than the final movie, the filter effect appears at a larger scale than in the final image (see the Pointillize filter example at left). Processing at the final movie's frame size allows you to see the true results.

Preview　　*Final Movie*

• Processing at your final movie's frame size is a must (but not the only requirement—see next page) if you want to reduce the compiling time for your final movie.

Build/Play

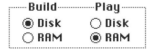

These buttons are the equivalent of "modes" (see previous page) but sit in the audio side of the Preview Options dialog box. When the video mode is "Effects to disk," you can separately determine how Premiere 3.0 will handle audio—either on your hard disk or in RAM. The four radio-style buttons provide three different combinations.

☞ *This only affects previews from the Preview command.*

• Build to Disk/Play from Disk

For audio-only projects, this is the best choice. Audio is processed and saved to hard disk as a temporary file. Premiere then plays the file from disk during the preview. For this option to be feasible with previews that include video, you'll need a top-speed hard drive. *Two* fast drives is better yet (see the tip two pages ahead).

☞ *This is also good choice for video movies with 16-bit stereo sound since the audio data rate is so high. It's useful for long previews, too, if all of the audio exceeds available RAM.*

• Build to Disk/Play from RAM

This is generally the best choice for all but audio-only projects. It's like the prior option, except Premiere progressively loads the file into RAM during playback. With enough RAM, the preview's smoothness can improve since there's less data to access on disk as the preview plays. You also get the advantage of temporary files being created on disk to save time down the road.

☞ *If you don't have enough RAM, you'll get a dialog box announcing that fact—instead of playback. One minute of 22 kHz mono sound requires 1.3 megabytes of RAM.*

• *Build to RAM/Play from RAM*

Premiere entirely handles the preview's audio in RAM here. With enough RAM, you can take advantage of the more rapid compiling that silicon provides. The disadvantage is Premiere doesn't create any temporary audio files on disk that may reduce compiling later.

 This choice requires no more RAM than the prior option.

▶ Temporary File Issues

 3.0

By now you probably know that *Make Snapshot* scratch movies as well as previews triggered from the Preview command (in *Effects to disk* mode) store temporary files on your hard disk. *Unchanged* segments won't have to be re-compressed for later previews or your final movie— potentially saving you plenty of time during your project.

Premiere 3.0 gives you a visual clue to the status of your temporary files. As it compiles temporary files, thin grey bars above the Construction window time ruler appear that correspond to each segment.

The upper half of the temporary file bar represents processed video. Alternating greys indicate each temporary file. The lower half shows processed audio.

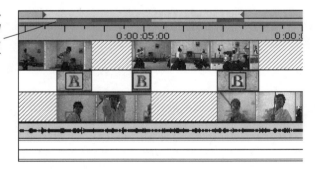

As you edit your project, some of those time-saving files may disappear! So you're forewarned, here are the actions that can produce that unfortunate turn of events.

 Command-Shift-Option-click the temporary file bar to deliberately delete all temporary preview files, which can be handy if you need to clear out more hard disk space.

• *Any* changes to previewed areas of your project will delete at least some temporary files. The slightest adjustment to a filter or transition, for example, will trigger new CPU work. Moving or editing clips will too.

• If you decide to alter video or audio settings in the Preview Options dialog box, Premiere has to delete *all* temporary video or audio files built by prior previews.

If some temporary files are still alive when you're ready to compile your final movie, you'll save compiling time only if the following is true: Options in the *Preview Options* dialog box (Command [) match the options in the *Project Output Options* dialog box (Command]) which Premiere uses to compile the final movie. The crucial options are image size (or "Process at" if turned on), frame rate, type, and all audio options.

One more temporary file tip: If your Mac has multiple hard drives or disk partitions, you can select which disk or partition is home for the temporary preview files. That can help tight storage situations and ensure Premiere uses your fastest drive. Normally, Premiere places the files in a new folder wherever your project's file exists. If you prefer another location, select "Scratch Disks..." in the Preferences submenu of the Edit menu.

Adobe Premiere™ Preview Files

Use the bottom two pop-ups to change the location of your temporary preview files.

☞ *If you have two hard drives, storing audio and video temporary files on separate drives can improve disk-based previews with both material.*

Scratch Disks	
Temp/Captured Movies:	*Same as Application* ▼
Video Preview Temps:	*Same as Project File* ▼
Audio Preview Temps:	*Same as Project File* ▼

[Cancel] [OK]

Whew! We've covered a lot of advanced preview territory. If you're a Premiere 3.0 user, you can gleefully leap over the next section.

▶ **2.0's Other Options**

Five options remain in Premiere 2.0's Preview Options dialog box, several of which significantly affect preview performance. Let's quickly see what each option can do.

(2.0) *These controls in the lower half of 2.0's Preview Options dialog box influence preview speed and quality.*

📖 *For more about the Video Filters check box, see page 114.*

☞ *All five check boxes at right affect only scrub and tap previews, not scratch movies.*

Cache: | **Everything** ▼ |

☒ **Video Filters**
☒ **Colored Borders**

☒ **Dithered**
☐ **Coarse**
☐ **Every Frame**

Cache

The pull-down menu determines the preview elements Premiere 2.0 will try to throw into RAM for smoother playback than from hard disk.

• "Everything" directs Premiere to try to load *all* preview data (clip content and effects) into available RAM. If your Mac is full of RAM and your previews are small and brief, this option may be for you.

• If RAM is tight, try "Effects Only" to stand a better chance of fitting at least some of the data into RAM.

Insufficient RAM in either above case will force the preview to play from hard disk. Or you can insist on that by choosing "Nothing." That's a good option if you have a wickedly fast Mac and do not want to wait for Premiere to process the preview into RAM.

Colored Borders

Color borders can accent Premiere's transitions, as you'll see next chapter. Typically, showing borders during a preview only minimally influences speed. If you need to squeeze all fat out of your preview, however, turn this off.

See page 132 for more about transition borders.

Dithered

If your monitor displays fewer colors than the color depth of your source clips, dithering can make clips appear to have more colors or greys. However, the improved appearance will be at the expense of extra processing time.

Coarse

Turn on this option to show images at half resolution. Having 75% fewer pixels to process can be a godsend for clips loaded with effects, especially when a faster frame rate is more important to you than preview resolution.

Here's the difference between coarse and regular resolution in the Preview window.

Every Frame

Normally, your Mac skips frames if it's not fast enough to match a preview's intended frame rate. With this setting, *every* frame of a preview will play. You may end up with slow motion, but you can visually check all frames.

☞ *This option is available only if the Audio check box is off.*

Congratulations! We've covered every preview option. Only a few settings affecting scratch movies remain.

▶ A Few More Scratch Settings

Compression settings can make a *huge* difference in scratch movie performance. Appendix A (page 328) covers compression settings thoroughly, but look below for quick advice that's tailored to scratch previews.

This is Premiere 3.0's Compression Settings dialog box, but similar settings are in Premiere 2.0's Project Output Options dialog box.

Select a fast-working compressor for previews, such as Apple's Video. If you're using hardware compression, your board's compressor is the best choice.

For previews, you can usually ignore the key frame setting.

Compression Settings

Compressor
Video
Color

Place a clip on the clipboard to view here

Quality
Least   Low   Normal   High   Most

Motion
Frames per second: 15
☐ Key frame every ____ frames
☐ Limit data rate to ____ K/Second

Cancel   OK

To reduce the file size and potentially raise the playback frame rate, set the image quality as low as you can tolerate. Many previews don't need "final" quality.

The frame rate here only affects movies made with the "Make Movie..." command. Other previews use the rate in the Preview Options dialog box.

Also check a related option in the Project Output Options dialog box (Command]). Make sure the Output is set to "Work Area as QuickTime Composite." That directs Premiere not to waste time re-compressing already compressed source clips. The disadvantage is your preview may end up with a smorgasbord of compression settings (hence frame rates), depending on how the source clips were compiled. But for early checking of your masterpiece, that's typically not a problem.

📖 *For more about the QuickTime Composite output setting, see page 287.*

That's all there is to know about previews. When you need to produce a storyboard or plaster your Premiere project *on paper*, look at the last section of this chapter.

Printing to Paper

Dare we also consider *print* amidst dynamic media? If your audience is full of hard-copy devotees—whether out of necessity or preference—Premiere gives you the opportunity to print the content of almost any window. We'll focus on the Construction, Project and Clip windows since they're the usual printout targets.

☞ *If Premiere's printing abilities don't meet your project needs, remember you can always use a screen capture utility to grab window views.*

Unfortunately, the rules of the printing game differ for each window—and the manual offers little help. You can chew up a lot of time (and trees) trying to get the results you want. To save you and the environment from such misery, let's look closer at the print possibilities.

▶ A Time-Line for the Pages

The Construction window translates fairly well to paper. You can see each thumbnail-sized clip and sense how tracks of the sequence fit together. And Premiere obligingly can print your entire production even when your work extends beyond the visible area of the window. To print the window successfully, consider these tips.

WYSIWYG the Window

Premiere prints the Construction window with the same time scale and display options that are on your screen. So be sure to configure the window to what you want before going farther along the printing path. Unfortunately, there's no way to change page margins, headers (you're stuck with "Construction Window") or footers (none).

📖 *For more about display options for the Construction window, see page 68.*

Visit Page Setup

Select "Page Setup…" in the File menu before printing. Consider reducing the image and orienting the page horizontally to fit a wider swath of time-line on each page. Among the many check box options (which vary depending on your printer and printer driver) *turn off* "Graphics Smoothing" for slightly cleaner movie bitmaps.

Print Thy Window

With the window displayed appropriately and Page Setup confirmed, you can print with confidence. Make sure the Construction window is active, then choose "Print Window…" in the File menu.

The dialog box you'll then see depends on your Chooser-selected printer. Keep in mind two caveats:

• Since Premiere gives no hint where page breaks will fall (or how many pages cover the entire sequence), you'll have to guess which pages to specify for partial print jobs.

 Color/Grayscale

• Be sure to turn on "Color/Grayscale" for the clearest thumbnail images on almost any Postscript printer.

▶ Views Out the Project Window

For more about the Project window's display, see page 32.

(2.0)

Printing the contents of the Project window is similar to printing the Construction window. If you print with the Project window in either icon view, however, you'll only print what's *visible* in the window. And you won't see much information about each clip.

For most users, therefore, "by Name" will be the sole Project window view destined for paper. Only here can you document important clip data and comments. You can print *every* listed clip, even those visible only by scrolling the window. And in Premiere 3.0, you can sort the window's contents by any column before printing.

The key to a successful By Name view printout is *to set the window's width correctly*. Too narrow of a Project window will obviously hide some content, such as a comments column. But in Premiere 2.0 there's a paradox: If you drag the window *too wide*, you also may cut off content. That's because Premiere prints the window no wider than an arbitrary width—about 4.5 inches. Page orientation, reduction percentages or other printing tricks have no impact on this limitation.

Too wide or narrow of a Project window in 2.0's by Name view may amputate important content.

☞ *Choose a vertical page orientation in the Page Setup dialog box to fit a longer list of clips per page.*

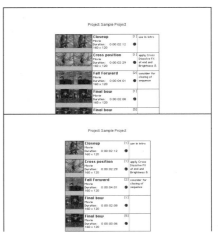

▶ Storyboarding the Clip Window

One frame on one page—that's all you get by printing the Clip window directly. Moooo!

Printing the Clip window only centers the *currently visible frame* on the page. No window elements or other frames will appear—just one image.

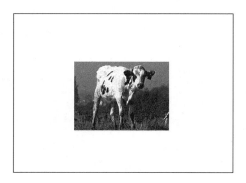

To show more than one frame per page, you could have Premiere build a numbered PICT file series with this output setting in the Output Options dialog box:

You could then arrange the exported PICTs in a graphics or page-layout application. This make-shift technique isn't very elegant, but possible in a pinch.

3.0

Premiere 3.0 offers a more direct solution: a handy "Storyboard Image…" command that prints a simple arrangement of selected movie frames. The feature even includes adjustable controls for columns, rows and spacing. Printing a storyboard involves three simple steps.

📖 *See page 56 for more about applying place markers in the Clip window.*

1 Call up the clip you want to print in the Clip window. Then set In and Out points and *numbered* place markers (0–9) on the frames you want to print. (You can export up to twelve frames at a time this way.) Note that you may also use the Storyboard feature from the Construction window to export a work area segment. The frames, however, will be based on place markers in the Construction window *time-line*—not place markers within an individual clip.

2 Select "Storyboard Image…" in the Export menu of the File menu to see the dialog box below.

Use the three slider bars at the bottom of the box to adjust the storyboard layout shown on the miniature page to the right.

Click the "Page Setup…" button to set the usual formatting parameters. One quirk exists: Depending on your layout, enlargement percentages (amounts above 100%) may actually reduce the size of your image. Keep an eye on the layout graphic at right to be sure of what you're getting.

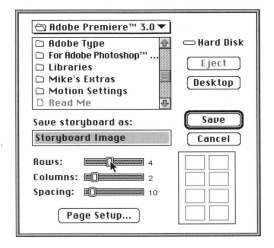

3 After setting the storyboard layout, name and save the new file. Premiere will create one or more PICT files (depending on whether the selected images fit on one page) that you can open and further enhance in a graphic application, such as Photoshop. To print the storyboard immediately, open the PICTs in Premiere and print from the Clip window.

Storyboard Image

▶ **Onward to Greater Heights**

Now that you have a good reading on your current project's flight status, it's time to try your hand at spins, rolls and other movie embellishments. The next chapter will transform you into a wizard with Premiere's transitions. Buckle your seat belt!

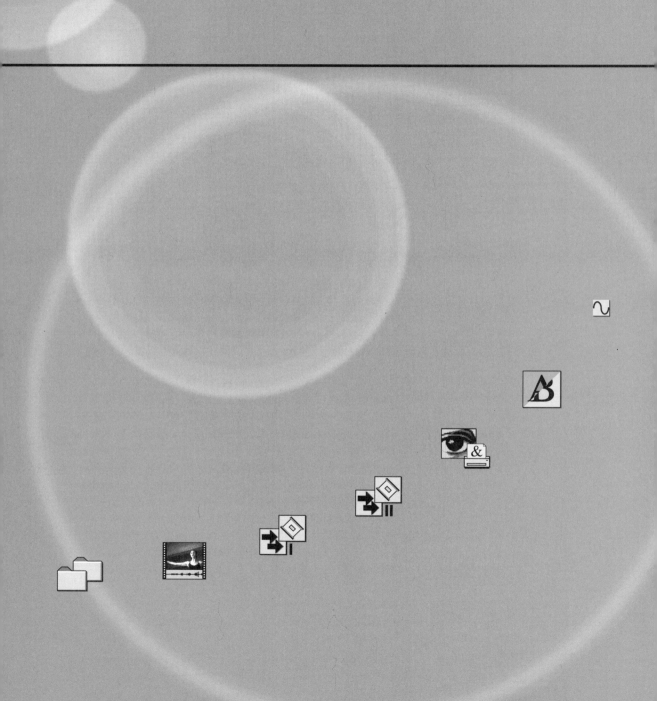

6

Adding Visual Transitions

A simple *cut* is often the best visual transition from one clip to the next. When your project needs more pizzazz or expressiveness, however, Premiere has dozens of other tempting flavors available—each with a variety of options.

Ahead you'll see how to place, fine-tune and manage such effects. We'll also tour each transition to help you choose from the mind-boggling array of creative possibilities. Last, we'll take transitions beyond the standard fare—in case you're ready for more elaborate acrobatics.

Working with Transitions

Transition Acrobatics

Working with Transitions

Before diving into the creative aspects of Premiere's transitions, let's master the more practical matter of applying them efficiently. This section shows you how to add a transition to your project and then customize its action. The pages also provide a hot tip that will help you stay on top of the wide range of available effects.

Before we begin, note that Premiere 2.0's "Special Effects window" and "FX Track" are called "Transitions window" and "T Track" in Premiere 3.0. For the purposes of these pages, 3.0's labels are used even though the advice applies to both versions (unless otherwise noted).

☞ Transitions versus filters...newcomers to Premiere often confuse the two. Transitions affect the visuals between two clips. Filters alter only one clip.

▶ Transition Placement

You don't need anything extra in Premiere to apply the most common (and often most powerful) transition—a cut. Simply butt two clips together—head to tail—in the same video track. Bang! During playback, the image will instantly switch from one clip to the next.

To add a smoother visual transition between two clips, you need to work with Premiere's Transitions window. That long window holds Premiere's entire stockpile of visual transitions, arranged alphabetically.

If the Transitions window isn't visible on your screen, select it in the Windows menu (or type Command 6). When the window is active, each icon animatedly demonstrates its effect.

☞ Type the first letter or two of any transition's name to select it quickly.

☞ To save screen space, you can narrow the window to show only the icons.

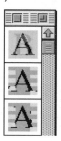

Follow three steps to add a transition to your project.

1 Place one clip in the A video track and the other in the B track so they overlap for the duration you want the transition to last. Usually, keep the overlap short and sweet—a few seconds—but the ideal length depends on what you want to communicate. The nature of a transition also is a factor—what may be too brief an overlap for a Cross Zoom, for example, may be just right for a Cross Dissolve. You'll gain a better feel for this as you work with various transitions.

2 Choose a transition in the Transitions window and drag it into the T track between the two clips.

The T Track highlights as you drag a transition into position. The transition automatically sizes itself to the overlap between the clips for the smoothest effect.

☞ *If you're building an edit decision list with Premiere, be careful which transitions you select. Some may not translate well into high-end systems. See page 337 for details.*

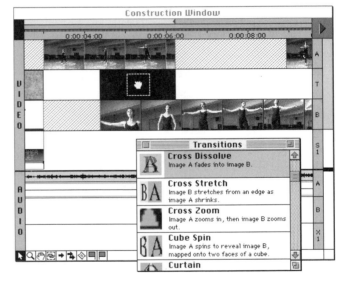

Premiere automatically sets the transition to flow from track A "down" to B (or B "up" to A) based on whichever clip is first in the overlap area. If there's no overlap or both clips start at the same time, Premiere defaults to the A to B direction. But you can change that (read on).

3 Double-click the transition's icon that you dragged into the T Track. That opens a dialog box for previewing and fine-tuning the effect (more about this dialog box a few pages ahead). Some of the same controls also sit on the transition's icon so common adjustments

will be more convenient. The controls will not be visible, though, if the icon is too short (or too small due to Construction window display options chosen in 3.0). They also will not appear if "Full Effects" is off in Premiere 2.0.

That's all you need to do for most transitions. Of course, many other editing adjustments are possible. (You aren't off the hook, yet.) All editing tools and techniques explored in Chapters 4 and 5 also work on transitions.

For example, if you want a transition to be a different duration than two overlapping clips, you can drag its edge in the track to shorten or lengthen it—just like any clip. As always, the Info window will happily show you the precise stats as you work.

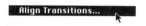

If you later decide to replace that transition with another one, instead of adjusting the duration again, do this: Copy the new transition (Command C), select the old transition in the T Track, and then choose "Paste to Fit" in the Edit menu (Command U). The new transition will fit into the exact same space, saving you work. Neat!

As you further edit your project, some transitions may become misaligned with their clips. Premiere provides a time-saving "Align Transitions…" command ("Check FX Alignment…" in 2.0) in the Project menu that can check the alignment of all transitions in your project. After you issue the command, Premiere stops at the first transition that's out of whack with a clip in the A or B video tracks. At that point, you'll see the following dialog box.

A vertical guideline appears in the Construction window to indicate the problem area. Besides "Cancel," the alignment dialog box gives you three options at that point.

☞ This feature evaluates a transition's alignment to the edge of an A or B clip, but not to any place markers.

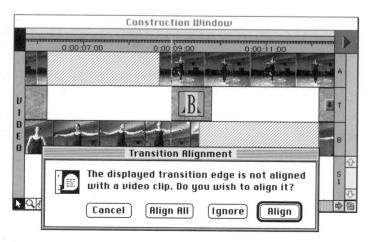

• Click "Align" to align the current transition.

• Click "Ignore" to move on without any changes.

 *If necessary, increase the Construction window's time scale to check closely spaced areas.*

• Click "Align All" to align all transitions without further stopping. If some of your clip edges are within a few pixels of each other, however, this may lead to unexpected results. In that case, it's worth the extra time to check each alignment individually.

▶ Fine-Tuning the Settings

Adjusting a transition's settings is the key to tailoring the effect to your creative needs. You can accomplish most of the fine-tuning from one dialog box. To access the box, double-click the transition's icon in the Construction window. Or choose "Transition Settings" in the Clip menu (Command E) after selecting the transition. In Premiere 2.0, "Effect Settings…" is the command's name.

Available controls within the dialog box depend on which transition you choose. The Band Wipe example at right includes all possible controls.

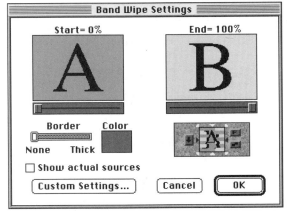

Let's explore the whiz-bang power each control offers.

Preview Windows & Sliders

The left Preview window in the dialog box shows the first frame of the transition (represented by the "A" graphic); the right window shows the last frame ("B"). Drag the slider that's under either window to preview the transition from beginning to end—from 0% to 100%.

Besides previewing, you can use sliders to *limit the range of the effect*. For example, you may want a Clock Wipe transition to end vertically as a split screen rather than sweeping around to the twelve o'clock position.

To end the Clock Wipe transition at the six o'clock position, drag the End slider to 50%.

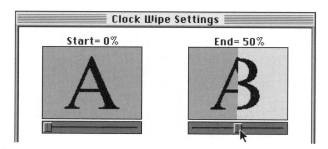

You can move *both* sliders simultaneously by holding down the Shift key while dragging. "Freezing" a transition at the same start and end percentage offers several cool effects (no pun intended) that we'll explore toward the end of this chapter (page 150).

Show Actual Sources

Start= 0%

Turn on this check box to see your clips instead of the simple A and B graphics in the dialog box. The clips will not play in the box like a movie, but you'll at least see still-image clip frames that correctly correspond to the start and end of the transition.

Border/Color

You can add a border along the edge of most transitions if you like. Dragging the slider right gradually increases the border's thickness, as shown below.

Note that the preview shows the border's actual thickness, not its relative size to your movie frame. Thick borders therefore appear thinner at full-screen size.

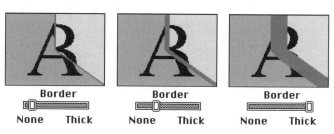

If you want a color border instead of the drab default grey, double-click the Color box to select a border color with Apple's standard color picker. Premiere 3.0 also has its own color picker design. The picker you see in 3.0 depends on your choice in Premiere's General Preferences dialog box.

3.0

For more about using each color picker, see page 241.

The next five controls appear in the transition's icon in the Construction window and the Settings dialog box.

Track Direction

Reverse the flow of the transition with this button—either down (from track A to track B) or up (from B to A). This is handy when the direction Premiere initially assigns is not what you desire.

Orientation

Many Premiere transitions can strut their stuff in several orientations or from different starting points. If the transition is capable of such tricks, small triangles will be visible around the effect's icon that you can click. Active triangle(s) are red. For example, the Clock Wipe transition at left will start at the right upper corner.

Forward/Reverse

The *action* of most transitions is reversible with this small button. For example, you can have the Clock Wipe transition move counter-clockwise (reverse) instead of clockwise (forward) to reveal the next clip. This differs from the Track Direction button, which determines the order of clips—not the transition's *movement*.

Anti-Aliasing

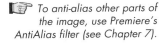

The anti-alias control smooths the transition *edges*—not the entire image. Click the button to choose from off (the default), low or high. The small button indicates your choice with the jaggedness of its icon.

☞ *To anti-alias other parts of the image, use Premiere's AntiAlias filter (see Chapter 7).*

If you select a border for the transition's edge, the border will anti-alias too.

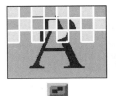 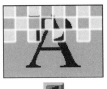 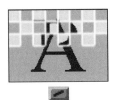

Custom Settings

☞ *Option-click a transition's icon in the T Track to go directly to the Custom Settings dialog box.*

If this button is visible, click it to access custom settings for the transition. Premiere 2.0's *Channel Map* transition was the first to offer such extras. Premiere 3.0 expands that idea much further by providing custom settings for several different effects. We'll explore the power of custom settings as we examine each transition in the next section of this chapter.

▶ Managing All Those Transitions

Adobe Premiere™ Plug-Ins

Cross Dissolve

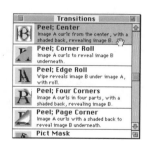

Premiere lists transitions alphabetically in the Transitions window. That's fine when you already know *what* effect you want *and* its name. Without those two items, however, the intuitive-looking Transitions window suddenly becomes *very* intimidating. The number of transitions is so great (over 60 in Premiere 3.0) that trying to recall what's available taxes even the most dedicated user.

Here's a solution: *Rename* the transitions. Each transition is a separate plug-in file that sits in Premiere's Plug-Ins folder. You can open the folder and alter the names of those plug-ins without any problem—and that will change their order in the Transitions window. This little secret gives you two opportunities for reorganizing the window's long alphabetical list.

1. Put Favorite Transitions First

Add a space or two in front of the names of favorite transitions you rely on most frequently. They'll appear at the top of the Transitions window.

2. Group Transitions By Category

In addition to (or instead of) adding spaces, organize effects *by category* so selecting a transition will become much easier. To cluster effects in the Transitions window this way, insert a consistent category name *before* each plug-in's name. For example, the five transitions that "peel" a clip away could be renamed as below:

Current name	New Name
Center Peel	Peel; Center
Page Peel	Peel; Page Corner
Page Turn	Peel; Corner Roll
Peel Back	Peel; Four Corners
Roll Away	Peel; Edge Roll

Use the categories this book provides or create your own. Either way, your transition decisions will become more manageable. And you'll reduce the odds of forgetting about a rarely-used (but occasionally crucial) effect.

Now that you can apply, tailor and keep on top of all of Premiere's wonderful transitions, let's take a comprehensive tour to see what each special effect offers.

Transitions in Review

Dissolves (below)
Cross Dissolve • Dither Dissolve
Additive Dissolve
Non-Additive Dissolve

Wipes, Stretches, Slides (p. 136)
Barn Doors • Center Merge
Center Split • Clock Wipe
Cross Stretch • Curtain • Funnel
Inset • Pinwheel • Push • Quad Slide
Quad Stretch • Quad Wipe
Quarter Slide • Quarter Stretch
Quarter Wipe • Radial Wipe
Random Wipe • Slide • Split • Stretch
Swap • Wedge Wipe • Wipe

Irises (p. 140)
Iris Cross • Iris Diamond • Iris Points
Iris Round • Iris Square • Iris Star

Bands & Blocks (p. 141)
Band Slide • Band Wipe
Checker Grid • Grid • Origami
Slash Slide • Sliding Bands
Sliding Boxes • Triangles
Venetian Blinds • Checkerboard
Mixed Stretch • Mixed Wipe
Random Blocks • Spiral Boxes
Zig-Zag Blocks

Peels (p. 144)
Center Peel • Fold Up • Page Peel
Page Turn • Peel Back • Roll Away

Spins & Swings (p. 145)
Cube Spin • Multi-Spin • Shutter Slide
Shutter Wipe • Spin • Spin Away
Swirl • Doors • Swing In
Swing Out • Multi-Spin Swirl

Zooms (p. 147)
Cross Zoom • Zoom

Maps (p. 148)
Channel Map • Displace
Luminance Map • Texturize • Three-D

Other Transitions (p. 149)
Direct • Take • PICT Mask
Paint Splatter

Are you ready to begin the grand tour of all Premiere transitions? As trumpeted earlier in this chapter, this section organizes the transitions by *visual category* (see left) rather than the purely alphabetical manner of Premiere's Transitions window.

Our visit to each transition includes a brief description and five-frame illustration of the effect. Icon-based controls are also shown so you'll know ahead of time what orientations and directions are possible—without having to drag the icon into the Construction window. For transitions with custom settings, you'll also see the range of values you can use—to get a good idea of the effect's extra potential. All of this information will help you to compare transitions before deciding which to use.

If you're fairly sure you want a transition that peels the first image away to reveal the second image, for example, check out all "peels" together. Yes, peels may seem like an odd name for a category of Premiere transitions. But such labels descriptively break down what would otherwise be one large collection of wipes.

Transitions or custom settings that are new to 3.0 sport the **3.0** icon used throughout this book. The few transitions Premiere LE lacks are also flagged with **LE**. Note that the tour also covers the fourteen extra, exclusive, exciting transitions in this book's Goodies Disk! (Is that enough of a plug?) They have this icon: **P**

So sit back, relax and take some time to browse this fourteen-page comprehensive visual reference. It's not necessary to digest every transition now unless you're really gung ho. However, at least a quick look will prepare you to come back to these pages for urgent help when you're in the middle of a deadline-driven project. Even if you're a Premiere veteran, this section may remind you of a few forgotten transitions that may be of assistance at a later date—or some effects you never realized existed in the first place. Enjoy!

▶ Dissolves

Dissolves are probably the second most common transition aside from cuts. All dissolves share the same trait—one image slowly fades away as the other gradually appears. Dissolves can:

- add a classy touch to titles and graphics

- convey a change in time or place between two clips

- hide flaws and minor discontinuities between clips—"Dissolve what you can't resolve" is an editing truism.

Another common use for dissolves is to fade a clip to or from black—such as at the beginning or end of a movie. Keep in mind you don't need a black clip to do that. Just leave the A or B video track *empty* (be sure to point the dissolve's Track Selection arrow appropriately) and place your clip in the other track.

To fade to or from white or a solid color, create a color matte for the empty track segment (see page 280).

Cross Dissolve

The first image fades out as the next image fades in.

Dither Dissolve

A dithered pattern of pixels dissolves the first image to reveal the next image.

3.0 Additive Dissolve

The second image appears to fade in *over* the first image.

3.0 Non-Additive Dissolve

Neither image fades, so this isn't a true dissolve. The first image stays at full strength, but increasingly lighter pixels within it switch to the second image.

▶ Wipes, Stretches & Slides

Wipes feature a line or shape that "wipes" away an image to reveal the next image. Stretches and slides are similar except they stretch or slide one of the images during the transition's progression. Since these transitions are very directional, for most of them Premiere gives you several choices for their orientation and starting point.

Barn Doors   The first image divides and wipes away to reveal the next image. You can orient the effect vertically or horizontally.

Center Merge   The first image splits into quadrants that converge towards the center to reveal the second image.

Center Split   The first image splits into quadrants that wipe to the corners, revealing the second image.

Clock Wipe   The first image wipes away like a clock to reveal the second image. Eight starting points are available.

Cross Stretch   The first image shrinks away from the selected side as the second image stretches across. You can orient the effect vertically or horizontally.

 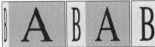

3.0 **Curtain**   The first clip is split and pulled to each side like a curtain to reveal the second clip.

Funnel   The first image is sucked out to the selected side to reveal the second image.

Inset   A growing rectangle wipes over the first image from a selected corner, revealing the second image.

 Pinwheel

[Custom Settings...]

An adjustable number of wedge-shapes widen radially to reveal the second image. Click the "Custom Settings..." button to set from 2 to 32 wedges.

Push   The first image is pushed from the selected side to reveal the second image.

 Quad Slide   The first image slides away in quadrants, revealing the second image.

 Quad Stretch   The first image stretches away in quadrants, revealing the second image.

Quad Wipe   The first image wipes away in quadrants, revealing the second image.

 Quarter Slide   The first image slides away in consecutive quarters, revealing the second image.

Quarter Stretch The first image stretches away in consecutive quarters, revealing the second image.

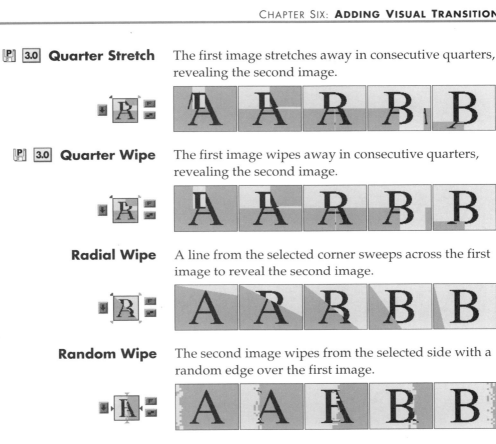

Quarter Wipe The first image wipes away in consecutive quarters, revealing the second image.

Radial Wipe A line from the selected corner sweeps across the first image to reveal the second image.

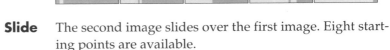

Random Wipe The second image wipes from the selected side with a random edge over the first image.

Slide The second image slides over the first image. Eight starting points are available.

Split The first image splits in the middle and slides away. You can orient the effect horizontally or vertically.

Stretch The second image stretches over the first image. Eight starting points are available. If you choose a corner, the second image zooms in from the selected corner.

Swap　The two images swap positions as they move halfway to opposite sides and then return to center.

Wedge Wipe　Two wipes sweep radially in opposite directions to reveal the next image. Eight starting points are available.

Wipe　The classic wipe—a line moves across to reveal the second image. Orient it horizontally, vertically or diagonally.

▶ **Irises**　Irises expand a simple shape from a single point to reveal the next clip. You can move an iris's center origin point anywhere in the frame by dragging the small white *handle* in the Start window of the Settings dialog box. In fact, when you drag the handle all the way to the frame's side, you often achieve a completely different shape effect.

Start= 25%

 Iris Cross　A cross expands over the first image to reveal the second.

Iris Diamond　A diamond expands to reveal the second image.

Iris Points　Triangular points expand from four sides over the first image to reveal the second image. This is the only iris that doesn't have a handle to drag the effect off-center.

Iris Round

A circle expands over the first image to reveal the second.

Iris Square

A rectangle (with the clip's aspect ratio) expands over the first image to reveal the second image.

Iris Star

A five-pointed star expands over the first image to reveal the second image.

▶ Bands & Blocks

These transitions feature band- or block-shaped regions that move or accumulate to reveal the next clip. Bands transitions appear first below, followed by their blockier **3.0** cousins. In Premiere 3.0, you can customize most of these transitions by clicking the "Custom Settings…" button. Specifying very large custom values, however, may bog down Premiere's processing.

Band Slide

Interlaced bars of the second image slide from opposite sides over the first image. You can orient them horizontally, vertically or diagonally. In Premiere 3.0, click "Custom Settings…" to set from 2 to 1000 bands.

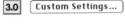

Band Wipe

Interlaced bars of the first image wipe away to opposite edges, revealing the next image. You can orient the effect horizontally, vertically or along opposing corners. In 3.0, click "Custom Settings…" to set from 2 to 1000 bands.

P 3.0 Grid

[Custom Settings...]

In a band-like pattern, a grid fills to reveal the second image. Click the "Custom Settings..." button to set from 2 to 32 grid segments in each direction.

P Origami

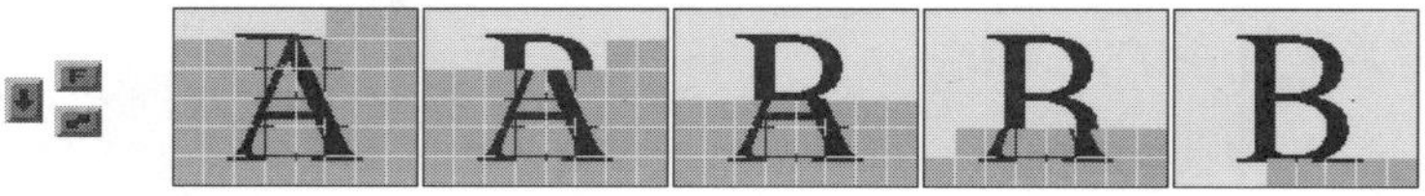

In a band-like pattern, consecutive triangles appear that reveal the next image.

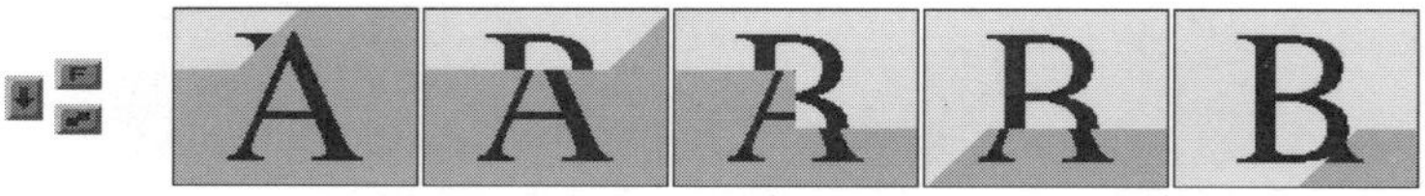

3.0 Slash Slide

Slashes rain on the first image to reveal the second image. Eight start points are available. Click the "Custom Settings..." button to set from 4 to 500 slashes.

Sliding Bands

Sliding bars progressively widen to reveal the second image. You can orient the effect horizontally or vertically.

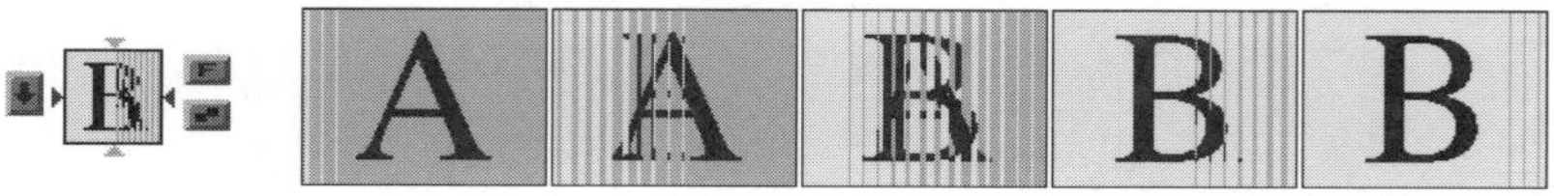

Sliding Boxes

3.0 [Custom Settings...]

Sliding bands—not sliding boxes like the name implies—move across from the selected side and coalesce into the second image. In Premiere 3.0, click "Custom Settings..." to set from 2 to 1000 slices.

Venetian Blinds

3.0 [Custom Settings...]

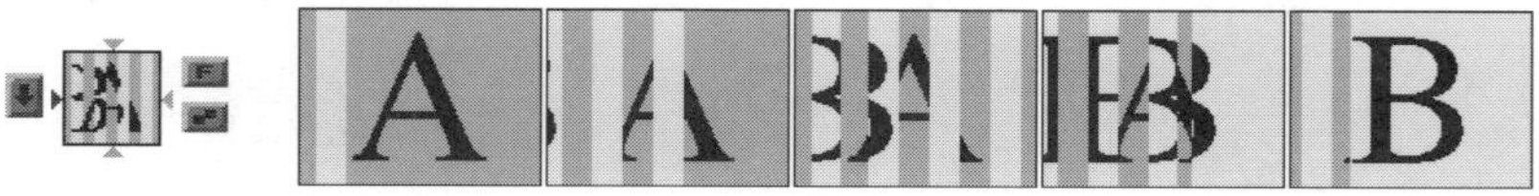

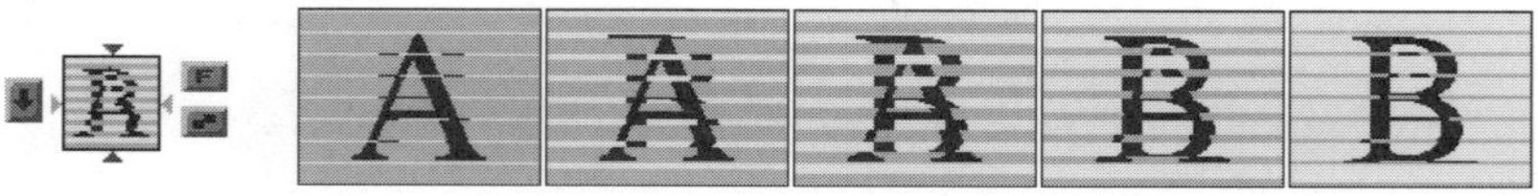

Full-width bars widen to reveal the second image. You can hang the blinds horizontally or vertically. In 3.0, click "Custom Settings..." to set from 2 to 1000 blinds.

Checkerboard

`3.0` [Custom Settings...]

A checkerboard pattern progressively reveals the second image. In Premiere 3.0, click the "Custom Settings..." button to set from 2 to 32 slices horizontally (more slices are possible vertically).

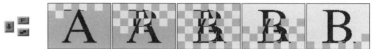

`3.0` **Checker Grid**

[Custom Settings...]

This is similar to Checkerboard (see above) except a grid appears at first. Click the "Custom Settings..." button to set from 2 to 32 slices in each direction.

`3.0` **Mixed Stretch**

[Custom Settings...]

A patchwork pattern of alternating grids stretch and widen to reveal the second image. Click the "Custom Settings..." button to set from 2 to 32 grid segments in horizontal and vertical directions.

`3.0` **Mixed Wipe**

[Custom Settings...]

This is similar to Mixed Stretch (see above) except no stretching of the images occurs—just a wipe. Click the "Custom Settings..." button to set from 2 to 32 grid segments in horizontal and vertical directions.

Triangles

Alternating triangles reveal the next image.

Random Blocks

Small random boxes gradually reveal the second image.

Spiral Boxes

The second image is progressively revealed by a spiral wipe of boxes. In Premiere 3.0, click the "Custom Settings..." button to set from 2 to 32 boxes horizontally (more slices are possible vertically).

3.0 Custom Settings...

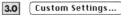

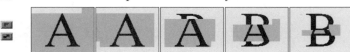

Zig-Zag Blocks

The second image is revealed by a zig-zag wipe path of blocks. In Premiere 3.0, click the "Custom Settings..." button to set from 2 to 32 blocks horizontally (more blocks are possible vertically).

3.0 Custom Settings...

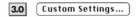

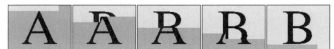

Peels

In a variety of ways, these transitions peel away the first image's surface to reveal the next image. Most give the peeling image an opaque, shadowed back, but some show the image right through—like curling film. Due to their edge-like nature, Premiere does not provide a control to anti-alias these transitions.

Center Peel

The first image peels away to the four corners from a center puncture to reveal the second image.

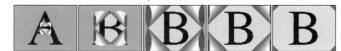

3.0 Fold Up

The first image progressively folds itself in half repeatedly to reveal the second image. The folding image shows through on its back.

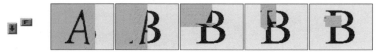

Page Peel

The first image curls away from a selected corner to reveal the second image.

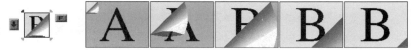

Page Turn

This is just like the Page Peel effect, except the curling image shows through on its backside.

Peel Back

Quarters of the first image peel away to each corner sequentially to reveal the second image.

Roll Away

The first image rolls away from the selected side to reveal the second image. The rolling image shows on its back.

▶ **Spins & Swings**

The first seven members of this group are "spins"—they rotate the first image in some manner to form the transition to the next image. They're followed by three other transitions which "swing" the new image like a door over the prior image. There's enough variety in this bunch to make any viewer (including the moviemaker) dizzy. Premiere LE users take note: Several of these transitions are not a part of your Premiere package.

⚙ **Cube Spin**

The two images appear to be on adjacent faces of a cube that rotates from the first image to the second image. Repeating this over several clips, each originating from a different side of the cube, can further solidify the illusion.

3.0 **Multi-Spin**

An adjustable number of second clip rectangles spin in over the first clip. Click "Custom Settings…" to set from 1 to 32 rectangles horizontally (more are possible vertically).

[Custom Settings…]

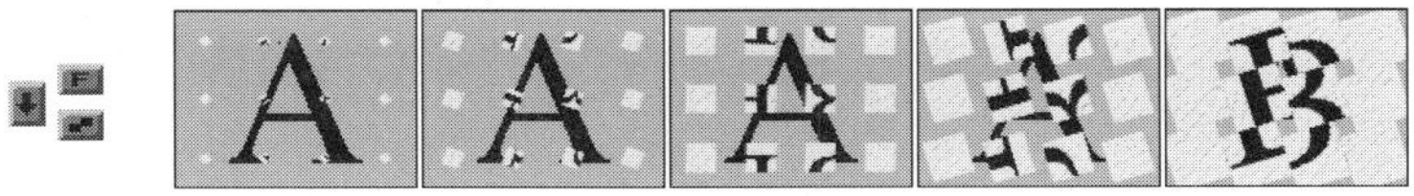

Shutter Slide The first image splits into four quadrants which slide away with a spin, revealing the second image.

Shutter Wipe The first image splits into four quadrants which wipe away with a spin, revealing the second image.

Spin The second image appears to spin along an axis at the center of the first image. You can orient the spin axis horizontally or vertically.

Spin Away This is similar to the Spin transition (see above), but the second image appears in perspective as it rotates—giving a more convincing feeling of depth. You can orient the spin horizontally or vertically.

Swirl An adjustable number of rectangular *pieces* of the second image spin in as a cluster from the center to cover the first image. Click the "Custom Settings..." button to set from 1 to 32 rectangles horizontally (more are possible vertically). Enter 1 for both values to produce a single spinning image. You also can set the spin rate. The default, 100%, is one rotation. Astronomical values are possible for very fast spins—exceeding what's possible with Premiere's motion settings.

Custom Settings...

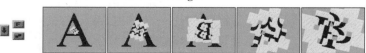

Doors Two doors that split the second image swing together over the first image. The doors can be oriented to swing horizontally or vertically.

 Swing In An inward second image swings from a selected side to cover the first image.

Swing Out An outward second image swings from a selected side to cover the first image.

▶ **Zooms** These effects zoom an image in or out in perspective. Just two are available, but they cover most zooming needs.

Cross Zoom The first image zooms in to pixel-by-pixel level, followed by the second image which zooms back out to normal size. The Premiere 3.0 version of this transition includes adjustable start and end handles. You can drag the handles to independently set the zoom's vanishing point in each direction (center is default).

Zoom The second image zooms in from a vanishing point to cover the first image. It also includes a handle for setting the zoom's vanishing point.

▷ **Maps**

Maps are somewhat different creatures than other Premiere transitions. They can produce interesting visual effects that may be worthy of playback *throughout* a segment's duration, not just as a transition. Some maps create results you can also achieve with Premiere's Transparency Settings (Chapter 10's focus), but applying the effects as transitions is often more accessible.

🔄 **Channel Map**

Use this transition to mix and match color channels from two different clips—mostly for exotic color effects. You can also assign a clip's color channel (or greys) to the *alpha channel*. Used with a movie, the new alpha channel will form a dynamic mask to superimpose over other clips.

📖 *See page 158 for how to work with the Channel Map.*

Greys of an A track movie (left image) are sent into the alpha channel of a B track clip (middle). That's then superimposed over a third clip (far right).

3.0 **Displace**

This transition uses red and green channels in one track's clip (which is called a "displacement map") to *shift* or *displace* pixels in material from the other track.

📖 *See page 159 for much more about Displace.*

The fragmented still-image (left) displaces pixels in the middle clip, producing the shattered image at right.

🔄 **Luminance Map**

Greys of the first image expose the second image. It's most effective for images with a wide range of greys.

The left clip and middle clip are in Tracks A and B. Placing this transition between them results in the far right image.

3.0 **Texturize**

This effect maps the first image on top of the second image. The second image is therefore more subtle than the first image, unless you reverse the effect.

The far right image is the result of this transition between the first two clips.

Three-D

Viewed through 3-D glasses, this transition can add a feeling of depth—one image plays ghost-like over the other. It accomplishes that by mapping the first image to the red RGB channel and the other to blue. (Now if only we all had 3-D glasses…)

▶ **Other Transitions**

Here are the remaining transitions in Premiere. Although listed last, they're very useful for everyday projects as well as snazzier movie ventures.

Direct

3.0 ☞ *Premiere 3.0 users should instead apply the Take transition described below.*

This transition plays B track clips instead of overlapping clips in the A track. Use it when you don't want to trim an A clip to produce an *insert* or *cutaway* to B material.

3.0 **Take**

In Premiere 3.0, Take is a fast alternative to the Direct transition. It also plays B track clips regardless of what's above in the A track. However, Take doesn't have to compile frames to do that (unless filters or other effects in the B clip require compiling). That's why it's faster.

PICT Mask

☞ *Even if you select a grey-scale image, the PICT mask will be black or white.*

After dragging this transition into the T Track, a window opens for you to select a still-image PICT file as a mask. The mask defines which portions of each clip will appear. Monochrome PICTs produce the most predictable results.

Black areas in the PICT show the first clip; white pixels reveal the second clip (but you can reverse that). Anti-aliasing is also available for the edges.

Paint Splatter

This wild effect reveals the second image through drippy paint splats that accumulate on the first image.

📖 *See page 161 for how to modify the Paint Splatter effect to create custom pattern effects.*

With some simple hacks in ResEdit, you can customize this effect with your own series of PICT shapes. The next section will show you how— together with several other power techniques for creating new transitions.

Transition Acrobatics

If you're hungry for *more* effects, this section is for you. You'll see how to freeze, combine, multiply or hack Premiere's existing collection of transitions. With these techniques you'll gain several new ways to move from one image to the next—as well as some intriguing visual effects applicable to a wide range of projects.

▶ Frozen Effects

Let's try the simplest technique first. You can "freeze" the action of transitions to produce *insets* and various *split screens*. Although similar results are possible with Premiere's motion settings or transparency settings (the subjects of Chapters 8 and 10), using transitions is often quicker for basic compositions. Here's the scoop:

1 In the Construction window, align the two clips you want to show together in the A and B tracks. Then drag a transition between them, making sure it extends the full length of both clips. Use iris or zoom transitions to create insets. For split screens, various wipe transitions are ideal (as you'll see on the next page).

Align two clips and a transition— the first frozen step.

Note: Example clips at right are alone in the tracks for clarity. In a real project, of course, other clips and transitions would likely surround the segment.

2 Double-click the transition to open its Settings dialog box. Then hold down the Shift key as you drag a preview slider to lock both sliders at the *same* percentage. The percentage you select determines an inset's size or a split-screen's location.

In this Zoom transition example, the Shift key was held down to move both sliders simultaneously to the 50% point.

☞ Turning on the "Show actual sources" check box can help with positioning.

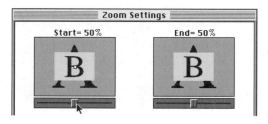

Start= 50%

For more about transition controls, see page 131.

3 If you're working with a zoom or iris transition, use the handle in the Start preview window to move the inset to a desired location in the frame. Other controls in the dialog box also may need attention, depending on the effect you want to achieve. For example, you may want to click the Track Direction button to put the A clip in the inset. Or perhaps you want to add a color border around the inset with the Border slider and Color box.

4 Click OK in the Settings dialog box when you're done. Then preview the results.

Below are three examples of insets you can create.

Here are insets produced by freezing iris transitions or the Zoom transition.

Iris Round   Iris Square   Zoom

Notice that the last example—Zoom—shows *the entire clip at reduced size* in the inset window. However, iris transitions show *part of the clip at full-size* in the inset.

If your subject doesn't fit in an inset or split-screen—or is elsewhere in the frame—you'll need to use Premiere's motion settings. See Chapter 8.

Three more examples are below, using frozen wipe transitions to create a split-screen.

Many varieties of split-screens are possible with frozen wipes.

Wipe   Wedge Wipe   Radial Wipe

If you need a different split-screen than what's shown here, create a garbage matte. See page 264 for details.

The first example—the Wipe transition—can split the frame horizontally or vertically at mid-point, third-point or anywhere else in the frame. (Keep in mind that a similar transition—Slide—also can split the frame this way, but it will show the *same* side of both images next to each other.) The other examples above show how the Wedge Wipe transition splits slightly offset from the corners, unlike Radial Wipe's purely corner-bound appearance.

▶ Back-to-Back Transitions

This second technique is fairly straightforward, too. Almost any wipe transition applied twice (back-to-back) can appear as a new single transition. Simply butt two clips together in the A or B track. Then place and align a wipe transition under each clip, as shown below.

The two clips and two copies of the Spin Away transition are placed sequentially.

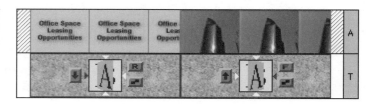

The key is to set the second transition's controls to complement the action of the first transition. For example, notice the Track Direction button in the second Spin Away icon is the opposite of the first Spin Away copy. The opposite starting point triangle is activated too. Depending on the effect, you may need to switch the Forward/Reverse button also.

With the controls as shown above, back-to-back Spin Away transitions can produce the following results.

Spin Away gives a feeling of depth as the clip plane rotates. Other swinging transitions such as Doors, Swing In and Swing Out can produce similar effects.

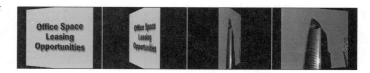

The above example uses black as the transition background. Of course, a clip you are transitioning to or from can instead be in the other track. But if you are using this technique to form a stand-alone segment, a simple clip such as a cloud scene or solid color matte will work effectively for the background, too.

If you prefer that your clip images remain more stable and only the transitional element moves, try the back-to-back technique with other wipes, such as:

Band Wipe

In Premiere 3.0, the Band Wipe transition is even handier than in 2.0 because you can set the number of bands with the Custom Settings dialog box. Be sure to set the Track Direction button to the opposite direction in the second transition so the second-half of the effect flows in the same direction as the first-half.

Here, the Band Wipe effect has two bands. Notice the clip images do not move as the transition progresses.

Pinwheel

This new Premiere 3.0 transition provides a psychedelic look when set to a high number of wedges and placed back-to-back. Of course, fewer wedges also are effective but less exotic.

This Pinwheel example shows 32 wedges, the maximum number possible.

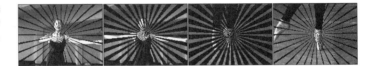

Rather than using the same transition in a back-to-back fashion, let's see how applying more than one transition *to the same segment* can produce new effects.

▶ Effects on Other Effects

There are thousands of ways to combine two different Premiere transitions. Fortunately, choosing a combination isn't so mind-numbing when you realize that certain transitions work together more effectively than others. Although this section by no means presents the only marriages made-in-heaven, here are a few strong prospects.

Fading Transitions

For a subtle touch to the end of any wipe-style transition, fade out the effect towards its end. You could use one of Premiere's dissolve transitions to produce the fade, but there's an easier way: Take advantage of the fade lines that S track clips offer.

First overlap the two clips you want to transition in the A and B tracks. Then drag a transition into the overlapping area in the T track. Next (here's the new part) place a copy of the B clip into the S track, trimming its length to match the transition. Last, adjust that clip's

📖 *For more about how to fade superimposed clips, see page 258.*

fader to start at 0% opacity and conclude at 100%. Altogether, your Construction window tracks should look something like below.

This Construction window layout can successfully fade the end of any selected transition.

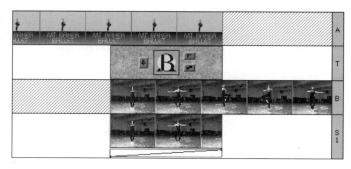

With this arrangement, the S clip becomes more visible as the iris transition expands. That gradually blends together outside and inside areas of the iris shape.

With the Iris Round transition, the result is akin to an exploding QuickTime nova.

Wiping an Iris or Zoom

Another interesting combination is to wipe an expanding iris or zoom transition. For example, you could apply a Clock Wipe to an expanding Iris Round, as shown below.

This combination produces a quasi-spiral effect.

3.0

To combine two such transitions, you need to compile the same clips twice. Premiere 3.0's virtual clips feature greatly simplifies this—if you follow these steps:

1 Arrange the two clips you want to show in the A and B tracks of the Construction window—well past where your movie will extend in the time-line. This area will become your virtual clip "pasteboard."

2 Drag a wipe transition (such as Clock Wipe) in the overlapping area between the two clips. (Make sure the Track Selection arrow points down). Then using the

📖 *For more about creating virtual clips, see page 78.*

Marquee tool, select the transition segment and drag (with Shift-Option keys down) to create a virtual clip without any audio.

Use 3.0's Marquee tool to select the transition segment, as shown at right. Then create a video-only virtual clip by holding the Shift-Option keys down as you drag the block selection.

3 Place the virtual clip at the desired location in your movie in the B track. Then copy the first clip that was in your "pasteboard" area and paste that copy in the A track above the virtual clip. Finally, drag an iris or zoom transition between the two, such as an Iris Round. That's all—go ahead and preview the effect.

When you're done, the Construction window should look like this.

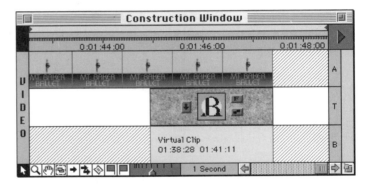

2.0 Premiere 2.0 users also can follow the above process even though virtual clips are not available. For the second step, *compile* the segment in the "pasteboard area" to build a new source clip. (To do that, place the yellow work area bar over the segment and issue the "Make Movie…" command from the Project menu. Be sure to set the Output pop-up menu to "Work Area" in the Project Output Options dialog box.) After compiling the clip, substitute it for the virtual clip in the third step above.

☞ *Be sure to compile with the None compressor and the highest image quality so the clip's image is not altered.*

If you prefer to wipe a "frozen" iris or zoom (the effect we explored at the beginning of this chapter section), you'll need to open the iris or zoom transition's Settings dialog box and move the two preview sliders to the same percentage. An example of such results is below.

The frozen Iris Round transition defines the inset and the Clock Wipe wipes it.

A similar approach is to use one of the swinging transitions to "open" an inset. For example, a frozen Zoom transition could form a window within the movie frame that the Doors transition opens.

After this sequence, zoom the inset window to full-frame size for a snazzy way to follow the title.

Perpendicular Bands

The last effects combination we'll explore works well with band-like transitions, such as Venetian Blinds, Band Wipe, and Sliding Bands. Use the same process described earlier for wiping an iris or zoom transition—with one exception: Instead of applying a *different* second transition, *use the same effect twice*—orienting the second effect *perpendicular* to the first.

Change the second effect's orientation by clicking the perpendicular set of triangles in its icon.

3.0

[**Custom Settings...**]

In Premiere 3.0, you can additionally use a band-like transition's Custom Settings to tailor the number of bands that appear in each direction.

Let's quickly look over a few examples of the technique. Combining horizontal and vertical orientations of the Sliding Bands transition produces this result:

The Sliding Bands combination reveals the next clip through an interesting moving texture.

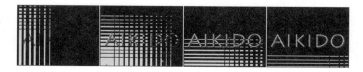

3.0

Premiere 3.0's new Slash Slide transition is also a good candidate for this effect. Set it to slash from two corners, for example, for a very active transition.

Consider this when you need a very aggressive transition.

Applying a Venetian Blinds transition in both orientations at once builds a nicely evolving grid transition.

Remember that 3.0's Custom Settings for this transition can further tailor the grid effect.

▶ Virtual Clip Mirrors

3.0

This next technique doesn't produce a new transition. But it uses a transition and Premiere 3.0's virtual clip capabilities to create a cool double-mirror effect. The key is to nest a virtual clip within itself. Here's how:

📖 *For more about creating virtual clips, see page 78.*

1 Place a clip in Track A. Use the Marquee tool to select all or part of it, then drag to create a virtual clip (with Option-Shift keys down to leave out audio).

2 Place the virtual clip in the B track directly under the first clip. Then drag a Zoom transition between them. The Construction window should look like below.

The virtual clip lies nested in the same segment that originally created the virtual clip.

3 Double-click the Zoom icon to open its Settings dialog box. Set the preview sliders to the same start and end value, such as 75%. Adjust other transition controls in the dialog box if desired, then click OK.

Now preview the results. Barbershop mirrors! You'll end up with an image within the same image, for as many iterations as Premiere allows your virtual clip to go.

To change the iteration depth, visit "Virtual Clips…" in the Preferences submenu of the File menu. You can go up to 64 levels, but the compiling time may be monstrous.

Although this mirrors effect may never be useful to you, treat it as inspiration (or titillation) for experimenting with other transitions and nested virtual clips.

▶ Unfolding the Channel Map

Now let's take a few moments to plot our path with the Channel Map. This transition has plenty of creative potential that may not be immediately obvious.

After you drag the Channel Map transition into the T track, the following dialog box appears.

All four pop-up menus hold the same choices that are shown in this last menu. The menus allow you to selectively combine channels in a variety of ways for the movie output.

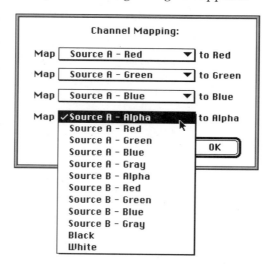

At first blush, you can use this to create advanced (or crazy) color effects. As shown above, the first three pop-up menus can map any channel from clips in Track A or B to each color channel of the output. With the right set of clips, that can produce interesting color collages.

The far right image is the result of mapping two color channels of the left image with the greys of the middle image.

You also can align copies of the *same* clip in Track A and B, apply different filters or other effects to each copy, and then recombine them with the Channel Map into a single modified image. Surprising results can occur.

There's another compelling purpose for this transition, too. The bottom pull-down menu sends an image component to the output's *alpha channel*. Eureka! That's how you can add an alpha channel to *any* visual clip in Premiere.

An alpha channel is an extra, invisible layer of an image that acts as a mask to define which parts of the image will be transparent or opaque. Grey values in the alpha channel define the transparency of pixels in the clip when it's superimposed over other clips.

3.0 ☞ *Premiere 3.0's Track Matte key type can produce similar moving masks—although not normally based on a single color channel. See page 272.*

When you apply the Channel Map's alpha abilities to a movie clip, you can produce an alpha channel that *changes* over time. That's called a *moving mask* or a *traveling matte*. Their dynamic nature invites all sorts of creative experiments with superimposed clips—a topic we'll explore further in Chapter 10. Before we move on, here's a quick peek at the idea to whet your appetite.

Greys of a B track animation are sent to the alpha channel of this segment's output. Other pop-up menu's of the Channel Map transition are left alone to retain the Track A image.

When compiled (with 3.0's virtual clips or 2.0's Make Movie command) and superimposed (in this case, over another gradient clip), you have a moving mask.

▶ Displacement Map Shifts

Let's explore the Displace transition a bit further. It's similar to the Displace filter in Photoshop. Like the Channel Map transition we just visited, Displace's potential isn't obvious at first glance.

This transition's purpose is to shift pixels in one track's clips based on color intensities of the material in the other track (which is called a "displacement map").

The red intensity in the displacement map controls how far pixels shift horizontally in the other image; the green intensity controls vertical shift.

With this transition and the appropriate displacement map image, you can sag a clip's image downward like a cloth held by its top corners. Or you can bevel or bulge a clip outward—or fragment a clip's image like shatters of glass. The possibilities are endless. Although the fancy name "displacement map" is used in this context, the map can really be *any* clip.

See this book's Goodies disk for displacement map examples that you can experiment with on your clips. Photoshop also ships with several examples—try those in Premiere.

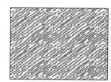

The textured still-image (left) displaces pixels in the middle clip, producing the altered image at right.

Here's one other spiffy example: Use a high-contrast movie of a person or other entity moving across a flat-color background as the displacement map. (Apply Premiere's *Brightness & Contrast* filter or the *Extract* filter to the clip if necessary to produce a high-contrast image that isolates the subject and background.) With the Displace transition, the high-contrast entity will end up as a transparent, lurking presence in the other track's clip.

With this transition, the high contrast hawk in one clip (left) displaces pixels in the middle gradient clip, creating a more mysterious hawk at far right.

Besides this basic shiftiness to Displace's character, keep in mind you can control the effect in several ways by accessing the transition's Custom Settings.

Enter a scale which multiplies the intensity of the pixel displacement.

Turn on the check box to have the intensity of the displacement map's blue channel lighten or darken the visible image.

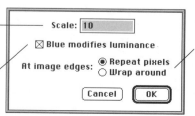

Decide how to treat new edge pixels that are pulled into the shifted image. "Repeat pixels" extends the color of the former edge pixels. "Wrap around" gives the new pixels the color of pixels on the opposite side of the frame.

▶ Custom Paint Splats

We've reached the last technique of this chapter. (Whew!) In either version of Premiere, you can create custom pattern transitions based on the *Paint Splatter* transition. All you have to do is draw a pattern progression in a paint program and make a few ResEdit tweaks to the Paint Splatter plug-in that's featured on page 149.

ResEdit

Although the thought of hacking with ResEdit strikes fear into many users, it's really no problem as long as you work with copies of files. Here are the steps.

1 Using a paint program, create a set of black and white 320 x 240 PICT images that progress from almost all white to almost all black. They can be organic shapes like Paint Splatter or a more regular pattern. Use as many frames as you want, although 25 or less is best (Paint Splatter uses 9 frames).

Frames appear here around each image in this progression for clarity but should not be part of your pasted PICT in ResEdit unless you want a one-pixel border around your movie.

☞ *The transition based on this illustration is "Origami." You'll find it on the book's Goodies disk.*

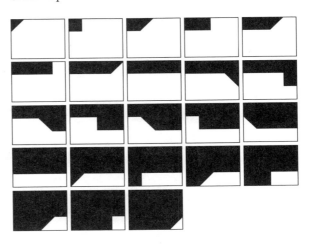

Paint Splatter copy

2 In your Mac's Finder, make a copy of the Paint Splatter effect plug-in that's in your Premiere Plug-Ins folder. Give the file a new name that describes your new transition.

Origami

3 Open your newly-named transition in ResEdit. Select the *ICNc* resource, then choose "Clear" in the File menu to delete the resource entirely. Next, double-click the *PICT* resource to open its window. Choose "Select All" and then "Clear" to delete all existing PICT resources. Keep the PICT window open for the next step.

If you are using Photoshop 2.0, set clipboard preferences to 1-bit. In Photoshop 2.5, you must copy from a 1-bit document.

4 Switch back to your paint document that holds your PICT images. Copy the first PICT in your pattern (the mostly-white frame). Then switch to ResEdit and paste the image in the empty PICT resource window. Repeat this process one-by-one for all of your images. The last image should be your almost-black PICT. Keep in mind the PICT resources in ResEdit must be numbered sequentially from 128 (which ResEdit does by default).

In the PICT view of the ResEdit window, each image you paste will look squished since it has to conform to the available resource squares. But that won't affect your final results.

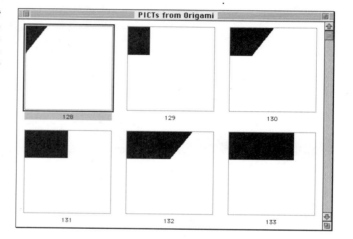

5 Close the PICT resource window. Then double-click the *TEXT* resource icon and open resource number 1000 (which should be the only item). This holds the description that appears in Premiere's Transitions window. Change the text to briefly describe your new effect.

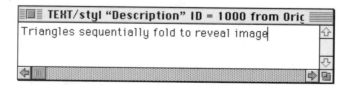

6 Close the TEXT box and save the new effect. Then quit ResEdit and drag the new plug-in into your Premiere Plug-ins folder. Congratulations, you've just authored a new piece of software—at least sort of. (Time to switch careers—ooops, just kidding.)

Adobe Premiere™ Plug-Ins

That's it! The next time you run Premiere, you'll have the new transition available in the Transitions window—using the frames you created.

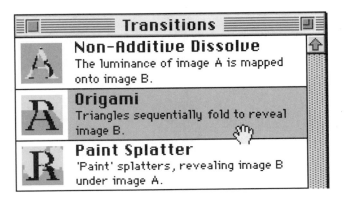

▶ Fading to Filters

Believe it or not, the transitions we've just finished exploring only scratch the surface of Premiere's creative effects. Take a break and then get ready to soar some more. We'll explore Premiere's powerful filters next.

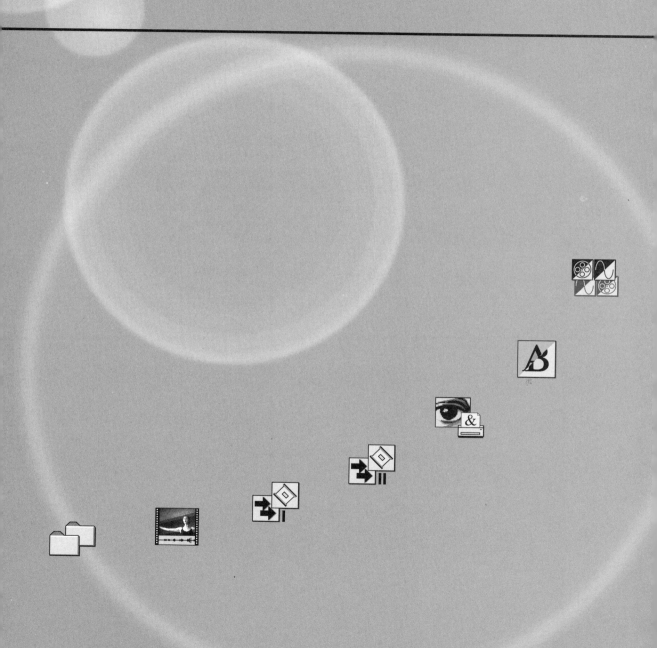

7

Applying Digital Filters

Premiere's digital filters aren't a prerequisite for quality QuickTime results, but when applied wisely they can magnify the communicative power of even the most straightforward movie. This chapter explores filters thoroughly to help you take advantage of such magic.

First we'll cover every angle of applying filters to all or part of a clip. Then we'll visually tour and assess all of Premiere's four-dozen-plus filter specimens (so you don't have to spend a week or two doing that yourself).

The creative possibilities of Premiere's filters will make you dizzy, but these pages will keep you in control. Hold your hat as we try a few *loop de loops*!

Filter Techniques

☞ *Premiere's filters modify a single clip. Transitions work between clips. Both species create special effects.*

Before we go bananas exploring Premiere's tantalizing filter effects, let's first nail down the *process* of applying filters to a clip. This topic isn't as flashy but is the key to achieving fresh, professional results with filters. Along the way you'll also see how to preview filters accurately, how to filter just part of a clip and how to manage the growing list of filters Premiere provides for you.

▶ Adding Filters to a Clip

Hitching filters onto a clip requires only a few steps that you'll quickly pick up. Keep an eye out for time-saving tricks as we go through the process. Since you'll likely apply filters often, your time-savings will add up fast.

☞ *If you're building an edit decision list, forget about filters. See page 337.*

1 In the Construction window, select a clip. Then choose "Filters…" under Premiere's Clip menu (Command F). Or use this handy shortcut: Place the arrow cursor (the Selection tool) on the clip. Then hold down the Option key and your mouse button to get a

To apply a new filter, select "Filters…" in the pop-up menu.

pop-up menu. Select "Filters…"—if it's a virgin clip, that's all you'll see in the menu.

2 In the Filters dialog box that appears, choose a filter from Premiere's many offerings. The left scroll box alphabetically lists the available flavors for your clip.

The Filters dialog box shows all available Premiere filters. If you're working on a sound clip, the Available list will only contain audio filters.

☞ *Type the first letter or two of an available filter's name to select it quickly. You can use arrow keys to move up or down the Available or Current list.*

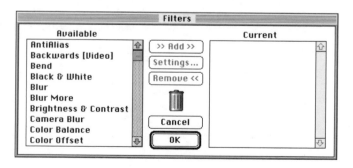

To apply a filter to your clip, move the item into the Current box. The quickest way is to double-click a filter's name—or just drag it over. But you also can select the filter and click the box's Add button or tap the Enter key.

To remove a filter from the Current list, select it and tap the Delete key or click the box's Remove button. Or drag and dump the unwanted filter into the prominent trash can in the dialog box's center.

3 Most Premiere filters have adjustable settings. After adding such a filter to the Current list, a new dialog box will eagerly appear for fine-tuning. Applying the Brightness & Contrast filter, for example, calls up this box.

As you adjust filter settings, the preview window will instantly show the results. Click OK when you're done.

Premiere 3.0's version of this dialog box appears at right, but 2.0's is similar.

Premiere 3.0 users can rejoice over the new Zoom tool and Hand tool that sit next to a filter's preview window. Use that duo to give you a close-up of the filter's effect.

To zoom the preview image larger, choose the Zoom tool and click in the image where you want to zoom. You can zoom up to ten times size. To zoom back towards the original size, Option-click with the Zoom tool.

Double-click the Zoom tool *icon* to see the image at *actual* size (the size of the source clip). To indicate you're at that true size, Premiere 3.0 will outline the plus or minus sign in the zoom cursor.

Use the Hand tool to shift the zoomed image portion that appears in the preview window. Double-click the Hand tool *icon* to return the image to original size.

Here's one more preview shortcut: Press the spacebar while using the Zoom tool to switch temporarily to the Hand tool. Press the Command key while using the hand to switch temporarily to the zoom.

☞ *If RAM is tight or the General Preference setting for these tools is turned off, the tools won't be available. See page 298.*

4 Add more filters to the clip if desired. To do that, repeat the previous two steps. You can combine any number of filters—in any order—for interesting (and

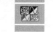

sometimes bizarre) results. You also can apply the same filter repeatedly to INTENSIFY a particular effect. The only limiting factor is your time. More filters will take more time to fine-tune, preview and compile.

As you add more filters, you may need to adjust an earlier one. To re-visit a filter's dialog box, double-click the filter in the Current list. Or select the filter and click the Settings button.

☞ The Settings button appears active for any selected filter, but only works for adjustable filters.

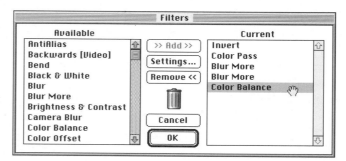

You don't have to add filters in order. Premiere is forgiving if you prefer to select filters ad hoc. You can rearrange the Current list anytime by dragging filters up or down with the mouse. The *final* order of filters, though, is very important. Premiere applies filters to a clip in the order shown in the Current box. Depending on the filters, the order will greatly influence your results. For visual evidence of this fact, look over the examples below.

Using the Invert filter first or last determines whether the original clip—or the results of other filters—are inverted.

Invert
Emboss
Brightness & Contrast

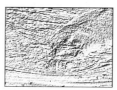

Emboss
Brightness & Contrast
Invert

Applying the Solarize filter after Tiles modifies the original clip image and the tile edges.

Solarize
Tiles

Tiles
Solarize

5 When you're done adding and adjusting filters, bless the Filters dialog box with your OK. The filtered clip will then sport a racy blue stripe along the top of its Construction window thumbnail—your clue that filters have been applied to the clip.

As you continue to edit a project in the Construction window, you'll find yourself frequently re-visiting filter settings (since getting settings right the first time is rare for most of us mortals). The speediest way to do that is to use the pop-up menu shortcut described in Step 1 three pages back. (Hold down the Option key and mouse button with the arrow cursor over the clip.)

☞ Use the pop-up menu to quickly answer "What filters went on which clips?" In complex projects, that question will arise frequently as you work.

Besides *Filters*, the pop-up menu will list every filter you've applied to the clip. Selecting a filter directly in the pop-up menu will avoid a longer trip through the Filters dialog box to reach a filter's settings.

▶ **Pass the Filters, Please**

The five-step process we just walked through applies filters to *one* clip at a time. If you have several clips that need the same filters and filter settings, the one-by-one approach would quickly become dreary. A serious Premiere limitation? Not really, because the "Paste Special..." command can ride to your rescue.

In a nutshell, here's how: Apply filters to one clip and massage the filter settings as desired. Then select and copy the clip in the Construction window (Command C). Now select another clip you want to filter similarly and trigger "Paste Special..." in the File menu (Command H).

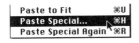

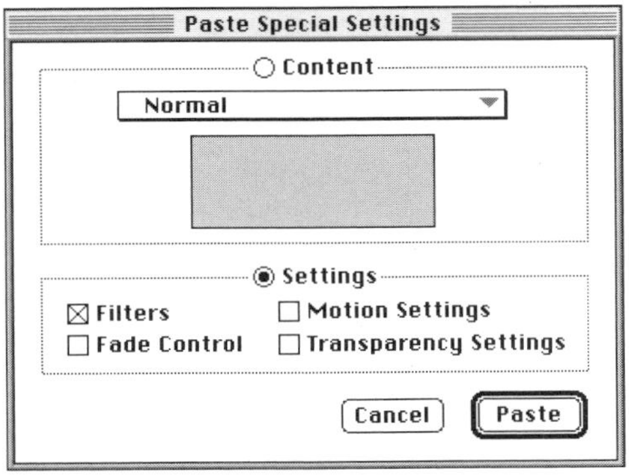

The Paste Special Settings dialog box can quickly transfer the filter settings of a copied clip to a selected clip. For this task, you can ignore the "Content" half of the dialog box.

📖 For more about using the "Paste Special..." command, see page 87.

At a minimum, turn on the Settings button and the Filters check box, as shown above. Then click the Paste button or hit your Return key. Presto! The second clip now has identical filtering.

To paste the same filter arrangement repeatedly, select another clip in the Construction window and choose "Paste Special Again." In Premiere 3.0, you also can select *several* clips with the Track or Multi-Track tool and then issue "Paste Special…" or "Paste Special Again." That will apply the copied filter settings to *all* selected clips at once. Click relief at last!

▶ **Secrets of Filter Previewing**

Knowing the three secrets of filter previews will further speed your filter efforts. They solve problems that aren't immediately obvious, but can (painfully) slow you down.

Secret #1: Previewing the Preview-less

The built-in preview in a filter's dialog box is the quickest way to see the visual impact of filter settings—as well as the cumulative effect of any previous filters.

This Brightness and Contrast filter was applied after the Pointillize filter. The Brightness & Contrast filter's preview image therefore shows the effects of both filters.

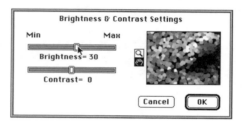

Unfortunately, built-in previews are available in less than half of all Premiere filters—including many of the most popular ones. To preview the preview-less filters, you can rely on Premiere's regular preview methods (described in Chapter 5). But there's a sneakier alternative that's often more convenient—especially if you're still working in the Filters dialog box. *Simply add the Color Balance filter after any filter that lacks a built-in preview.* Then use *its* preview image to see the results of prior filtering.

In this example, neither the Tiles or Sharpen Edges filters have a preview window. The Color Balance filter does, however, and has no effect on the clip at its 100% default settings. This trick also works with the Brightness & Contrast filter and other filters with default "neutral" settings.

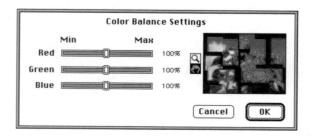

Secret #2: Size-Sensitivities

No matter which preview you set your sights on (a filter's built-in preview or a separate preview image), remember this: many Premiere filters are *size-sensitive*. If the preview image is a different size than your final output, *size-sensitive filters will not preview WYSIWYG*. Let's use the Pointillize filter to illustrate this size phenomenon.

In the half-size (120 x 90) Preview window (left image), Pointillize elements appear twice the size of what's compiled in the final 240 x 180 movie (right).

What happened? Premiere applied the filter *directly* to the preview image. It didn't process the filter with the clip's *original* image and then scale the results to fit in the smaller preview image. What you see in a preview may not always be what you get in your final movie.

In Premiere 3.0, you can avoid the problem if you set the "Process at" option in the Preview Option's dialog box to your final output size. In Premiere 2.0 or 3.0, you also can accurately preview size-sensitive filters by:

⊠ Process at: 240 h 180 v

 For more about the "Process at" option, see page 117.

• using the "Make Movie…" command to compile the segment into a preview movie at your final output size

• setting the Preview window (at least temporarily) to your final output size before triggering a preview

All of these methods require additional compiling time, however. If you're desperate for greater preview speed, you may have to just stay aware of the size issue as you work with previews. Later in this chapter, we'll flag all of Premiere's size-sensitive filters (with the icon at left) to help you avoid such nasty visual surprises.

Secret #3: A Different Preview Frame

 For more about setting place markers, see page 56.

This last secret is short and sweet. In Premiere 2.0, to see a different frame in a filter's built-in preview, you have to temporarily change the clip's In point. In Premiere 3.0, however, simply attach a "0" place marker to the frame you want to see. That frame will appear in the filter's built-in preview instead of the In point.

▶ **Variable Strength Filtering**

📖 *For more about using the Razor tool, see page 80.*

Frequently, you may need to vary a filter's strength within a clip. Maybe the clip has to integrate well with surrounding material. Maybe you only want to filter part of a clip. Perhaps you just seek another expressive dimension for your movie composition.

Let's solve the easiest situation first: filtering only part of a clip. The solution is straightforward. In the Construction window, slice the clip with the Razor tool where you want the filter(s) to begin and end. Then select the clippette and apply filters to your heart's content.

Now for the greater challenge: *gradually* varying filter settings during a clip. The problem is that Premiere filters generally are an all-or-nothing proposition. Most filters apply their power to a clip at a constant level—they're *static*. Only a few Premiere filters, such as Mosaic and Mesh Warp, are *progressive*—offering start and end settings so you can gradually vary their strength.

To become a variable virtuoso with static filters requires extra work. You have to slice the clip into pieces and give each one incrementally different filter settings. You also have to use the Cross Dissolve transition to blend the pieces smoothly. Here's the seven-step process:

👉 *Turn on "Snap to edges" (Tab key) to align in a snap.*

1 Place a copy of the same clip in the A and B video tracks of the Construction window, precisely aligning their In and Out points.

2 Drag the Cross Dissolve transition into the T track (the F/X Track in 2.0) between the two clips, aligning it along the clips' left edges. Then drag the transition's right edge so its duration is one second.

Depending on the smoothness you want, you can use a different interval than one second for the transition.

3 Select the B track clip and apply a filter (or combination of filters) to it. For this example, the Posterize filter was chosen and set to 32 colors, as shown below.

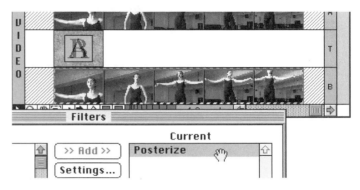

4 Now use the Razor tool to slice the A Track clip to match the right edge of the Cross Dissolve transition. Then apply your chosen filter(s) to the remainder of the A Track clip, incrementing the filter settings as desired. Below, the A clip is posterized to 24 colors.

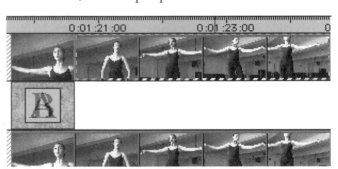

5 Paste a copy of the Cross Dissolve transition to the right of the original in the T track. Then point the copy's Track Selector button upward. Depending on your Construction window display, the button may not be visible in the track. You may have to double-click the transition first to call up its Settings dialog box.

6 With the Razor tool, slice the B Track clip at the two-second mark (or where the second Cross Dissolve transition ends if you're using different intervals). Then select the B clip portion that's right of the razor cut and apply filter(s) at incrementally different settings.

7 Continue to slice both clips into two-second pieces, incrementing their filter settings further. Then copy and paste alternate versions of the Cross Dissolve transition (with a downward and then upward Track Selector button) until you reach the end of your segment. Such a Construction window arrangment will follow the white arrow path shown below. Upon finishing, preview your quasi-progressive filter results.

The slices in one video track should fall at the mid-point between slices of the other track. The Cross Dissolve transitions should alternately flow down then up, as shown by the white arrow.

Whew! Coercing a static filter to be progressive requires several steps and some time, but can lead to high quality movie results. Now let's turn our attention to hurdling over a different Premiere filter limitation: applying filters to only part of a clip's image.

▶ Filtering Part of the Image

Premiere's visual filters affect the entire clip image. Unlike Photoshop, a marquee to select part of an image is not available. As always, a few ways have been cooked up to get around this problem. To filter only part of a clip's image, consider either of the following approaches.

Freeze a Transition
This first option is accessible to all Premiere users (including those with LE). You can "freeze" a transition's effect to define a filtered area within a clip's image. Chapter 6 also covers this technique. In brief, here's a recap:

For more about "freezing" a transition, see page 150.

Align copies of the same clip in the A and B video tracks. Then drag a transition into the T track for the segment's entire duration. Iris and Zoom transitions supply useful regular shapes, but other transitions can successfully define more exotic filter boundaries.

In this example, the Iris Round transition is placed between two copies of the same clip.

👉 *For a custom-shaped filter boundary with this technique, use the PICT Mask transition. See page 149.*

Double-click the transition to view its Settings dialog box. Then freeze the transition's action—set its Start and End values to the same percentage by Shift-dragging one of the preview sliders in the dialog box.

In this example, the Iris Round transition is frozen at 50%.

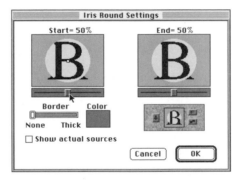

Finally, apply filter(s) to one clip, leaving the other clip alone. Also click the transition's Track Selection button if necessary to change where filtering appears. Brightness & Contrast and Posterize effects surround the subject at left.

Use Transparency Settings

This second approach to filtering part of a clip's image is much more versatile and takes advantage of Premiere's *Transparency Settings*. Although that's the subject of Chapter 10, here's an early preview if you can't wait.

1 Drag and align copies of the same clip into a video track and an S track (the Super track in 2.0).

Copies of the same clip sit aligned in the A track and a superimposing track.

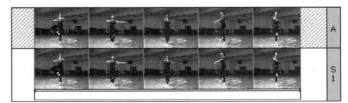

Key Type:

2 Select the S Track clip and choose "Transparency Settings…" in the Project menu (Command T). The dialog box that appears holds several ways to superimpose part of a clip's image—either as a static mask or a moving mask. Chapter 10 delves into the choices in detail. The idea to remember now, though, is to superimpose just *the image portion you want to filter*. Then click OK.

📖 *For more about alpha channel mattes, see page 269.*

3 Apply one or more filters to the S track clip. Then preview the segment. Portions of the filtered clip will appear superimposed over the untouched clip. In the example at left, Blur More and Brightness & Contrast filters limited to the clip's outer regions. The oval shape is a simple alpha channel matte that you can create with Premiere's Title window—more about that ahead.

▶ Managing Filters

Here's a final issue to chew on before we visit each filter. In the Filters dialog box, the long alphabetical list of available filters can intimidate instead of inspire. Most users will have to stay on their toes to remember (or find) a particular filter. The problem becomes worse if you throw Photoshop or third-party filters into Premiere.

To manage the filter scene better, try the same trick that's suggested in the previous chapter for transitions: *rename* the plug-in files. Each filter is a file sitting in Premiere's Plug-Ins folder. Giving them new names can re-sort their order in the Filters dialog box. So you can:

1. Put Favorite Filters First

Add a space or two in front of the names of filters you rely on most frequently. They'll appear at the top of the Available filters list.

Current name	New Name
AntiAlias	Blur; AntiAlias
Blur	Blur; Basic
Blur More	Blur; More
Camera Blur	Blur; Camera
Gaussian Blur	Blur; Gaussian
Radial Blur	Blur; Radial

2. Group Filters By Category

To cluster related filters together in the Available list, precede each filter name with a category name. For example, you could re-label Blur filters (which are alphabetically scattered all over) as shown at left.

As you peruse the rest of this chapter, you'll gain a better feel for filter groupings that may work well for you.

Filters in Focus

It's time to explore the nooks and crannies of every Premiere filter. Get ready for plenty of filtered movie examples and a close look at each filter's settings. And watch for several fruitful filter combinations.

The filters are organized in the following pages by what they *do* (see the list at left). Yes, the classification scheme may seem a bit arbitrary and some filters fail to fit neatly into one category. But this approach is a step ahead of a purely alphabetical list. Here you can more easily compare related filters based on your general intent and then decide which one to use.

In time-tight projects, a filter's impact on movie compiling speed can also be a deciding factor besides aesthetics. (Alas, sometimes there's never enough Mac muscle available.) Especially slow Premiere filters therefore earn the following watch icon to warn you ahead of time: Perhaps Photoshop-style hardware acceleration of all Premiere filters will someday appear. Meanwhile, apply slower filters judiciously when deadlines loom.

There's one other unique icon to watch for in the pages ahead. As you discovered earlier in this chapter, preview windows that are smaller than your final movie's frame size will not show size-sensitive filters accurately (unless you take one of the steps mentioned on page 171). So those potentially contrary filters are also flagged for your protection with this symbol: ☆☆

Of course, filters that are new to Premiere 3.0 wear the 3.0 icon used throughout this book. Also, the handful of filters that Premiere LE lacks receive this icon: (LE)

Let these pages be an handy excuse to wander down some filter avenues on your own. Using the techniques of the first half of this chapter, see how each filter works on a variety of clips. Their creative potential is endless!

▶ Brightness & Contrast Filters

Brightness & Contrast
Gamma Correction
Levels

Most projects will benefit from this first batch of Premiere filters which adjust brightness levels in your clip. Use the *Brightness & Contrast* filter to adjust all pixels at once, or turn to the *Gamma Correction* filter to tweak only a clip's middle-greys. Premiere 3.0 also has a *Levels* filter—a more sophisticated version of the first two offerings. On the next page, let's see how each filter shines.

Brightness & Contrast

Use this filter to adjust brightness and contrast in a clip. Slightly increasing both values, for example, may bring out more texture (especially in muddy captured clips). Of course, you also can push the filter's sliders to extremes to produce high-contrast clips or other wacky results.

Plagued with slightly dark clips from a VideoSpigot? Here's your solution.

The image at far right has brightness and contrast moderately increased to emphasize the ear-wagger.

Contrast can alter the influence of other filters, too. For example, increasing the contrast *before* applying the Color Replace filter can better define affected color regions. Or slightly decreasing contrast before using one of the Sharpen filters can moderate its sharpness.

Gamma Correction

This filter lightens or darkens a clip's middle-greys—the *gamma*—without significantly affecting strong shadows and highlights. Middle-greys typically provide visual detail in a clip. Tweaking this filter often goes hand-in-hand with using the Brightness & Contrast filter.

A gamma range of 0.1 to 2.9 is available. 1.0 is the default. Our friend at far right has a gamma of 0.8 to lighten the bovine middle-greys.

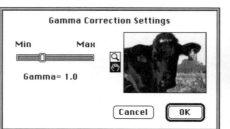

3.0 Levels

Premiere 3.0's Levels filter is like having Brightness & Contrast, Gamma Correction and Color Balance filters all rolled into one. Once you're comfortable with Levels, you may even want to kiss those three filters good-bye.

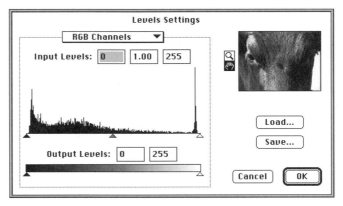

Photoshop users will recognize this filter's dialog box. It's a slightly watered-down version of the Photoshop filter that goes by the same name.

The Input Levels histogram charts the brightness of pixels in the clip's image. Towards the left side of the histogram are the image's darker pixels (typically the shadows). Lighter pixels (highlights) are plotted to the right. Numerically, the darkest possible value is 0 and the lightest is 255. The height of each vertical line shows how many pixels in the image have that brightness value.

To *increase contrast* in your clip, move the triangles under the histogram. Slide the black triangle right to darken the shadows. Drag the white triangle left to brighten the highlights. To produce a high-contrast clip, move the black and white triangles close together. The preview will show the results as you do this. If you prefer, enter values directly in the text boxes above the histogram instead of maneuvering the triangles.

☞ *Unlike Photoshop, there's no way to toggle back and forth between new and original Levels settings.*

To *alter the middle-greys* (midtones) in your clip without significantly tweaking shadows or highlights, drag the grey triangle—the *gamma*. Be careful, though, this can alter the extent of visual detail in the clip.

To *decrease contrast* in your clip, use the Output Levels control at the bottom of the dialog box. Drag the black triangle right to lighten shadows. Slide the white triangle left to darken highlights. Or enter numbers in the two text boxes. For example, if you set the black triangle to 100, all darker pixels in the clip will lighten to the 100 value.

You also can *cross* the black and white triangles to *opposite* sides of the Output Levels control to produce wild color effects like the Solarize filter.

Normally, adjustments affect the entire RGB image—all color channels—at once. But you can use the pop-up

Load...

Save...

menu at the top of the dialog box to alter individual color channels. To give the clip a stronger red cast, for example, switch to the red channel and then adjust the Input Levels triangles inward. Manipulating individual color channels to extremes is the path to exotic, radioactive images.

When you've reached the right combination of triangle adjustments, click the Save button if you want to store the setting for use on other clips. Call up such saved settings later with the Load button.

▶ Color & Greyscale Filters

Color Balance
Tint
Hue & Saturation
Color Replace
Color Pass
Posterize
Invert
Solarize
Color Offset
Black & White
Extract

To change a clip's complexion, look to these filters for help. Perhaps you need to correct "ill-luminated" shots or the color by-products of other filters. For wholesale hue adjustments, *Color Balance*, *Tint* and Premiere 3.0's new *Hue & Saturation* filter each provide a somewhat different solution. Need to replace one or more colors with a single color? Then use the *Color Replace* filter.

Five other Premiere filters are more unusual color manipulators. *Color Pass* leaves a selectable number of colors alone in your clip—converting the rest of the image to greyscale. *Posterize* reduces all pixels in a clip to a few colors. *Invert* and *Solarize* flip colors to the opposite side of the color wheel. And *Color Offset* creates convincing depth illusions (with a pair of 3-D glasses).

If you're aiming for purely greyscale results, use the *Black & White* filter to convert all colors in a clip to greys. Or try Premiere 3.0's new *Extract* filter to control more precisely the range of greys that will appear.

Color Balance

Use this filter to alter hues in the entire image. All you have to do is change the relative intensities of the RGB color channels. For example, if a video clip suffers from the blues, push the Blue slider left to cheer up the clip.

Premiere 3.0's dialog box is shown. From 0% to 200% is possible for each slider. In Premiere 2.0, the sliders' range is narrower: 0% to 100%. All default at 100% strength.

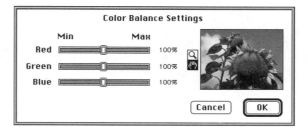

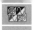

Tint

This is the color acetate of Premiere filters. It superimposes a selectable hue *on top of* the entire clip. That tends to subdue contrast more than if you use Color Balance.

The original clip (left image) is tinted (middle) versus color balanced (far right). Notice how the Tint filter alters all image areas, including black regions.

When Tint's dialog box appears, first click the Color box to choose a tint color from a color picker. Then adjust the Level bar to determine the tint's strength.

Zero percent provides no effect; 100% completely obscures the image with the tint color.

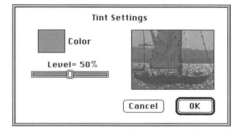

3.0 Hue & Saturation

This Photoshop-derived filter gives you a third way to manipulate all colors in an image at once.

Default values for the filter are shown. Although the function of this filter overlaps other filters we've seen over the previous few pages, some users may prefer this filter's approach.

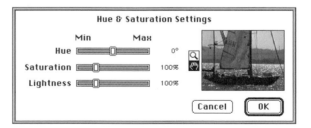

The Hue slider rotates the clip's colors around a color wheel. For example, to change a clip's colors to the opposite side of the color wheel, push the Hue slider all the way right (180°) or left (–180°). Positive values rotate around the color wheel *clockwise* from the original color.

The Saturation slider adjusts the intensity of the clip's colors. You can set it from 0% (a greyscale image) to 400% (sizzling hot colors). The Lightness slider alters underlying greys in the image, affecting brightness.

Color Replace

Color Replace changes selected "target" colors in your clip to a single "replace" color. When used subtly, you can selectively brighten muted colors or cool oversaturated colors. Applied more brazenly, it's your avenue to Tron-like color effects.

Click either color box to select a color with a color picker. Or click in the Clip Sample image to suck the Target color with an eyedropper. Option-click in the image to set the Replace color.

☞ *On eight-bit monitors, you may have to click in the image more than once for a desired color (due to dithering).*

After selecting a Target and Replace color, move the Similarity slider right if you want a broader range of target colors from your initial choice. Turning on the Solid Colors check box also can be helpful. It plasters the replacement color *opaquely* onto the targeted pixels. More importantly, though, it's the only way you can target and replace black or greys in the image.

☞ *To infuse more than one Replace color into your clip, apply the filter repeatedly.*

 Color Pass

The Color Pass filter retains a selectable number of colors in a clip while converting all others to shades of grey. This effect is one way to emphasize the subject in a scene.

In its Settings dialog box, there are two ways to define which colors "pass" through the filter unaltered. You can click the Color box to bring up a color picker. Or you can move your cursor into the Clip Sample image. Just like the Color Replace filter, the cursor will turn into an eyedropper that can suck up any clicked color.

Move the Similarity slider right to preserve an expanded range of similar colors.

Turn on the Reverse check box to flip the effect: your chosen color(s) turn grey, leaving other colors intact.

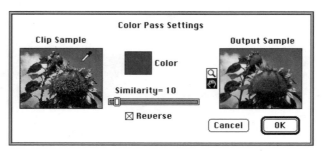

Posterize

This filter reduces the number of colors in a clip's image. Only the most prominent colors survive—you select how many. Any other colors change to the closest surviving color. This effect is most powerful on natural images, not titles or graphics that may already have only a few colors.

Use the slider in the Settings dialog box to tell Premiere how many colors to retain—from 2 to 32. Low settings produce large, flat color regions. Higher values create more subtle effects.

Invert

Invert automatically flips all colors to their opposites—as on a color wheel. Black and white pixels also reverse. Therefore, shadows will appear raised and highlights will become new shadows. Sometimes that's the face-lift your material may need. But it's also a handy fixer-upper of certain other filter effects. For example, Invert can eliminate the large black areas created by the Find Edges filter.

Here's an unaltered image (left) and its inverted cousin (right).

☞ *To selectively change an inverted color, apply the Color Replace filter afterward.*

Solarize

This filter is an adjustable version of the Invert filter. Instead of color flipping the entire image, you can switch just a portion of the colors. That can produce an effect like film that's been *partially* exposed during developing.

Only the most prevalent colors survive unaltered towards the maximum setting. A 100% threshold is the same as applying the Invert filter.

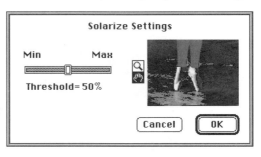

Color Offset

This filter offsets a color channel without altering the rest of the image. Use it to create 3-D movies and weird ghost-like effects. To viewers peering curiously through flimsy 3-D glasses, shifting the red channel slightly left recedes objects; to the right pushes objects forward.

First select a color channel and offset direction. Then push the offset slider. Small shifts (2-5%) produce a realistic depth illusion that doesn't boggle the eyes.

☞ *To shift diagonally, apply Color Offset twice to a clip—once to shift left or right, and again to shift up or down.*

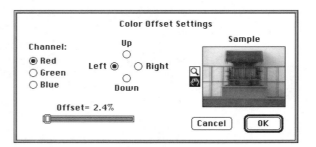

Black & White

This filter performs one simple task: It strips color out of a clip, leaving only shades of grey. This is how you can slip in greyscale clips within a color segment, for example, or create a greyscale background with a color version of the same clip superimposed on top.

3.0 Extract

The new Extract filter in Premiere 3.0 is a more sophisticated greyscale creator than the Black & White filter. Besides converting a clip to greys, you can selectively convert greys to black or white—in effect altering the dynamic range of your clip's image. It's essentially the greyscale cousin of 3.0's Levels filter.

In Extract's dialog box, the histogram charts the distribution of greys in the clip. Toward the left are darker greys; lighter greys are plotted to the right. Numerically, the range is 0 to 255. A column's height shows how many pixels in the image have that grey value.

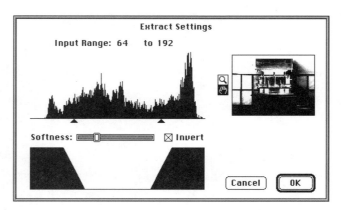

☞ *Turn on the Invert check box to invert the clip image like a film negative, as shown below.*

To adjust the range of greys, slide the two triangles under the histogram. If the Invert check box is turned off, pixels that sit *between* the two triangles are converted to white. All other pixels becomes black. For example, moving the right triangle to the left turns more of the light pixels in the image black.

But everything doesn't have to be so absolute. You can use the Softness slider to allow at least some greys to survive (in fact the default setting already does that). If you move the slider farther right, more greys appear.

Dragging the Softness slider right produces a wider range of greys that are not mapped to black or white. That's reflected by a less-steep slope in the diagram that's below the slider. The "valley" represents black; the top plateau is white. Slopes are the greys in the altered image.

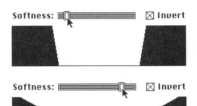

▷ **Blur Filters**

AntiAlias
Blur
Gaussian Blur
Blur More
Camera Blur
Radial Blur

☞ *To soften a superimposed clip's edges, use the Smoothing pop-up menu in Transparency Settings. See page 263.*

This side-by-side comparison of the same clip at near true size reveals subtle blur differences. The filters are all size-sensitive.

★☆

☞ *Note that the Blur filter keeps the edges of high-contrast details slightly sharper than the AntiAlias filter.*

Blur filters are image softening specialists. To different degrees, they blend pixels together so that high-contrast areas—such as the "jaggies" along angled lines or object edges—appear smoother (but less focused).

The filters have three common uses: They can soften imported graphics that aren't already anti-aliased. They can tone down video or scanned-image noise. And they can mute busy backgrounds for superimposed clips—keeping the viewer's eye on the main subject.

The first four Blur filters are not adjustable, but as a group offer a range of softening power. *AntiAlias* and *Blur* are most subtle, followed by *Gaussian Blur* and *Blur More.*

Original *AntiAlias* *Blur* *Gaussian Blur* *Blur More*

Blurs are your entry into interesting molten metal effects. Try applying the filter combo at left for liquefied results. Use Gamma Correction to strengthen the details in the filtered clip. You also may need the Brightness & Contrast filter (or 3.0's new Levels filter) to balance the image. Then tweak the Tint filter to the desired color— liquid gold, bronze, mercury, copper or even a hot plasma-like look.

Camera Blur

Unlike the previous blur filters, this new 3.0 filter is *progressive*—it can change over the duration of the clip. Use this filter to simulate a camera lens focusing or unfocusing on your clip. Or freeze it at the same Start and End percentage to create a greater blur than other blur filters can provide.

Adjust the sliders to set the Start and End blur levels. To lock the filter to a single percentage, hold down the Shift key as you drag. At 100% strength, the clip image will have no detail.

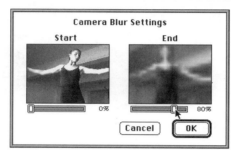

Radial Blur

Radial Blur is the most exotic blur filter. Applied subtly it softens, but at more extreme settings it's intergalactic. The filter blurs a clip radially, from any point in the scene that you define. It can produce two types of radial blurs. *Spin* is a concentric circular effect like a rapidly rotating camera. *Zoom* is like a fast zoom with a camcorder—the blur radiates from a single point.

Set the Amount from 1 to 1000. For a Spin blur, the Amount is the degrees of rotation that will occur in both directions—so 180 degrees is a full circle blur. For a Zoom blur, the Amount is how far the blur radiates outward.

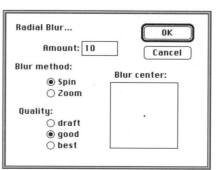

Use the Blur center box to do something camcorders cannot—have an off-center origin point for the blur. You can thus aim the blur at a particular element within your scene. Click anywhere in the box to set the new center.

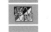

Radial Blur has the dubious distinction of being the slowest Premiere filter. That's why there's a *Quality* control. Reducing the quality to *Draft* reduces the wait, but the blur will be coarser. *Best* improves on *Good* towards a clip's outer edges, especially on large-frame clips.

Here are three Radial Blur examples applied to the same title clip—all blurred from their center.

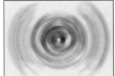

Spin 90, good   Zoom 30, best   Zoom 90, good

▶ Sharpen Filters

*Sharpen
Sharpen More
Gaussian Sharpen
Sharpen Edges*

These cousins of the Blur filter family perform a complementary task—they sharpen clips by *increasing* the contrast between adjacent pixels. You'll notice the effect most in image areas with significant color differences.

A common use for these filters is to sharpen fuzzy video clips. On titles, graphics and other images with strong contrast, applying any of the stronger filters in this group will produce a neon-like pixel fringe.

Another comparison of the same clip at near true size—this time for Sharpen filters. All of these filters are size-sensitive.

☞ *Lessening a clip's contrast with the Brightness & Contrast filter beforehand can moderate the sharpening of these filters.*

Original   Sharpen   Sharpen More   Sharpen Edges   Gaussian Sharpen

Applying Sharpen Edges twice to a natural image can produce a buzzing maze of pixels. Consider superimposing the same clip (but unfiltered) on top of the filtered mayhem to selectively add back natural elements.

From left to right is a hippo clip, the same clip with the Sharpen Edges filter applied twice, and the original hippo superimposed back over the filtered clip.

▶ Stylize Filters

Crystallize
Pointillize
Mosaic
Replicate
Tiles
Emboss
Find Edges
Pinch
Spherize
Mesh Warp

Consider these filter specimens when you need to turn a humdrum clip into a very unusual segment. Photoshop veterans will recognize many of these filters.

The first five members cluster a clip's pixels into a pattern of cells. *Crystallize* creates crystalline shapes. *Pointillize* transforms a clip into a dynamic pointillist painting. And *Mosaic, Replicate* and *Tiles* form different effects using a rectilinear set of cells. Note that the random nature of all but the *Mosaic* and *Replicate* filters means the cells will jiggle and bounce their way from frame-to-frame (even during still-image clips).

Other Stylize filters attack other geometries. *Emboss* and *Find Edges* manipulate object edges. *Pinch* and *Spherize* stretch a clip's surface elastically. And *Mesh Warp* is the wildest clip twister of all—allowing you to warp portions of your clip over time on a controllable grid.

☞ *Sharpen filters (see the prior page) also are edge manipulators, although not as much as Emboss or Find Edges.*

 ☆☆ **Crystallize**

This filter clumps a clip's pixels into a vibrating mass of single-color polygons. You can set the cell size from 3 to 999 pixels.

From left are 6 and 30-pixel settings on a 320 x 240 clip. Adding Sharpen Edges afterward (far right image) can send the facets into another world.

 ☆☆ **Pointillize**

This filter transforms your clip's image into a buzzing swarm of randomly placed dots—like an animated pointillist painting. Black is the background color. Use the dialog box to set the cell size from 3 to 999 pixels.

☞ *Use the Color Replace filter if you desire a different background color.*

Here are examples of 5, 10 and 40 pixel settings on a 320 x 240 clip. Notice how large cell sizes can look like molecular mayhem.

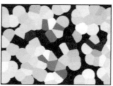

Mosaic

Mosaic divides the image into a grid of squares. This filter is especially enticing because it's *progressive*. With different Start and End percentages, you can gradually change the pixellation over a clip's duration.

Control the size of the grid with the percentage slider. The filter assigns to each square the average color of all pixels that the square covers. Turning on the Sharp Colors check box increases the color saturation and alters the grid's proportions (far right image).

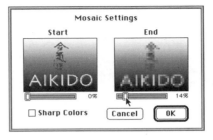

For an extra dimension to the grid, try applying either the Sharpen Edges or Find Edges filter after Mosaic.

Here's a four-frame sample of a clip with the Sharpen Edges filter applied after Mosaic. The edge effect changes as the Mosaic intensity reduces.

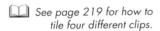

Replicate

This filter splits the frame into a grid of tiles and displays the entire image in each tile. For example, setting the slider to two produces four identical quadrants. Premiere 3.0's version (shown below) is progressive, offering Start and End settings. Premiere 2.0 has just a single slider.

The images multiply as you move the slider right. Shift-drag to lock both sliders to the same value. High values can often produce great background textures (far right image).

📖 *See page 219 for how to tile four different clips.*

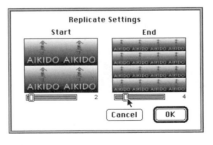

 Tiles

This filter divides a clip's image over a collection of square tiles. Unlike the Replicate filter, only part of the image rests on each tile. The tiles can be stationary in a grid like a bathroom floor, or they can bounce around like a Scrabble set in an earthquake.

Specify how many tiles should vertically be in your clip. As many as 99 are possible.

👉 *Divide your output's vertical dimension by six to figure out how many tiles will fit without obscuring the clip. 120 x 160 movies, for example, can show up to 20 tiles vertically.*

Set the maximum percent (of a tile's size) that a tile can bounce. From 1% to 90% is possible. A greater offset produces more random rattle.

Choose what should fill the space between the tiles. Background and Foreground Color are usually the same—black. Inverse Image flips the pixel grout to the opposite side of the color wheel.

The first two images are 4 and 10 tile settings, both with a 10% offset. Applying Tiles twice with a 90% offset (far right image) creates tiles within tiles that really begin to rattle.

Team up this filter with the Cross Zoom transition to ignite a QuickTime explosion, as shown below.

Applying the Cross Zoom transition from 0% to 50% sends tiles of the image flying past the viewer's eye.

Emboss

Emboss creates a raised or stamped look in a clip by toning down colors and outlining edges with black. The black outlining turns most images very dark, but fortunately Premiere offers the following easy solutions to that darkness problem:

Note that inverting reverses the embossed shadows.

• You can add the Solarize filter afterward to turn black to white and selectively invert other colors. Also add the Color Balance or Tint filter if you need a different hue.

• If you do not want to reverse the shadows, use the Tint or Color Replace filter alone. You can create molten gold, silver, bronze or copper clips this way, especially if you soften the image with a Blur filter.

• You also can superimpose part of the original clip over the dark embossed image (using Premiere's Transparency Settings—more about that in Chapter 10).

Find Edges

If Find Edges turns your clip too dark, look over the lightening techniques described above for the Emboss filter.

This filter is a transplant from Photoshop. Wherever it senses an edge in an image, it traces it. Color edges get color traces. Grey edges receive a white trace. And light edges receive black. Applied once, this filter usually transforms most clips into a maze of neon strokes against a black background.

The left clip has Find Edges applied once. Applying the filter twice (middle) magnifies the outlining effect. Add Blur and Invert filters to soften and lighten the edges (right).

Pinch

Inspired by Photoshop, Pinch pushes clip pixels inward or outward from a clip's center point. You can specify the amount from –100% to 100%. Large negative percentages, such as –100%, give a fish eye lense-look to a clip.

These title clip examples are pinched at –100%, 40% and 100%.

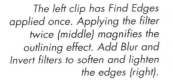  

Spherize

This filter stretches a clip's pixels over a circular area inside the clip (an oval on 4:3 aspect ratio images). At full strength, it becomes a half-sphere or cylinder. Progressively applying this filter can pulsate the image.

Enter an amount from –100 to 100 to determine the extent of image curvature—from convex to concave.

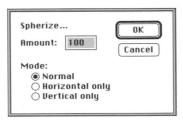

Select Normal to produce a half-sphere. Horizontal only and Vertical only map the pixels onto a half-cylinder.

The first two titles are Normal mode at –100 and 100 Amounts. The far right example is Vertical only mode at 100.

Mesh Warp

Mesh Warp is your own fun house of distorted mirrors. By dragging points on a mesh that overlays your clip, you can warp the clip's image. Best yet, the warp can be progressive since Premiere provides start and end settings.

Mesh Warp can be progressive—the filter's effect will evolve smoothly over the clip's duration if start and end settings are different. Besides more serious uses, it provides a great opportunity to wangle shots of your friends and relatives.

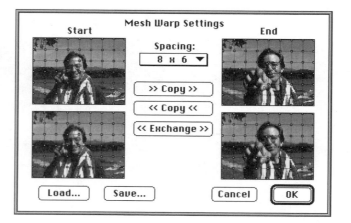

Let's go through the steps of creating a unique warp. The four grid boxes in Mesh Warp's dialog box can be confusing at first but become clearer after you try them.

Be sure to set the grid first. Changing it erases your work.

1 First use the central pop-up menu to choose from a 4 x 3, 8 x 6 or 12 x 9 grid spacing. The 12 x 9 grid offers the most fine-grained warping control but can be more tedious to manipulate.

End

2 While *holding down the Shift key*, drag mesh points in the *top* image boxes. As you do this, points in the lower boxes will move to identical positions. The goal is to position points *around the area where you want distortion to occur*, such as around a particular subject, title or graphic. You won't see warping yet, but this will give you more control in the next step. To start (or end) with an *unaltered* image, leave the Start (or End) box alone.

3 Now drag mesh points in the *bottom* box—*without* pressing the Shift key—to create warp distortion. The further you drag a point from where its companion sits in the upper box's mesh, the more warping occurs (see right). To *eliminate* distortion at a particular point, click the same point in the *top* image box while pressing the Shift key. That will force top and bottom mesh points to match again so no distortion will appear there.

End

4 Click OK to your warped creation and then preview it. Premiere will compile a smooth progression from the Start to End image, such as the example below.

The warp distortion smoothly evolves over the clip's duration.

Before slowing down from warp drive, keep in mind that the dialog box also offers a few more conveniences.

• Use the Copy buttons to copy distortion settings from one end of the clip to the other. Click the Exchange button to flip Start and End settings.

• You can save warp settings as files for future use on other clips. Click Save to name and store the warp. Click Load to retrieve your earlier warp files.

▶ Fluid Filters

Bend
Ripple
Wave
ZigZag
Twirl

This group of filters can create fluid-like flows within your clip's frame. That type of effect is particularly suitable for background textures, but sometimes it can add just the right distortion to a clip's center of interest.

Choose from five fluid effects. *Bend* and *Ripple* dynamically undulate your clip in a variety of controllable patterns. *Wave* goes a step further by providing a virtual pond and a bag of rocks to toss. *ZigZag* and *Twirl* also create a fluid look, but are static in nature.

Bend

The Bend filter dynamically stretches an image from the edges of the movie frame. The center of the image stays relatively stable. Along the clip's edges, pixels will elastically undulate in whatever direction you set. You can even independently adjust what happens along horizontal and vertical edges.

Set the direction of the wave's movement—Left, Right, In or Out horizontally; Up, Down, In or Out vertically.

Choose from a circular, triangular, square or a sine wave shape. The sine wave produces the most fluid effect.

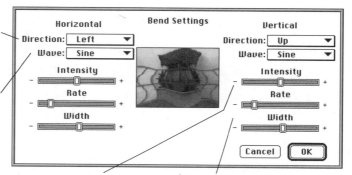

The Intensity slider determines the strength of the bending action (the height of the wave). The lowest setting halts all bending.

Rate sets how fast the bend moves along edge of the clip. Width sets the wave's width from crest to crest.

Here are sine, circle, triangle and square wave examples, all with medium intensity and width.

Extremely narrow widths can produce interesting dynamic textures. Great width *and* intensity really churns the pixels. Use only with a bottle of Dramamine nearby.

The top four examples feature sine, circle, triangle and square bends at medium intensity but a very narrow width.

Here are sine, circle, triangle and square bends at maximum intensity and width.

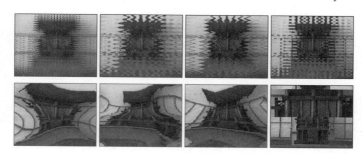

Ripple

Ripple also bends an image and even has a similar dialog box as the Bend filter. But Ripple operates differently. The undulations are more coordinated for a water or wind-like effect (hence the Ripple name). At moderate sine wave settings, images appear to float on a rippling pond.

There's an additional element that the Bend filter lacks—the Fill Color box. You can assign a specific color to new pixels that are drawn inward from the edges of the image. This can further increase the wave illusion.

To select a fill color, click the Fill Color box to use a color picker or click in the preview image. See the Bend filter on the prior page for details about other settings in the dialog box.

☞ *Since the preview is in motion, clicking on a color in it can be tricky. Temporarily slide intensity settings all the way left first to freeze the preview.*

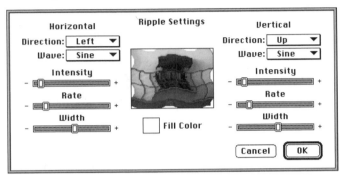

At extreme settings, this filter can do much more than simulate a rippling pond. It can produce many bizarre effects if you are willing to experiment a bit. Here are a few examples to give you an idea of the potential:

• Turn one ripple direction *off* (such as vertical) by sliding its Intensity slider all the way right. Then work with the other ripple direction, as shown below.

A high width, low intensity sine wave gently rolls (left image). High intensity and width makes pixel taffy (middle). Triangle waves at high width and intensity fold the image (right).

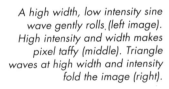

• To produce dynamic background textures and vibrations, set up triangle waves in both directions with a very low width and very high intensity setting. Hummm!

 Wave

The Wave filter is essentially a more controllable Ripple filter. You can influence just about every quality of its wave action. So it can produce an even wider range of distortions (gulp!) than the Ripple filter. Chaotic, flowing

textures for backgrounds are possible at extreme settings. At moderate levels it's a virtual pond and bag of rocks. Of its three wave types, sine is most organic—a rolling wave—but triangle and square waves are also intriguing.

Here are eamples of sine, triangle, and square waves at default settings.

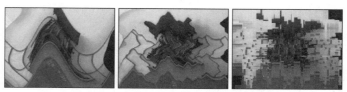

Unlike a real pond, the water never settles down with this filter—it just keeps on rippling. But we'll use the pond analogy anyway below to help you better understand the individual settings of the Wave filter.

Drop from 1 to 100 pebbles (generators) in the pond. Each produces a concentric wave pattern. Crashing waves of many pebbles, of course, are complex.

Wavelength is the distance between wave crests. Amplitude is the wave height. Both can be from 1 to 9999 pixels. Premiere will randomly use values within the min./max. range. Greater range makes greater turbulence.

☞ *To have matching waves on more than one clip, turn off Random Start Phase and set the wave generator to 1. Minimum and maximum values for wavelength and amplitude should be set the same, too.*

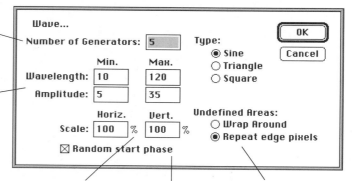

You can separately scale wave components. Setting vertical to 0% ripples waves horizontally, like wind blowing across a flag.

Turn on Random Start Phase for more chaotic results. Off ensures a consistent pebble action during the clip—hence more uniform waves.

These buttons tell Premiere how to treat the new pixels it pulls into the image from the edges. Repeat edge pixels extends the colors of the existing edge pixels. If edge pixels vary in color, a banding effect can result. Wrap Around gives new pixels the color of the edge pixels on the opposite side of the image.

You have to experience this filter first-hand to appreciate its power. But here are a few interesting examples that may help you form a Wave settings strategy.

The left image has default sine waves, except amplitude is set to 10 min./15 max. The middle image's waves stretch higher. At far right are square waves (at default settings) applied twice.

ZigZag

This filter drops a rock into the center of your liquid clip image. The rock forms a radial wave from the image's center in one of three selectable patterns. Unlike previous Fluid filters, though, ZigZag doesn't ripple—it's static.

The three ZigZag variants are very similar. *Pond Ripples* slightly elongates the waves toward the upper left and lower right corners—as if the pond is in perspective. *Out from Center* provides purely concentric ripples. *Around Center* adds a swirl to that—as if the pixels are beginning to flow down the digital drain.

Here are examples of Pond Ripples, Out from Center, Around Center—all at default settings.

Enter values for the Amount and Ridges to control the lift and frequency of ZigZag waves.

Amount sets the height of the tallest wave, from 1 to 999 pixels. Moderate amounts (such as 5 to 10% of the height of your clip) are most convincingly liquid. An amount greater than your clip's height throws the wave crest off the screen.

Enter how many wave ridges will appear—from 1 to 999. Large values simulate a high frequency wave vibration, like below.

 Twirl

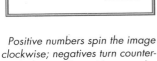

Twirl funnels a clip's image into a central digital drain. It develops this effect by rotating the central area of the image more than the edges. The range of acceptable angles is from -999 and 999 degrees.

Positive numbers spin the image clockwise; negatives turn counter-clockwise. These title examples are (from left) 90, 360 and 999 degrees.

Use this filter instead of Radial Blur if you want the twist but not the blur.

▶ Size Filters

Image Pan
Crop
Resize

These three filters are only in Premiere 3.0. Use the first two, *Image Pan* and *Crop,* to define which pixels within your clip will appear in the final output. Rely on the *Resize* filter to improve the output of any overly-large clips in your project.

[3.0]

📖 *For how to use the Image Pan filter to produce rolling credits, see page 246.*

Image Pan

Here's the niftiest new filter in Premiere 3.0 for many users. You gain the power to pan, tilt or zoom *within* a clip. That's a great way to create rolling credits or to simulate a camera pan or zoom. You also can use the filter to crop clips as well as scale images up or down to match your final frame size. Let's see how Image Pan works.

The dialog box opens with the first and last frame of your clip shown. Each frame has a crop rectangle with handles. Enter numbers in the text boxes or drag the rectangle's handles to define the image portion you want. You also can move the entire crop rectangle by clicking inside it and dragging. In this example, the 320 x 240 clip is cropped to follow the subject's movement.

Use the Copy buttons to copy a crop rectangle from one side to the other. The Exchange button switches both rectangles at once.

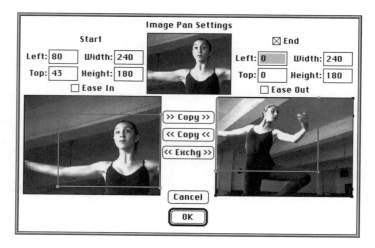

To crop the clip without any panning or other movement—based solely on the boundaries of the Start rectangle—uncheck the End check box. Otherwise, Premiere will create a smooth progression during the clip from the Start to the End rectangles. That sequence will preview slowly in the top image. Turn on the Ease In and Ease Out check boxes to have Premiere gradually begin or end the movement (like a proper camera pan).

Note that if you establish crop rectangles that are different in size or proportion than your final output, Premiere will stretch or distort the image to fit. Done deliberately, a progression from a very narrow crop rectangle to a very wide one can rubberize your clip.

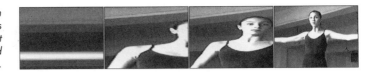

The Image Pan effect starts with a 3 pixel width stretched across the frame (left image). That progresses to an undistorted image by the end of the clip.

 Crop

Use this filter to rid your clip of video fringe noise or any other unwanted edge elements. Premiere will stretch the remaining image to fill the frame. This filter is best for trimming just a few pixels from the edges. For more extensive cropping, use the Image Pan filter.

Use the slider bars to trim out unwanted material. You can work by pixels or percentage—click the buttons at the bottom. Up to 20 pixels (or 20% of the image) can be lopped off of each side.

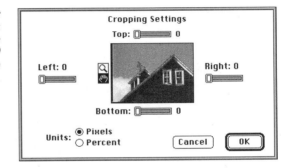

3.0 Resize

Do you have a source clip that's different in frame size than your intended output, but the clip is the correct aspect ratio? Then consider applying this filter. It will give you *slightly* better-looking output than what QuickTime normally produces when it scales the clip during the Make Movie compiling process.

▶ **Visual Odds & Ends**

Backwards (Video)
Horizontal Flip
Vertical Flip
Roll
Ghosting
Posterize Time
Field Interpolate
Video Noise
Convolution Kernel

Nine more visual filters! None of these remaining entries fit into the previous categories. Read on to see how their purposes range from the very practical to the surprising.

Backwards (Video)

This filter plays a clip in reverse. Basic but very practical. Watch out for one odd problem, however. Any filters applied to the clip *before* Backwards (Video) are ignored by Premiere. So always apply Backwards (Video) *first* in your filter list to avoid this quirky behavior.

Horizontal Flip/Vertical Flip

These two filters reverse a clip's *image* horizontally or vertically. The sequence still plays forwards—unless you've also applied the Backwards (Video) filter.

Here's a fun trick with either filter: split-screen symmetry. Align copies of the same clip in Tracks A and B. Place the Wipe transition in the T Track between them and "freeze" the Wipe at 50% vertically to split the screen. Then apply the Horizontal Flip filter to one of the clips. The effect works best with well-defined subjects.

Roll

This filter continually pushes a clip to a selected side, filling the vacated area with the same image. Each consecutive frame moves a few more pixels.

Select the direction that you want the image to roll.

☞ *For the same effect, but more control, use the Push transition between copies of the same clip in A and B tracks.*

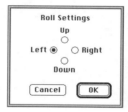 

Ghosting

After applying this filter, each frame of the clip shows a "ghost"—a transparent image of the prior few frames. The current image also becomes semi-transparent.

The ghosting effect works best with moving elements that have a simple, stable background.

 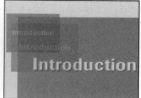

Posterize Time

Despite all the advice in this book for increasing a movie's frame rate, here's a filter that undoes it all. This filter purposely forces your clip to *skip* frames during playback! For example, enter 15 in the dialog box if you're producing a 15 fps movie and want to have a particular clip appear like 1 fps. It's a quick way to produce a choppy stop-action effect.

There's one red flag to watch out for, however. As with the Backwards (Video) filter, any filters applied to the clip *before* Posterize Time will be neutralized. So always apply Posterize Time first in your filter list.

Field Interpolate

If your video digitizer grabs only half of the horizontal scan lines to capture full-frame clips and you're aiming for full-frame output, this new Premiere 3.0 filter can be handy. It creates the missing odd or even scan lines by averaging the data from adjacent scan lines. That can smooth full-frame images considerably, especially if there's fast motion within the frame.

Video Noise

Video Noise scatters a very small amount of video noise into your clip's image. That's one way to blend a squeaky clean clip with captured clips that suffer from noise. The effect is so subtle that you may need to apply this filter more than once to the same clip.

Convolution Kernel

This new Premiere 3.0 filter will be familiar to Photoshop users—it's similar to Photoshop's *Custom* filter. You enter values into a mysterious grid of boxes to produce a new image-processing wonder.

This filter works based on a mathematical process called convolution (hence the name). The unaltered clip is at far right.

To save a kernel setting, click the Save button. To load saved kernel files into the boxes, click the Load button.

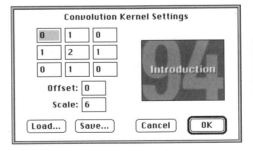

Premiere uses the numbers you enter to increase or decrease the brightness levels of pixels in your clip. That's how Brightness & Contrast, Blur, Sharpen, Emboss, Invert and many other filters work—they adjust brightness values. So you can use the Convolution Kernel to create custom blurs, embosses, and more!

As Premiere calculates a pixel's brightness, the value in the center box acts as a *multiplier*. Enter from -999 (very dark) to 999 (glaringly bright). Surrounding boxes represent adjacent pixels. For example, the box below the center box is for the pixel below the one Premiere is currently evaluating. Enter numbers in any, some or all of these boxes to multiply the brightness levels of other pixels.

More math: the number you enter in the Scale box divides the sum of brightness values in the pixel grid. And the Offset is a value that's added to Scale's results.

This book's Goodies Disk includes several Convolution Kernels to get you going in your filter experiments.

As you can see from the previous two paragraphs, the math really doesn't give you a feeling for what this filter can produce. Unless you're Steven Hawkings, the only way to understand how the numbers interact is to experiment hands-on and to look at examples.

Here are four of the Convolution Kernel files that are in the book's Goodies Disk. Clockwise from upper left are Bright Colors, Emphasize Edges, Heavy Blur and Fracture Edges. Note that large values are not necessary to produce useful results.

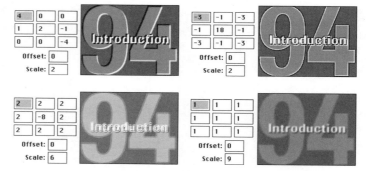

▷ Audio Filters

Backwards
Boost
Fill Left
Fill Right
Echo

Premiere's audio filters are convenient for simple audio adjustments. For more refined sound editing, rely on a dedicated sound editor such as Macromedia's *SoundEdit Pro* or Opcode's *AudioShop*.

Backwards
This filter plays the sound clip backwards. Now you too can find hidden messages in old Beatles songs.

Boost
Boost is like the loudness button on a car stereo. It amplifies weak sounds while leaving louder sounds alone.

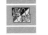

Fill Left/Fill Right

These two filters play the sound clip entirely through the left or right audio channel. That can be handy for spatial placement if viewers will have stereo speakers connected for playback. For one-speaker, mono-sound presentations, however, Fill Left will have no effect and Fill Right will completely silence the sound.

Echo

This filter provides an adjustable echo for your audio. That may add just the right depth and character to a dry narration or otherwise bland sound clip. The longer the delay that you set with the slider, the bigger the sound space will seem. Soft intensity is barely noticeable, but loud may be too much.

▶ MooVing on to Motion

Congratulations! You should now know much more about Premiere's wonderful world of filters than when you began this chapter. It's a never-ending journey—there's always more to discover.

Let's move on to a different category of special effects that Premiere can provide for your movie clips. *Motion settings* allow you to fly, zoom and tumble a running clip within another clip's frame. So catch your breath and then hold on for more acrobatics!

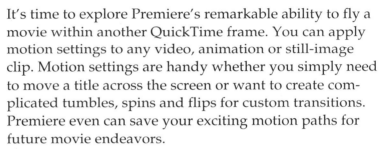

8

Flying with Motion Settings

It's time to explore Premiere's remarkable ability to fly a movie within another QuickTime frame. You can apply motion settings to any video, animation or still-image clip. Motion settings are handy whether you simply need to move a title across the screen or want to create complicated tumbles, spins and flips for custom transitions. Premiere even can save your exciting motion paths for future movie endeavors.

The first part of this chapter will take you through each motion control in Premiere so you can skillfully add zip to any clip. We'll then use this knowledge to solve a variety of practical (and creative) problems in projects. Let's get those clips movin'!

Exploring the Settings

Premiere's Motion Settings dialog box is chock full of powerful controls. After stepping through the basics of creating a motion path, we'll take each motion control for a spin. By the last page, you'll be able to roll, twist and flip a clip in a frame with ease.

▶ Creating Your Path

Let's jump right into creating a motion path. Besides learning the process, we'll see some of the differences between Premiere 2.0 and 3.0 versions. As always, the best way to digest these pages is in front of your Mac so you can experience each step for yourself.

1 Open the Motion Settings dialog box by selecting a clip in the Construction window and choosing "Motion…" from the Clip menu (Command Y).

Premiere 2.0 (top) and 3.0 (bottom) versions of the Motion Settings dialog box are similar. In either one, you set the motion trajectory in the large box. A straight path initially appears with two motion points—Start and Finish—from left to right. A preview of the clip's motion plays in the upper left corner of the dialog box.

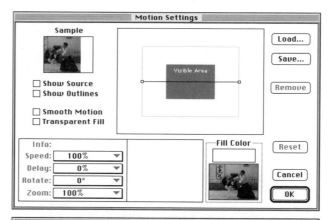

3.0 Three improvements in Premiere 3.0 are prominent. There's a time bar for setting the clip's speed along the motion path (instead of a pop-up menu). You can use text entry boxes or sliders to set a motion point's location, rotation, zoom and delay. And the preview window in the upper left corner is larger and can show composited clips and special effects.

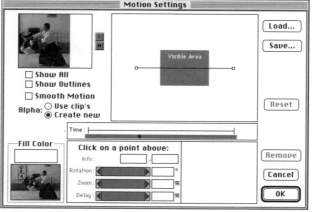

3.0

Premiere 3.0 has two other less obvious enhancements. Motion now occurs in sub-pixel increments—1/256th of a pixel—for smoother results, especially in full-frame, full-motion movies. And 3.0 can render two fields of image data per output frame, further reducing the chance of choppiness rearing its ugly head.

With these advances known, let's continue on with the process. After opening the Motion Settings dialog box, generally you should define a path with motion points and then set options for each point.

2 Click anywhere along the straight-line motion path to add a new motion point.

The cursor becomes a pointing finger when it's over the motion path. "Visible Area" is the region that will appear in your movie.

☞ *Are you creating a movie that's not in a 4:3 aspect ratio? The Visible Area rectangle will be inaccurate. You'll have to rely more on trial and error.*

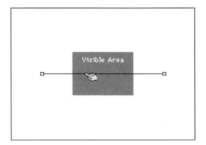

3 Drag the new point anywhere within the box to reshape the motion path.

As you drag the point, the clip's first frame appears as a visual guide. Note that you can drag a frame entirely out of the Visible Area along any side.

☞ *To view the frame that corresponds to the selected point, turn on the Show All check box (Show Source in 2.0).*

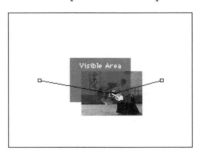

☞ *Since clips appear at a small scale in the motion path box, each pixel in the box typically represents more than one pixel of clip movement.*

Precise dragging of a motion point isn't easy, but you also can use the keyboard. Tap an Arrow key to move a selected point pixel-by-pixel. Hold down the Shift key to move five pixels per tap. In Premiere 3.0, holding down the Control key and tapping an Arrow key will move a motion point in 0.1 pixel increments.

As you position the point, its coordinates display in the lower half of the dialog box. In 3.0, you can also *enter* coordinates in the box to set the point's position. To center a frame along the motion path, for example, you would enter coordinates of 0,0 in the Info boxes. You can enter values in 0.01 increments if desired (further evidence of 3.0's sub-pixel positioning abilities).

Info: #1 is at [-10] , [-20.05]

4 Repeat the last two steps—create a new motion point and position it—as often as necessary to define your entire motion path. Keep in mind that you can move the Start and Finish points in the box, too. You can even place points rudely on top of each other.

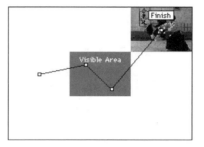

5 Now that the motion path is at least roughly defined, select each point and set options for it. Define its speed, rotation, zoom and delay using the controls in the bottom half of the dialog box (more about those controls in a minute). Then click OK.

That's the basic process. The clip will show a red line along the bottom of its Construction window thumbnail, proudly announcing that motion settings are present.

Here are three other caveats you should know about the Motion Settings dialog box.

• As motion points accumulate on top of each other or in a complex path, clicking to select a point (so you can apply options) can be a chore. Fortunately, you can advance from point to point *in order* by pressing the Tab key. Hold down the Shift key while tabbing to move in reverse.

• In Premiere 3.0, if the preview window saps too much speed from other controls (or you want to stop the action at a particular point) click the pause button at its right.

• To delete a selected motion point in either Premiere, select it and punch the Delete key. To remove *all* motion settings from a clip, click the Remove button.

Remove

▶ The Wizard of Speed and Time

Premiere 3.0 includes a nifty time bar for setting the speed of a clip along its motion path. Let's turn you into a wizard with this control before looking at other motion point options. If you're a 2.0 user, you can skip this section.

The time bar's length represents the entire duration of the clip. Besides Start and Finish motion points (left and right ends), Premiere marks each intermediate motion point you create. Each motion point appears on the bar as a vertical line—a time mark—showing the relative time the point will play.

The black arrow travels from left to right at constant speed. You can drag the arrow to preview a particular time.

This is the key concept: For a clip to reach an intermediate motion point sooner (speed up), drag the motion point's time mark left. To have more time pass before the clip reaches a motion point (slow down), drag the motion point's time mark right.

Let's look at a simple example. How do we ensure a tumbling clip reaches a particular motion point halfway into the clip's playback? Drag the motion point's mark to the middle of the time bar. As shown below, *time and space are independent* for a motion point. (Einstein, where are you?) A mid-duration motion point doesn't have to be *spatially* midway along its movement path.

As you click and drag a motion point's time mark, the cursor turns into a pointing hand and a black triangle appears above the mark. The percentage indicates the time bar location. In the trajectory box above the time bar, the motion point is selected and shows its frame, but spatially remains unchanged as you alter its timing.

☞ *Pausing the preview window is a good idea during adjustments so the time bar arrow isn't continually jumping around.*

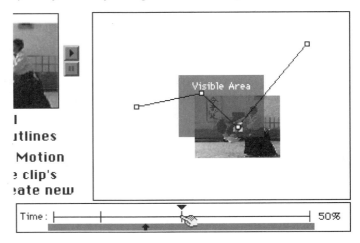

Remember, you're not changing the clip's overall duration or playback speed. You're determining how swiftly the clip moves along the motion path—*within* the clip's duration. Premiere uses percentages because the motion speed is always *relative* to the clip's duration.

You also can *add* motion points directly in the time bar. First move the cursor to an *empty* area of the time bar near where you want the new point. (The cursor will turn into a triangle.) Then click the time bar. The new point will appear as a time mark in the bar as well as a new point along your motion trajectory, as shown below.

Creating new motion points in the time bar allows you to conceive of your motion path temporally as well as spatially.

☞ *Keep the following in mind when working on complex motion paths: Clicking an existing point's time mark in the time bar is another way (besides using the Tab key) to select buried motion points in the path.*

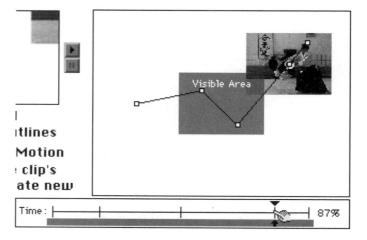

If you didn't click at the percentage desired, simply slide the time mark to a new position in the time bar. The percentage indicator will show your temporal position.

In this case, slightly adjusting the mark better balances the first intermediate motion point.

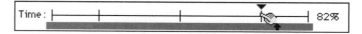

That's all you need to know to become a wizard of speed and time in 3.0. Premiere 3.0 users can skip ahead to *Other Options for Each Point* on the next page.

▶ **2.0's Speed Pop-up**

Premiere 2.0 has a pop-up menu for setting the speed of a selected motion point. From one to 400 percent is possible. Select "Other…" if you want to enter in-between values the pop-up menu doesn't list. If a previous motion point has a different speed setting, Premiere will gradually increase or decrease the speed to the value you set as the clip approaches the selected motion point.

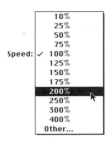

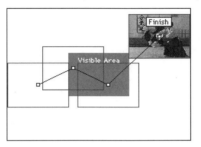

Premiere uses percentages because motion speed is always relative to a clip's duration. Choosing 200%, for example, means the clip will travel "twice as fast" at the selected motion point.

How fast is that? In relative terms, it's twice the speed of the 100% default. In absolute terms, the speed depends on the clip's duration. (Pretty slippery, eh?) Since speed is so hard to pin down, trial and error are usually necessary to produce the results you want. Consider the example below to aid your understanding of speed values.

The first two segments of this example motion path are equal in length. The speed assigned to the four points is (from left) 100%, 200%, 200% and 50%.

Here's what will happen: The motion will gradually accelerate from 100% to 200% in the first interval. In the second interval, the clip will maintain constant speed. That will play for half as long as the first interval (since it's double the speed, but an equal length path). In the last interval, the clip's motion will slow, reaching half the starting speed by the last frame. All of this action will occur within the clip's overall duration, which you set in the Construction or Clip window.

▶ Other Options for Each Point

Speed isn't the only variable you can set for a motion point. Premiere provides four other options: delay, rotation, zoom and distortion. Let's briefly look at each one.

In Premiere 2.0 (top), delay, rotation and zoom are set with pop-up menus. In Premiere 3.0 (bottom), you can directly enter a value for each option or use a "tractor tread" slider to adjust values incrementally. Distortion in both Premiere versions is set in its own special box.

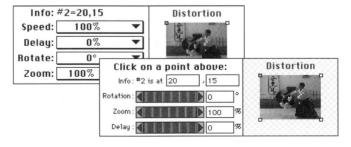

Delay

Assign a delay if you want to *pause* a clip at a selected motion point. In Premiere 3.0, a blue bar will appear along the time bar to indicate the delay's duration.

Delaying a motion point by 20% produces a thick blue bar in the time bar that's one-fifth of the clip's total duration.

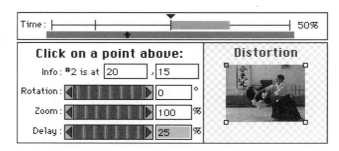

☞ *In Premiere 3.0, delaying the Start motion point by 100% freezes all motion—a time-saver when using motion settings just to zoom, rotate or distort a stationary clip.*

2.0

☞ *To freeze all motion in Premiere 2.0, move the Finish point on top of the Start point.*

3.0 ☞ *In 3.0, you can use the new Swirl transition to rotate a clip more than eight full rotations. See page 146.*

In this example, the selected motion point is assigned a rotation of –30°. Premiere displays the clip at that angle in the preview and motion path boxes. Premiere 3.0's dialog box is shown, but the display is similar in 2.0.

In the above example, note that 50% is the maximum delay you could assign to the selected motion point. Any greater would exceed the time that remains before the clip's playback is finished. Premiere 3.0 is logical—you can't delay longer than the time available until the next point. This is different than how delays work in Premiere 2.0—which can cause problems when you open 2.0 projects in 3.0 (more about that issue on page 216).

Premiere 2.0's Delay pop-up menu also assigns percentages, but the values do not correspond to any time logic. That's why a delay greater than 100% is possible for any point (although confusingly so). In fact, you can set the delay for any point as high as 400%. Hmmm.

Rotation

In Premiere 2.0, you can rotate a clip from –360° (counterclockwise) to 360° (clockwise)—two full rotations. Premiere 3.0 ups the ante four-fold by allowing rotation from –1440° to 1440°. That's eight full rotations.

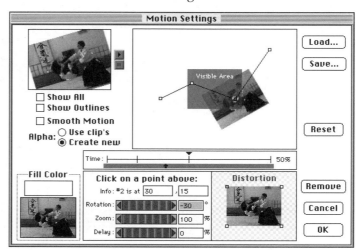

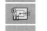

Note that to reach an assigned angle, a clip begins rotation at the *previous* motion point (unless, of course, there isn't one because you selected the Start point).

Zoom

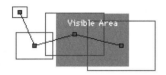

This option shrinks or expands the clip's frame size at the selected point along the motion path. In Premiere 2.0, the percentage can be from 1 percent to 400 percent. Premiere 3.0 can stretch slightly more—to 500%. As with rotation, zooming begins at the previous motion point—unless you selected the Start point.

Distortion

The Distortion box lets you drag any corner of the clip to twist and stretch it like a sheet of plastic. Together with

rotation and zoom controls, you can produce a variety of three-dimensional effects. As with rotation and zoom options, the distortion gradually builds from the *previous* motion point.

Dragging a corner handle twists the clip's image.

☞ *Turn on the Show All check box ("Show Source" in 2.0) to see the frame that corresponds to the selected motion point.*

Besides dragging corner handles in the Distortion box to wangle your clip, you can:

• *Shift the image*—To shift the entire image within the Distortion box, press the Shift key as you drag the image.

The shifting limits are the box's boundaries.

☞ *Shifting and spinning in the Distortion box is added to any movement or rotation assigned from other settings.*

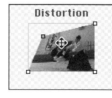 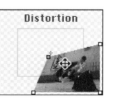

• *Spin the image*—Hold down the Option key and place the cursor over a corner handle of the clip image (the cursor will turn into a spin icon). Then drag to spin around the clip's center point.

As you spin, note that corner points must stay within the Distortion box. To accomplish this, Premiere alters the distortion if necessary (far right image).

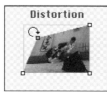 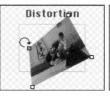 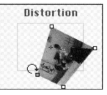

Any motion point with options applied appears red in the motion path box.

One last motion option note: Setting options one-by-one for every motion point can be monotonous. Luckily, Premiere provides two helpful shortcuts.

• You can copy all options from one point to another. Select the initial point and tap Command-C to copy it. Then select the motion point you want to paste the options into and type Command-V.

Reset

• Click the Reset button to return *a selected motion point's* options to default values—speed 100%, delay 0%, rotate 0%, zoom 100% and no distortion.

▶ Overall Motion Adjustments

Now let's examine other settings in the dialog box that aren't tied to a specific motion point. The first two we'll visit only alter the display of the Motion Settings dialog box—visual conveniences some users will prefer.

Show All ("Show Source" in 2.0)
The preview box normally shows only the clip's *first* frame. If you prefer to witness *all* frames of the clip, turn on this check box. In the motion path and Distortion boxes, you'll also see the correct frame that corresponds to a selected point. Of course, you pay a price for this help—the preview will play choppier and controls in the dialog box will become sluggish.

3.0

Premiere 3.0 gives you an extra bonus for turning on this check box: Filters, transitions or transparency settings modifying the clip will also appear in the preview. So it's much easier now to coordinate motions settings with other effects and superimposed layers of clips.

Show Outlines
Turn on this option to display a rectangular outline of the

Outlines can give you a good idea of the motion flow. For complex motion paths, however, crowded outlines may be difficult to comprehend.

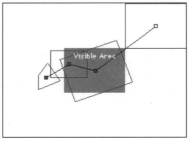

clip around each motion point. The outline will reflect any zoom or rotation options that are present along the motion path. Distortion effects will also appear, but only in 3.0.

The following three items in the Motion Settings dialog box can further enhance your clip's travels.

Smooth Motion

Turn on this check box to smooth a clip's motion around sharp-angled motion points. Smoothing is particularly apparent if your final movie will run at a high frame rate.

Alpha ("Transparent Fill" in 2.0)

In Premiere 3.0, if an alpha channel is already in the clip—such as a Premiere-generated title—the "Alpha: Use clip's" button will be active. (This is the same as "Transparent Fill" turned off in Premiere 2.0.) When you superimpose the clip with an alpha channel matte in Premiere's transparency settings (a Chapter 10 topic), just the alpha channel areas will serve as a mask.

📖 For more about alpha channel matte, see page 269.

With "Alpha: Use clip's" selected (that's "Transparent Fill" turned off in Premiere 2.0), a title flies over the background clip.

Turn on "Alpha: Create new" in Premiere 3.0 (or "Transparent Fill" in Premiere 2.0) if you prefer to superimpose *a solid clip frame* over the background material.

Turning on "Alpha: Create new" ("Transparent Fill" in 2.0) makes the entire motion clip opaque with a one-pixel soft edge.

Fill Color

If you prefer a solid color in the residual area around the moving clip, use this box. Place the cursor over the image to produce an eyedropper for grabbing an existing color within the clip. Or click the rectangular color box above to get a color picker for choosing the color.

This window always shows the clip's *first* frame. If the color you want is in a later frame, exit the Motion settings dialog box, temporarily trim the clip's beginning to the desired frame, and then return to this control.

▶ Traveling that Road Again

Motion Settings

You can save and re-use Premiere's motion paths for other clips or future projects—a tremendous time-saver. In fact, Premiere ships with nearly a dozen paths you can use as is—or alter them to create new paths. Just click the Load button in the Motion Settings dialog box and look in the Motion Settings folder within Premiere's folder.

To save your new motion travels, click the Save button to see the typical Save dialog box below.

Consider throwing the saved file into the Motion Settings folder so you can easily find it again.

Only Premiere 3.0 shows "Disk Free Space" at the bottom of the dialog box.

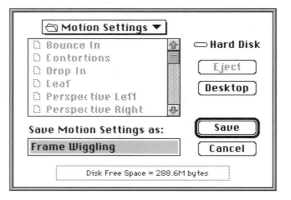

3.0

For Premiere 3.0 users who have upgraded from 2.0, here's one last tip: Motion settings opened in 3.0 that were created in Premiere 2.0 may need their *delays* adjusted. If you recall (see page 212), delays in Premiere 2.0 can be as high as 400%, but Premiere 3.0's cannot exceed 100%—and are generally much smaller. Fortunately, Premiere 3.0 alerts you to the potential problem.

Upon opening a motion setting file from Premiere 2.0 that has delays, Premiere 3.0 will (somewhat cryptically) alert you to the potential problem.

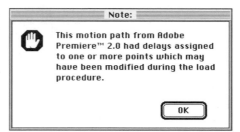

If you traveled through this entire section, you should now be much more of an expert at applying motion settings to clips. In the next section, we'll look over some intriguing examples to hone your motion abilities further.

Moving Experiences

Premiere's motion settings are more than another form of clip razzle-dazzle. They can solve a variety of movie problems. In this section, we'll first view several examples of their practical value for different projects. Then we'll look over a few whiz-bang ideas to give you a taste of what's creatively possible.

▶ The Right Place at the Right Time

This first technique is especially handy for solving problems with *insets*. In Chapter 6, we saw how you could "freeze" an iris transition to show an inset within the frame of another clip.

In this example, an Iris Round transition is frozen at 42% and positioned to highlight the ballet dancer's footwork.

For more about freezing a transition, see page 150.

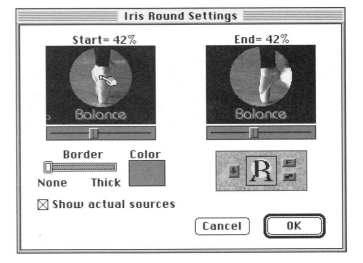

The freezing technique works fine as long as the portion of the scene you want to show in the inset matches the inset's position. That rarely happens, though, especially with a moving subject like a ballet dancer.

You can see the range of the dancer's movement in the B Track clip's thumbnails.

Motion settings can solve the problem. First select the inset clip (the B clip in this case) and open the Motion Settings dialog box (Command Y). Then create a motion path that keeps the subject within the inset's boundaries. You may need to zoom the clip to do that, too.

In this example, the clip is zoomed to 70% size and three motion points are placed near each other to correct for any off-center movement. In Premiere 3.0, turning on the Show All check box will show the inset in the preview box in the upper left corner—a great help for positioning decisions.

☞ Premiere 3.0's dialog box appears at right, but the same technique is also possible in Premiere 2.0.

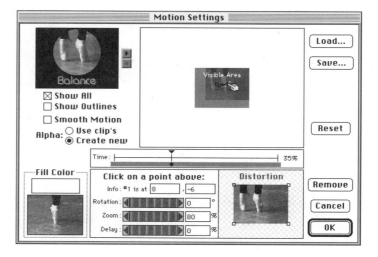

Similar to the above situation, you also can use motion settings to improve the positioning of *split-screen* clips.

Before and after results—the right example uses motion settings to shift the left clip further left and slightly downward.

📖 For more about creating split-screens, see page 151.

So keep Premiere's motion settings in your hip pocket when you're creating an inset or split-screen. With the right adjustments, you'll ensure your clip's action is in the right place at the right time—no matter how the footage was originally shot.

▶ The Clip Quartet

The Zoom control in the Motion Settings dialog box is a more precise pixel manipulator than Premiere's Zoom transition. Here's a straight-forward effect that takes advantage of the motion Zoom's accuracy: Play four *different* clips in one frame—by zooming the clips into quadrants. This is different than the Mosaic filter, which plays the *same* clip in several cells. To create the clip quartet effect, follow these steps:

1 In Premiere 3.0, arrange four clips in consecutive S tracks as shown below. Premiere 2.0 users should refer to the note at left.

Premiere 3.0's multiple S tracks are especially handy for this four-clip technique.

(2.0) *Since only one Super track is available in Premiere 2.0, you have to compile the segment (with the None codec and a matching color depth) after superimposing each clip. Then place the new clip in Track A and superimpose and compile the next clip...and so on until all four clips are included.*

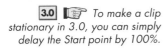

2 Open the Motion Settings dialog box (Command Y) for the first clip (in the A track). Zoom the Start and Finish motion points to 50% size. Then position the clip in the quadrant desired. The clip will not be in motion, so place the Start and Finish points on top of each other.

3.0 ☞ *To make a clip stationary in 3.0, you can simply delay the Start point by 100%.*

Here's an example of what the Motion Settings dialog box should look like. Be sure to turn on the "Alpha: Create new" button ("Transparent Fill" in 2.0). Then click OK.

☞ *No matter the frame size of the clip, location coordinates for the four quadrants are (from top left) –20,–15; 20,–15; 20,15 and –20,15.*

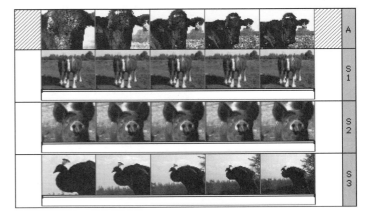

3 Repeat the second step for the other three clips, positioning each clip in a different quadrant.

3.0 👉 *To take advantage of 3.0's "Show All" feature, apply the key type before Step 2.*

Key Type: [Alpha Channel ▼]

4 In the Construction window, select each S track clip one at a time and open the Transparency Settings dialog box (Command T). In that dialog box (Chapter 10's focus), select the Alpha Channel key type in the pop-up menu and click OK. Then preview your results.

▶ More Zoom Magic

👉 *For more about Crop and Image Pan filters, see page 198.*

In the above technique, we zoomed a clip *smaller* to fit four clips into one frame. Zooming the other direction— larger— also can be useful for *cropping* clips, particularly in Premiere 2.0. Premiere 3.0 has the new Crop and Image Pan filters, which provides even better ways to crop shots.

Cropping can strengthen a clip's visual expression, particularly long shots that appear weak or distant in small movies. Cropping can also more accurately frame the area of interest and eliminate background distractions or fringe noise around the frame.

All you have to do is zoom a clip larger in the Motion Settings dialog box and position it so unwanted pixels are outside the visible area, such as the example below.

The captured video clip (left image) has a one-pixel fringe along its left and bottom edge. To crop that out, center the clip's Start and Finish motion points at 0,0 coordinates and set the zoom for both points to 102%.

Note that there's a disadvantage to zooming a clip larger (even slightly larger): the clip's sharpness will noticeably decrease. Premiere has to interpolate pixels between the source clip and the displayed frame.

▶ The Clip Parade

Ready for one more zoom enhancement? Let's march a parade of clips past the viewer's eye. With a simple use of Premiere's transparency settings (relax, Chapter 10 know-how

isn't necessary), we'll march more than one clip at a time within the frame. First we'll go through the process for Premiere 3.0 and then see how to adjust it for 2.0.

3.0

1 Line up three clips in consecutive S tracks, as shown below. Use additional tracks if you want to parade more than three clips.

The clips should be similar in duration and overlap to create a parade that marches in step.

☞ *You may need to use "Add/Delete Tracks..." in the Project menu (Command 3) to establish enough S Tracks.*

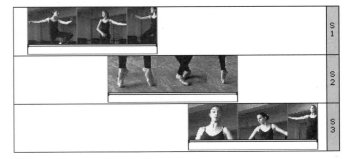

2 Select the first clip in the segment and open the Transparency Settings dialog box (Command T). Choose the *Alpha Channel* key type in the pop-up menu. Then click OK to close the dialog box.

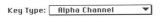

Key Type: **Alpha Channel** ▼

3 Open the Motion Settings dialog box for the first clip (Command Y). Define a motion path with five or six points that send the clip across the visible area with a gentle up and down movement. Then progressively zoom each point, as shown below. Last, give the box an OK.

In this example, each motion point from Start to Finish is zoomed to 20%, 30%, 50%, 70%, 80% and 100% size, respectively. Turning on "Show Outlines" can help your positioning. Be sure to turn on the Smooth Motion check box and "Alpha: Create new" button also.

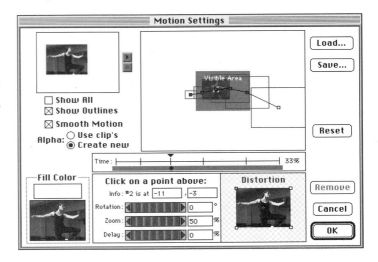

Settings
☐ Filters   ☒ Motion Settings
☐ Fade Control   ☒ Transparency Settings

4 Back in the Construction window, copy the first clip. Then select the clip in the *next* track and choose "Paste Special…" in the Edit menu. In the dialog box that appears, adjust the Settings as shown at left—then click the Paste button.

5 Select the clip in the next S Track and choose "Paste Special Again" in the Edit menu. Repeat this for any other clips in your parade. Then preview your results, which should look similar to below.

Depending on the duration of your clips and how closely you want them to march, you may need to fine-tune the overlap in the Construction window.

2.0 To parade clips in Premiere 2.0, follow Steps 1 through 3 for just the *first* clip in 2.0's one-and-only Super track. Then compile the segment (with the None codec) and place the new clip in the A track. Delete the original Super track clip. Next, place the *second* clip in your parade in the Super track so it overlaps the A track clip. Then compile the segment again. Repeat this process until you've compiled the entire procession.

▶ Bouncing Balls of Clips

Let's close this chapter with some Distortion box ideas to whet your creative appetite. Here's the first one: giving resilience to a bouncing clip. In Premiere 3.0, you can take advantage of virtual clips for this effect. Premiere 2.0 users can do it with extra compiling. Here are the steps:

1 Let's first shape a clip into a ball by freezing an Iris Round transition and making a virtual clip of the segment. (Premiere 2.0 users should compile the segment with the None codec instead.)

📖 For more about creating virtual clips, see page 78.

In an empty area of the Construction window, freeze the Iris Round transition into a large circle of the A clip. Then make a virtual clip of the segment.

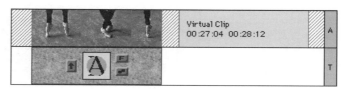

2 Open the Motion Settings dialog box for the virtual clip. Create a bouncing ball path, zooming up the clip's size as it progresses. Also use the Fill Color control to blacken the residual area outside the bouncing clip.

3 Now let's add resilience to the bouncing clip. At the motion point where the ball contacts the bottom of the clip, use the Distortion box to squish its shape. So the ball doesn't compress *before* contact (because Premiere will gradually increase distortion before the motion point), place a distortion-free motion point slightly before the contact point, as shown below.

In this example, the motion path gives the ball a single bounce. The "squish" motion point is selected so you can see the Distortion box settings below.

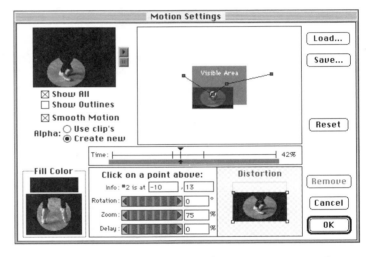

Click OK in the dialog box and preview your results, which should look similar to below.

Bouncing balls of clips! The ball's compression at contact adds a realistic touch—all due to the Distortion box control.

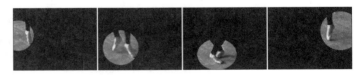

▶ **Distortion Box Reflections**

3.0

Now for our last motion trick of the day. This fun 3.0 technique illustrates how the Distortion box can team up with transparency settings to produce a convincing reflection of a clip. Although transparency settings is a Chapter 10 topic, we'll lightly touch on it here to walk through this effect.

1 Create four clips of equal length in 3.0. The first clip forms a background—drag it into track A or B. (This example uses a color matte, but a cloud scene or other background clips would work well, too.) Align the three remaining clips in consecutive S tracks, as shown below.

For this example, the S1 track holds a "table" surface—a Premiere backdrop file of marble. Track S2 has the ballet clip and S3 carries a copy of the ballet clip that we'll manipulate into a reflection.

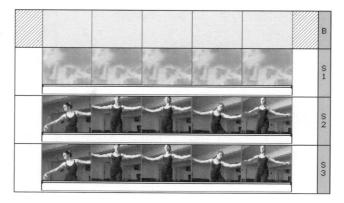

2 Open the Motion Settings dialog box (Command Y) for the S2 clip. Zoom the clip to 50% at the Start and assign a 100% delay. Then center the Start point in the upper third of the Visible Area as shown at left. Click OK to the dialog box.

3 Back in the Construction window, select and copy (Command C) the S2 clip you just modified. Then select the S3 clip and choose "Paste Special…" in the Edit menu (Command H). Turn on the Settings options as shown at left and click OK. That will paste S2's motion settings into the S3 clip.

◉ **Settings** ....
☒ **Motion Settings**

4 Open the Motion Settings dialog box for the S3 clip. Select the Start motion point. In the Distortion box, pull down and widen the top corners of the clip so it appears backwards and extends forward in perspective. Then click OK to close the dialog box.

The distorted clip will form a perspective plane in front of the original clip.

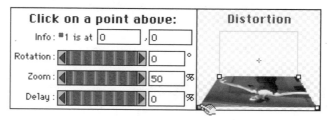

5 Use the "Paste Special…" command as described in Step 3 to copy and paste motion settings from the S3 clip to the S1 clip. Then open the Motion Settings dialog box for the S1 clip. Zoom up the Start motion point sufficiently so the "marble table" covers the lower portion of the visible area, as shown at left.

6 Back in the Construction window, hold down the Shift key and drag the entire fader line below the S3 clip to the middle—fading the entire clip to 50%. Use the Info window if necessary to guide your fading.

The faded clip will appear as a subtle reflection of the primary clip.

7 Open the Transparency Settings dialog box (Command T) for each S track clip, one at a time. Select the *Alpha Channel* key type in the pop-up menu. Then click OK to close the dialog box. That's all—go ahead and preview the results.

The center clip plays with its reflection accurately shown as a reflection in the marble.

Well, you've gained some additional ideas of how to take advantage of Premiere's motion settings. Use the examples as a starting point to create new moving experiences for your projects—the only limits are your imagination and your hard disk space.

▶ **To the Title Window**

With motion acrobatics behind us, let's aim closer to earth and create titles in Premiere—an essential element of most projects. Ahead you'll see how to master Premiere's Title window. Along the way, we'll animate text and have plenty of (practical) fun with titles and related effects.

9

Creating Titles & Graphics

Premiere's built-in Title window is a great convenience. You don't always have to run other applications to create text and graphics for your movies. And everything you produce in the window is smoothly anti-aliased and carries an alpha channel for superimposing. Even when you need pixel-level painting from a powerhouse like Adobe Photoshop, the Title window is a handy sketchpad for initially composing your screen ideas.

In this chapter, you'll see how to create new titles and work efficiently with the Title window's controls—including the many new features of Premiere 3.0. Then we'll explore text animation and other snazzy visual effects you can achieve with type.

Into the Title Window

Premiere's Title window is a very capable canvas for creating type and graphics for your movies. If you've used other drawing programs on the Mac, you have a head start in mastering this window. You'll soon run into unique tools and commands (and a few peculiarities), though, owing to the Title window's movie orientation. This section will sail you over those obstacles. We'll also explore simple ways of giving your titles some pizzazz with just a click or two of the mouse.

▶ Title Basics

Let's first review the basics of creating a title. Then we'll dive into each tool and command the Title window offers. Creating a title for your project is a four-step process.

1 Select "Title" from the New submenu in the File menu. A Title window will appear, as shown below. Two new menus also pop up on your Mac's menu bar: *Title* and *Font* (*Text* in Premiere 2.0).

Premiere 2.0 (back) and 3.0 versions of the Title window differ substantially in their palettes. Premiere 3.0 adds polygon, eyedropper and gradient tools. 3.0's window also initially shows dotted rectangles representing the NTSC safe areas for titles.

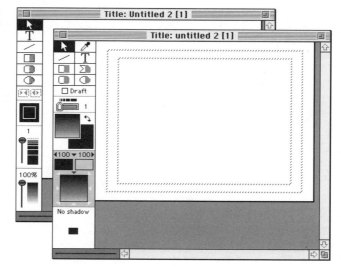

2 Create your title, using the tools at the top of the window's palette to enter text and draw shapes. Then enhance the elements as desired with the other controls. In Premiere 3.0 you can view a clip's frame in the window's background to help with positioning. You can also grab colors from the frame with the eyedropper tool.

3.0 ☞ *In 3.0, to reset all tools to default settings, type "R" while the Title window is active.*

3.0 *Premiere 3.0's ability to display a background frame greatly aids positioning, as shown by this title for a zoo promotional movie.*

For more about placing a frame in the background, see page 232.

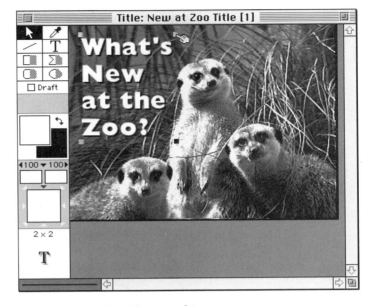

As you work with a graphic or text object in Premiere 3.0, the Info window (if it's visible) gives you key statistics. You'll see the location and size of the selected object as well as your changing cursor coordinates.

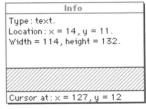

```
            Info
Type: text.
Location: x = 14, y = 11.
Width = 114, height = 132.



Cursor at: x = 127, y = 12
```

"Location" in the Info window refers to the upper left handle of the selected object.

Either version of Premiere is a smoothie—automatically anti-aliasing text and graphics in the window for a slick edge appearance. All objects also carry an alpha channel to simplify the superimposing of the title clip.

For more about alpha channels, see page 269.

3 Save the Title window by selecting the "Save…" command in the File menu (Command S).

4 Drag the Title window's contents into the Project or Construction window. To ensure that you drag the entire title, not an individual title object, hold down the Control key as you drag. (In 2.0, use the Command key.)

control

To superimpose a title, for example, drag it into an S track and use Premiere's Transparency Settings (more about that in Chapter 10). You also can adjust the fade line below the clip to fade the title in or out smoothly.

If you prefer that your fingertips do the walking, there are two alternatives to dragging the title into your project. You can choose "Add this Clip" from the Clip menu (Command J) or select "Import File…" in the File menu (Command I). Both will instantly plop your title into the Project window.

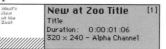

Once the title is in your project, it has a default duration of one second. That default is adjustable by choosing "Still Image…" ("Still Image Duration…" in 2.0) in the Preferences submenu of the File menu. The new duration will take affect the next time you open a Title window. Of course, in the Construction window you can always drag either edge of a title clip to change its duration, too.

You also can go back and alter the title anytime. To call up the Title window again, double-click the title clip's thumbnail—or select the thumbnail and trigger "Open Clip" in the Clip menu. Changes to the title will appear in your project after you save the Title window revisions.

Choose "Save…" for title revisions. "Save as…" creates a new file which you'll have to re-drag into your project.

What if your title needs a special touch Premiere can't provide? Simply export the title into Photoshop or another graphics application for more image processing. The two most convenient ways to do that are:

Export a PICT

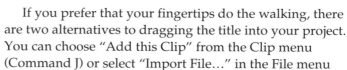

ZooTitle.PICT

With the Title window active, select "Frame as PICT…" in the Export submenu of the File menu. The PICT will match the Title image. You'll lose the alpha channel later, however, if your graphics program can't handle it.

Export a Filmstrip File for Photoshop

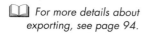

ZooTitle.film

Also in the Export submenu is "Filmstrip File…". This Photoshop-based approach can export multiple frames of the title image. And the alpha channel will stay with the file throughout the journey to and from Photoshop.

For more details about exporting, see page 94.

To export *special effects* with the title clip, such as Premiere's filter enhancements, you have to compile the segment first. Then from the new Clip window that appears, use either of the above commands.

That's all for the basic title-making process. Now let's step back and see how to configure the Title window environment properly before creating a new title.

▶ Configuring the Title Area

In Premiere 2.0, several commands for setting up the Title window are at the top of the Title menu. In Premiere 3.0, the same commands move into a single dialog box. To open that dialog box, make sure the Title window is active and then select "Title Window Options…" from 3.0's Windows menu (Command 1).

In Premiere 3.0, this dialog box consolidates several items that were formerly in the top half of 2.0's Title menu (far right).

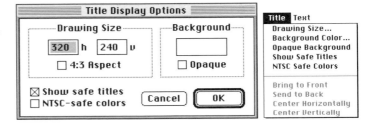

Let's briefly look over what each item can do.

Drawing Size

The Title window's default size is 320 x 240 pixels. If your movie output will be a different size, it's not essential that you match the size *as long as the aspect ratio is correct.* Premiere will scale the object-oriented title without a hitch when compiling your project. Working at the same size as your final output, however, often gives you a better feel for sizing type and deciding other title subtleties.

You can shrink the window to 60 x 45 pixels or stretch it to 2000 x 2000 pixels (assuming you have sufficient RAM). By keeping the 4:3 Aspect Ratio check box on, entering one dimension automatically produces the other.

3.0 ☞ *In Premiere 3.0, a General Preferences setting may limit you to 1024 x 1024 pixels. See page 297.*

Background Color

☞ *To quickly change the background color to black or white, type "B" or "W" anytime the Title window is active except when working with text.*

To change the background color from the default white, click the Background rectangle in Premiere 3.0. In 2.0, select "Background Color…" in the Title menu. Premiere 3.0 can work with Apple's standard color picker or its own color picker design. The one you'll see depends on your choice in the General Preferences dialog box. (We'll find out more about the pickers a few pages ahead.)

Normally the background color is transparent when you superimpose a title over another clip using an alpha channel key type. To make the background color opaque for superimposing work, turn on the Opaque check box.

📖 *For more about alpha channels, see page 269.*

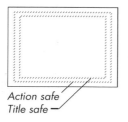

Action safe
Title safe

Show Safe Titles

Placing titles and graphics within safe areas is important for projects destined for television playback. Otherwise, television over-scanning may slip your work partially off-screen. For Premiere movies that will play only on computers, however, you can turn the rectangles off.

NTSC Safe Colors

Here's another check box targeted for television work. It automatically subdues any sizzling hot colors that you may choose in the Title window, reducing the chance of colors bleeding across television scan lines.

▶ A Frame for the Background

Premiere 3.0 offers another option that greatly improves your titling efficiency. As we saw a few pages earlier, you can display a selected frame from a clip in the background of the Title window. Positioning your title with such a reference frame is a snap. And with the newly available eyedropper tool, you can snatch a color from the background for your text or graphics.

Let's see how to place a clip's frame into the Title window's background. The process takes three steps.

1 Display the frame intended for the background in the Clip window. If the frame isn't the In point of the clip, you'll need to assign a "0" place marker to the frame.

Use the "0" place marker in the Clip window to target a different background frame than the clip's In point.

📖 *For more about setting place markers in the Clip window, see page 56.*

Clip: meerkats 2 [1]

00:00:00:12   In   Mark: 0
△ 00:01:04   Out   Goto: 1
                             2
                             3

2 Drag the clip from the Clip or Project window into the Title window. The Title window will highlight as you do this. After releasing the mouse button, the frame will land in the Title window's background.

The selected frame appears in the Title window's background.

Change the "0" marker's location anytime to see a different frame in the Title window—without having to drag the clip to the window again.

To remove the background frame, select "Remove Background Clip" at the bottom of the Title menu.

▶ Creating & Selecting

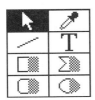

Now that you know how to configure the Title window, let's get into the nitty-gritty of creating text and graphics in the window. That means we'll focus towards the top of the window's tool palette (Premiere 3.0's appears at left, but most of the same tools are in 2.0).

If you're familiar with Macintosh drawing programs, you'll quickly acclimate yourself to these tools. Premiere's toolkit has a few quirks, however, so even experienced users should glance below for shortcuts and clarifications.

Selection Tool

Select any text or graphics object in the Title window with this tool. When the cursor is over an object's handle, it becomes a hand pointer. Dragging with the hand pointer resizes an object (except type) instead of moving it.

Keep in mind two other selection tips:

• In Premiere 2.0, you *can't select* all objects in the window at once (although you *can move* all objects at once by holding down the Command and Option keys as you drag an object). Premiere 3.0 remedies this glaring omission—simply choose "Select All" in the Edit menu. In 3.0 you can also select several objects at once by Shift-clicking. Holding down the Shift key also allows you to drag a marquee selection (marching ants) with this tool.

• In 2.0 or 3.0, to select objects one-by-one in the order they were created, press the Tab key (or for reverse order, press the Tab and Shift keys together). This is how you can select objects that are hiding under other objects.

3.0

While using other tools in Premiere 3.0, press the Command key to temporarily return to the Selection tool.

Type Tool

Use the Type tool to create and edit text. All text automatically anti-aliases as you complete each text block.

Adjust the style, size and justification of the text by selecting those attributes in the Title menu. Switch fonts with the Font menu. (In Premiere 2.0, all four attributes are submenus of the Text menu.) Unfortunately, in either Premiere version the *entire* text block will take on the attributes. To mix fonts, sizes or justifications, you have to create more than one text block.

☞ *To increase or decrease a selected text block's font size by one point, press Command-Shift-Greater Than (>) or Less Than (<). To change the block's size by five points, also hold down the Option key.*

What about leading—the space between lines of text? A hidden command for that lurks in Premiere. To increase or decrease a selected text block's leading by one point, press the Option key and tap the Up or Down Arrow key. For five points per key tap, also press the Shift key.

📖 *To kern text, see page 237.*

Line Tool

Draw straight lines with this tool. Press the Shift key as you drag to constrain the line to 45° angle increments.

Shape Tools

Use these tools to create rectangles, rounded rectangles, ovals and (in Premiere 3.0) polygons. Click the left side of a tool icon to draw a framed object. Click the right side to create a filled shape. Hold down the Shift key as you draw to coerce a rectangle or rounded rectangle into a square—or an oval into a circle.

☞ *Double-click any tool icon shown on this page to use it repeatedly without re-selecting it.*

In Premiere 3.0, you can quickly convert a framed object to an unfilled object (or vise versa). Select the shape and choose the "Convert to Framed" command in the Title menu (the command will be "Convert to Filled" if you selected a framed object).

3.0

To create a polygon in 3.0, click with the polygon tool to define corner points of the object. When you reach the last point, double-click it to tell Premiere you're done. If you're creating a filled polygon, Premiere automatically closes the polygon's shape before filling it.

☞ *An "o" near the cursor cross hairs indicates when you're near enough to a polygon's first point to close the shape.*

You can always edit the polygon points later by re-selecting the polygon and dragging its handles. You also can smooth a selected polygon by choosing "Smooth Polygon" in the Title menu. Select the command again to return the shape to sharper form.

Select a smooth or sharp polygon and drag its handles to change its shape.

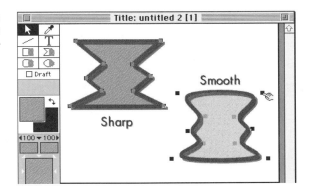

3.0

To create a filled object with a frame (like the polygons above), Premiere 3.0 differs significantly from 2.0. In Premiere 2.0, you only need to draw a filled shape and choose a different border color for it in the color swatch—like most draw programs.

To perform that trick in Premiere 3.0, the process is less intuitive—but ultimately gives you more graphics flexibility. First draw the object using the appropriate shape tool—framed or filled. Then, while the object is selected, choose "Create Framed Object" in the Title menu ("Create Filled Object" if you started with a framed shape). Premiere will automatically copy the object, create its opposite, and align the two together.

With a darker color for the framed object, for example, the two objects simulate a single filled shape with a border.

You won't see a filled object with a border right away because the two objects will have the same color. But Premiere finishes its routine by selecting the new object. So all you have to do is double-click the color swatch in the tool palette to change the object's color.

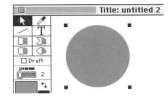 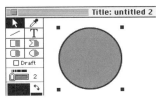

The advantage to this somewhat awkward duality is that you can graphically enhance each element individually. For example, as we'll soon see, you could give the border a different gradient or opacity than the filling. The disadvantage is you have to remember to select *both* objects when moving or altering the entire graphic.

Line Weight Slider

This tool is visible only when you select an un-filled shape or a line. Drag the slider to change the object's line weight—from one to 16 pixels. 3.0's tool at left looks different than 2.0's at right, but both work identically.

Before we move on to other title topics, remember one last object-creation note: Both Premiere versions have good ol' Cut, Copy, Paste, Clear, Duplicate and (yeah!) Undo commands in the Edit menu to help you create text and graphics. However, you can only copy and paste objects *in Title windows*—not Clipboard contents from other windows or applications.

▶ Moving & Layering

Repositioning objects in the Title window deviates in certain ways from standard Macintosh conventions. As always, you can drag a *single* object around with the Selection tool. Beyond that, though, the techniques tend to differ. Furthermore, Premiere 2.0 and 3.0 differ from each other. Refer below to clear up any confusion.

• *To move all objects at once*
In Premiere 3.0, choose "Select All" in the Edit menu and then drag any object. In Premiere 2.0, "Select All" isn't available for titles. The work-around is to hold down the Command and Option keys and drag any object.

3.0 • *To move several objects at once*
Premiere 3.0 follows the convention of most Macintosh applications: Click more than one object while holding down the Shift key, then drag. Or hold down the Shift key and drag to create a selection marquee, then drag the selected objects. Premiere 2.0 can't do either one.

• *To nudge an object*
Select an object and tap an Arrow key to move in one-pixel steps. Hold down the Shift key and press an Arrow key to advance five pixels.

• *To constrain an object's movement*
Like most Mac software, hold down the Shift key to limit object dragging to a horizontal or vertical direction.

Look for the next three adjustments in the Title menu.

Bring to Front
Send to Back
Center Horizontally
Center Vertically
Position In Lower Third

• *To move an object in front or behind another object*
Select "Bring to Front" or "Send to Back." Initially, Premiere layers Title window objects in the order they're created—with the latest object always sitting on top.

• *To center an object vertically or horizontally*
Choose "Center Horizontally" or "Center Vertically." In Premiere 3.0, centering several objects at once will center them *as a group*—not individually. Off-center objects within the group may therefore remain off-center.

3.0

• *To position an object in the lower third of the title area*
"Position in Lower Third" is a Premiere 3.0 exclusive.

▶ Visual Enhancements

Now let's add some sparkle to your text and geometric shapes by working with other tools and commands in the Title window environment.

Kerning

The two kerning buttons in the tool palette change the spacing between text characters. (In Premiere 3.0, the tools are visible only when editing text.) To kern, place the text cursor between two characters—or drag to select several characters at once. Then click the left button to tighten the spacing or the right button to widen the gap. You also can kern by holding down the Option key while tapping either the Left or Right Arrow key.

unkerned
kerned

☞ *To reset kerning to its original unaltered spacing, Command-click either kern tool.*

Shadows

In Premiere 2.0, only text can have a shadow— and the shadow's offset has to be the same number of pixels horizontally and vertically. Simply select a text block and drag the shadow slider to the offset desired.

3.0

Premiere 3.0 goes much further by allowing you to shadow *any* selected object—*at any angle*. Use the control box below—just drag the preview shadow anywhere in the box. As you drag, the pixel offset will numerically show on top. For a 45° shadow, hold down the Shift key. To eliminate a shadow, drag it out of the box or hide it under the solid object.

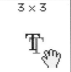

☞ *For shadows and other title enhancements that follow, in 3.0 you can apply them to several objects at once—an impossible task in 2.0.*

3.0 In Premiere 3.0, choose from three shadow styles by accessing the Shadows submenu in the Title menu. The shadow differences appear below.

The "Soft" shadow choice in Premiere 3.0 is most natural. It successfully recreates the dissipating light of real shadows. Premiere 2.0 provides only the "Single" and "Solid" shadows.

☞ *In Premiere 3.0, Option-clicking the shadow control box cycles through the three shadow styles.*

📖 *To adjust the opacity of shadows, see page 240.*

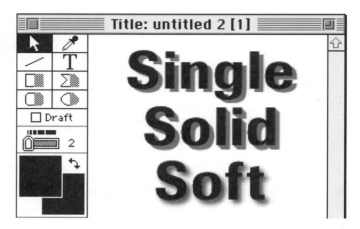

Color

Premiere 3.0 gives you two color swatches. Double-click the upper left box to choose a color for the currently selected object(s). Double-click the lower box to color the object's *shadow*. In either case, your click will pop up a color picker—Apple's or Adobe's—depending on a preference setting in the General Preferences dialog box. (We'll look at the two color pickers three pages ahead.)

To switch the two color swatch assignments, click the small curved arrow. To copy a color from one swatch to the other, simply drag the color into the other box.

Another way to select colors in Premiere 3.0 is to use the handy eyedropper tool. Click it anywhere in the title area to suck up the color that's underneath (including any color in a background clip frame). The color will immediately deposit itself into the *object* color swatch. To squirt a color into the *shadow* swatch, hold down the Option key as you click. To drop a *complementary* color into either swatch, also hold down the Shift key as you click.

2.0 Premiere 2.0 uses the standard-style control that we briefly visited earlier. Click the inner or outer rectangle to choose a fill or border color—like most draw programs. An alternative is to Option-click an object to set its fill color; Shift-Option-click to set its border color.

3.0 **Gradients**

Gradients are a new feature of Premiere 3.0. A combined gradient/opacity box powerfully controls the gradients but takes a few moments to understand. You can apply gradients to any text or graphic in the Title window.

To create a color gradient, follow these steps:

1 Select the object(s) you want to modify. Then click the upper left color swatch to modify the *object*. Or click the lower right swatch to modify the object's *shadow*.

2 In the gradient control box, click the small upper left color box to select a *start* color from the color picker. Then click the small right color box to select an *end* color for the gradient.

3 Click an arrow around the preview box to define the gradient's starting point. You can select any side of the box—or a corner for a diagonal gradient.

That's all of the steps—an example gradient is below.

The lower object has a color gradient that runs from left to right. You can see the object's gradient settings towards the bottom of the palette.

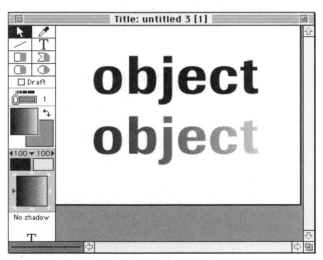

To eliminate a gradient, do either of these actions:

• Drag the color from the start color box to the end color box (or vice versa) to give both boxes the same color— thus no gradient.

• Click the center of the gradient preview box to visit your friendly color picker again. Then choose a new single color for the entire object or shadow.

Opacity

You can set the opacity of a text block or graphic object from transparent (0%) to completely opaque (100%). In Premiere 3.0, you can even create an *opacity gradient*, although it will have to share the same orientation as a color gradient. Finally, like color settings, shadows in Premiere 3.0 can have a completely different opacity than their mother objects.

To adjust opacity in Premiere 3.0, follow the first step of the gradient process described on the previous page. Then complete this second step:

2 To set a *constant* opacity for the selected object (or shadow), press the small black arrow at the top middle of the control to use a slider. To give the object (or shadow) a opacity gradient, press the two side black arrows to see a similar slider. The left black arrow sets the *start* percentage and the right sets the *end* percentage of the gradient.

In this multimedia example, the "Zoo Highlights" text block varies in opacity from 100% to 50% from left to right, allowing it to overlap the numerals. Its shadow also has a similar opacity gradient.

Premiere 2.0's opacity control, in contrast (no pun intended), is simpler because it only sets the opacity of an entire object. Opacity gradients or separate shadow settings aren't possible. Simply drag the slider to the percentage desired after selecting the object.

3.0

☒ Draft

👉 *Tap the accent key (') to toggle the Draft mode.*

Draft Mode

Congratulations! We've reached the last tool palette item, which is only in Premiere 3.0. To speed redrawing of the Title window, turn this check box on. It only affects the title's display, not the actual clip. CPU-intensive anti-aliasing and color/opacity gradients will no longer appear. They'll return when you uncheck the box.

▶ Picking a Color Picker

When you need to select a color in Premiere, like in the Title window, a color picker appears. Premiere 2.0 provides Apple's standard color picker. Premiere 3.0 adds a custom alternative. Let's briefly examine the two picks.

Apple's color picker offers a familiar color wheel. The picker allows you to specify a color numerically based on a RGB (Red, Green, Blue) or HSB (Hue, Saturation, Brightness) color model. Use the large vertical scroll bar at the far right of the box to control color brightness. Then click anywhere in the color wheel.

The top rectangle shows the new color you've selected. The lower rectangle shows the current color. If you choose to enter a color value numerically, from 0 to 65,535 is possible for each component.

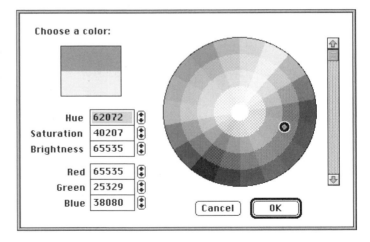

```
Choose a color:

         Hue          62072  ⬍
         Saturation   40207  ⬍
         Brightness   65535  ⬍

         Red          65535  ⬍
         Green        25329  ⬍
         Blue         38080  ⬍
                              [ Cancel ]  [ OK ]
```

The total number of colors shown, of course, depends on your screen's color depth. That's an inescapable fact for either color picker. An 8-bit monitor, for example, displays only 256 of the more than 16 million color candidates.

3.0

Now let's check out the Premiere color picker that 3.0 also lavishes on you. Unlike Apple's, it shows *all* available colors and brightness levels in one flat region. You don't have to scroll to adjust brightness levels—an advantage.

Just click in the color box—or *outside* of the box to choose any other colors on your screen, such as from a PICT file or other graphic. Numerically, however, Premiere's picker can only cope with RGB color values.

The far left edge of the color area features a continuous greyscale—from white to black. The rectangle displaying your choice is in the reverse position from Apple's—the lower swatch shows the new color you've chosen. The upper swatch shows any previously selected color.

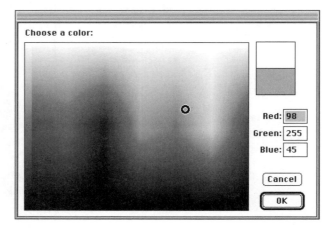

For more about the NTSC safe colors option, see page 232.

Here's another advantage of Premiere's color picker: If your color choice is outside the NTSC-safe color range, a small warning sign appears. The warning triangle will sit next to the swatch together with a small patch showing the nearest NTSC-safe color. Premiere will substitute the safe color for your wild selection if you turn on "NTSC-safe colors" in the Title Display Options dialog box.

If you have Premiere 3.0, what's your choice? To ensure your favorite picker always arises, select "General Preferences…" from the Preference submenu of the File menu. In the pop-up menu near the top of the dialog box that appears, pick your picker.

Say this ten times: Peter Piper picked a peck of color pickers.

General Preferences

Maximum image size:	2048 x 2048 ▼

Size changes take effect on restart.

Window at startup:	New Project ▼
Clip window shuttle control:	
Method for choosing colors:	Apple Picker / ✓Premiere Picker

Well, we've explored quite a bit of title territory, but we haven't yet reached Premiere's built-in text animator. In the next section, we'll tackle that feature and try several other useful techniques—title punchouts, special text effects and a shortcut for rolling credits.

Text Animation & Effects

Now it's time to move into more advanced title topics. Ahead you'll find out how to produce animated text in Premiere. We'll also collect a few Title window techniques that can pull you through sophisticated projects.

▶ Animation Can Do's

Premiere doesn't carry full animation capabilities like a dedicated animation application. However, you can change the size of text over time as well as stretch or contract text. With Adobe's Multiple Masters fonts installed in your Mac, you can also vary the weight, character width and optical scale of blocks that use those fonts.

You may wonder—Why not scale a title up or down with the Zoom transition or with Premiere's motion settings? You can do either, but animating text in the Title window is much cleaner. As a zoom or motion setting enlarges an image, *pixels in the image grow too.* (Anybody for Fatbit fonts?) The Title window, however, retains the full resolution of the font all the way through the sequence.

Be sure to work with outline fonts—Postscript or TrueType—for the cleanest text.

Before we step through the animation process, there's one basic Premiere limitation to understand: You can animate only *one line* of text at a time. If the text block you want to animate includes a carriage return to force another line, Premiere will tersely warn you that the return will be history if you proceed.

two lines

Both Premiere versions suffer from this text animation limitation.

If a text block wraps only because it's too narrow for the text that it holds, you won't get the above warning. But after animating the text, you'll get the same result: Premiere will reset the block's width to fit all characters on one line. (Premiere 4.0, where are you?)

two lines

The good news is you can endow a title with virtually any number of animated text blocks. So there's much you can achieve. Let's see how on the next page.

▶ Text Animation: The Process

Animating a text block requires three or four steps, depending on the animation complexity you desire. That may sound like a lot of steps, but you'll quickly get the hang of this process.

☞ *Animated text blocks tend to tighten, so try to leave kerning until after the animation is set.*

1 With the Selection tool, double-click a text block in the Title window. Or select a text block and choose "Text Animation…" from the Title menu. (In Premiere 2.0, that command is at the bottom of the Text menu.) The Animation Settings dialog box will then appear.

The selected text block will initially appear in the center of the window. Horizontal and vertical size sliders are available for all typefaces. If the text is an Adobe Multiple Masters font you'll also see weight, width and optical size sliders at the window's bottom (shown).

3.0 ☞ *In 3.0, dotted vertical lines along each side of the text block may also appear (shown). They represent the sides of the Title window.*

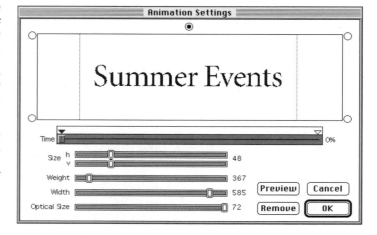

2 Click a direction button to set the *fixed point* from which the text block will animate. For example, the default center button (on top, as shown in the dialog box above) will animate the text from its center. Selecting a corner button will hold a corner of the text block at a fixed location as the animation occurs.

The first example shows the direction of a top center text animation; the second is an upper left corner result.

Sum̲me̲r̲E̲ve̲nts

Su̲m̲me̲r Events

☞ *100% in the time bar always represents the Out point of the title clip, regardless of the clip's duration.*

3 Now use the time bar in the middle of the animation box to set the type attributes to different values during the clip's playback. The left edge of the time bar (0%) represents the beginning of the clip. The time bar's far right (100%) represents the end of the clip.

First adjust the font attributes for the *start* of the animation. Make sure the time bar is at the 0% point (if not, click the triangle there or drag the slider far left). Then drag the font attribute sliders to the values desired.

In this example, the text will start at 0 point size (invisible).

To distort the text, hold down the Shift key and drag the two Size sliders independently.

The last part of this step is to move the time bar slider to the 100% point and set the text attributes for the *end* of your text animation.

This setting will make the text grow to 60 points by the segment's end.

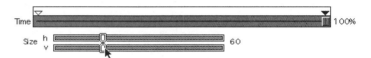

☞ *Split the Size sliders with the Shift key and set 0% and 100% points the same to distort text without creating animation.*

As you move the sliders, you'll see the changes in the preview window above the time bar. If you click the Preview button, the animation will play in the preview window.

[Preview]

4 You're done unless you want to add intermediate time points to create more complex text animations. To do that, move your cursor into the top half of the time bar—you'll see a small black triangle—then click where desired to define a new time point. If the triangle does not end up precisely at the right spot after your click, use the cursor (which turns into a pointing finger) to slide it right or left as needed. The percentage indicator at the right end of the time bar will update as you slide.

This time point is positioned precisely at the 50% point.

☞ *Multiple points near each other allow you to accelerate or decelerate changes—for softer, more natural movement.*

Then adjust the font attribute sliders to the values desired for that intermediate point. Premiere will automatically interpolate all values between the triangles. Continue adding as many points as needed. Then click OK to return to the Title window.

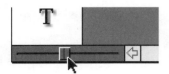

Back in the Title window, the text block will still be selected, but will show *white* handles at its corners. That's your clue that the text is animated.

To preview the animation in the Title window, drag the preview slider at the bottom left corner of the window. Or hold down the Option key and click the preview slider to play the animation. In either case, you won't see animation action in real time, but you'll get a reasonable idea of what you've accomplished.

To remove animation from a text block, select the block, go back into the Text Animation window and click the Remove button.

That's the entire text animation process. Take a spare moment and try it out a few times to get comfortable with the process. Then read below about a handy shortcut for a classic text item in movies—rolling credits.

▶ Rolling Credits via the Image Pan

Combining Premiere 3.0's Image Pan filter with the Title window is a natural for creating rolling credits. Let's go over how they can work together so you can add this classic movie-making element to your repertoire. All it takes is six easy steps.

1 Create a title clip that's the same width as your final movie output—but much taller—using the Title Display Options dialog box. For example, if you're producing a 240 x 180 pixel movie and you have approximately four screens worth of rolling credits to show (including a blank start screen), set the new Title window to 240 x 800 pixels or so.

To set the Title window to such an odd size, you'll need to turn off the 4:3 Aspect check box. You also can turn off the Show safe titles check box.

Title Display Options

Drawing Size: 240 h 800 v □ 4:3 Aspect

Background: □ Opaque

□ Show safe titles
□ NTSC-safe colors

Cancel   OK

In this example, the credits are placed on top of a solid color background. But you also could use this technique to superimpose the credits over another clip.

2 Type the full list of credits in the Title window. To start rolling with a blank screen, place the text at least an output screen's height down from the top of the Title window (check the Info window for the coordinates). Use the "Center Horizontally" command in the Title menu to align each text block. Then save the title file.

3 Drag the clip into a video track in the Construction window. Adjust its duration if necessary.

Don't worry that the title image looks out of proportion in the thumbnail. The next step will compensate for that.

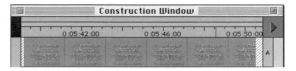

4 Apply the Image Pan filter to the clip. In its dialog box, set the Start rectangle to the height of your final output. Then drag the rectangle to the beginning (top) of the rolling credits. Next, click the Copy button to set the End rectangle to match. Then drag the End rectangle to the bottom of the credits to define the clip's last frame.

Here, Start and End rectangles are at a final output size of 240 x 180 pixels. The Start rectangle is at the top of the rolling credits, the end at the bottom. Ease In and Ease Out check boxes are on to smooth the movement.

📖 *For more details about the Image Pan filter, see page 198.*

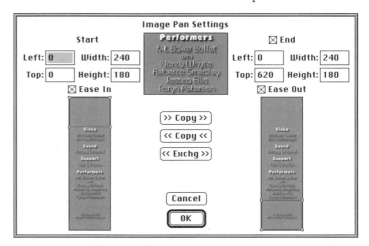

5 Click OK. Then preview the segment using any preview technique, such as *Make Snapshot*.

Magnifico—Rolling credits a la Premiere 3.0!

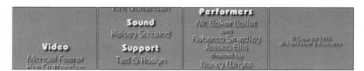

6 Fine-tune your work if necessary. Lengthen or shorten the clip in the Construction window to roll faster or slower. For very long rolling credits, consider placing a few such clips back-to-back. That's all, folks!

▷ Clear Punchouts

Let's briefly visit the bottom of the opacity slider in the Title window where there's a useful, if often overlooked, setting. In Premiere 2.0.1 or later, you can set the slider to "Clear"—in other words, zero percent. This setting has a special property that can be useful for some compositions.

In the Title window, clear appears the same as giving the selected object a white color with the color swatch.

In this example, the text block is given a clear opacity (0%). It appears white in the Title window just like the two horizontal lines, which actually are white with 100% opacity.

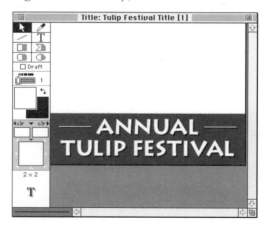

Now let's place the title clip in an S track to superimpose it over another clip, such as shown below.

The fader line at the bottom of the superimposed title clip is angled to gradually fade-in the title.

For more about alpha channel settings, see page 269.

When you superimpose the title—using an alpha channel key in Premiere's Transparency dialog box—the difference between clear and white objects becomes apparent. Clear objects *punch through* the title clip to reveal the background clip. White objects remain white.

Here are the results after superimposing the clip with an alpha channel key.

Notice how the text block shows the background clip image. The adjacent white lines, however, remain white since they did not have a clear opacity setting.

▶ More Fun with Titles

Let's explore a few more tricks with the Title window controls and then call it a wrap. Premiere 3.0 in particular, with its ability to control objects and shadows separately, offers some very powerful and easy ways to produce enhanced type. Below are over a dozen tasty text tidbits.

All of these text examples use Adobe's Imago Medium typeface at 36-point size in the Title window.

To import 3-D text from other applications into Premiere, see page 36.

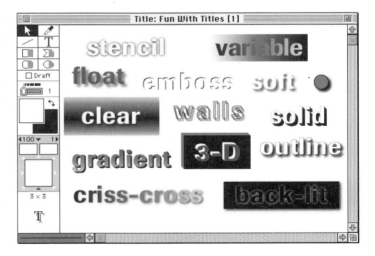

Although the effects are specified for greyscale results (to match this book), most are also very effective with color.

The next few pages explain the settings and offer related comments for each example, starting from the top of the window on down. Use these examples as a starting point to create your own intriguing type.

Stencil

Align white text over an identical text block that only shows a soft shadow. Top settings are: white, 100% opacity, no shadow. Bottom settings are: Text—white (or the background color), 1% (virtually invisible). Shadow—black, 100%, soft, 1 x 1 offset (to generate a shadow).

Variable

Give text the opposite gradient of its background. Text—black to white, 100%, no shadow. Background—white to black, 100%. Although the above specs produce a grey-scale gradient, it's also compelling with color.

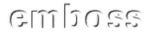

Float

This one's simple: Offset a soft shadow far enough to give a floating illusion. Text—any tone or color, 100%. Shadow—black, 50% opacity, 4 x 4 offset.

Emboss

Shift a solid shadow one pixel to the upper-left. Text—white, 100%. Shadow—black, 100%, solid; –1 x –1 offset.

Soft

This is a softer version of the "Float" effect since the text melds into the background and the shadow is lighter. Text—white, 100%. Shadow—black, 70%, soft; 3 x 3 offset.

(Bullet)

This lone bullet is just a reminder that graphic objects in the Title window are fair game for these effects, too.

Clear

Place "Clear" type with a soft shadow on two rectangles with opposite gradients. Type—black; clear opacity. Shadow; black, 70%, 2 x 3 offset. Background—top rectangle is middle gray to black; bottom is the reverse.

Walls

Build miniature walls of text with the outline type style and a solid shadow. Text—black, outline style, 100%. Shadow—black, 100%, 4 x 5 offset.

Solid

Premiere can produce simple three-dimensional effects (up to 16 pixels deep) with the solid shadow style. Text—white, 100%. Shadow—black, 100%, 5 x 5 offset.

Gradient

Give text an extreme opacity gradient over a strong shadow. Text—white, 100% to 1% opacity. Shadow—black, 100%, solid, 3 x 3 offset.

3-D

Here the white shadow appears as the most illuminated 3-D surface. Text—any mid-tone, 100%. Shadow—white, 100%, solid, –4 x –4 offset. Background; black rectangle, grey shadow, same offset as the text block.

Outline

This one is similar to the "Float" example, except an outline-style text block sits on top of white text—and is kerned to match the white text's spacing.

Back-lit

Invert the "Stencil" effect (described earlier) for a back-lit look. It's two text objects—black text centered over a separate soft shadow. Top settings are: Text—black, 100%, no shadow. Bottom settings are: Text—black, 1% (virtually invisible). Shadow—white, 100%, soft, 1 x 1 offset. Background—black rectangle, soft shadow, 2 x 2 offset.

Criss-cross

Apply opposite gradients to text and shadow for type that evolves over its length. Text—black to white (left to right), 100%. Shadow—white to black, 100%, soft, offset 1 x 1.

Whew! Much more is possible, requiring only some experimentation and time to discover. Have fun!

▶ Becoming Layers Aware

Now that you're a master with titles and graphics, let's find out how to superimpose them (or any other material) onto other clips. That's our last destination before compiling your final movie. So take a breather and then get ready for layers and layers of clips.

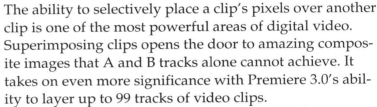

10

Superimposing Clips

The ability to selectively place a clip's pixels over another clip is one of the most powerful areas of digital video. Superimposing clips opens the door to amazing composite images that A and B tracks alone cannot achieve. It takes on even more significance with Premiere 3.0's ability to layer up to 99 tracks of video clips.

In this chapter, we'll first visit the superimposing basics, followed by tips and tricks for each "key type" that creates transparency in a project clip. Then we'll explore Premiere's ready-made tools for building background clip material—so you'll have plenty of visuals that can sit under your super clips.

The Super Process

Let's first walk through the steps of superimposing a clip. Then we'll check out the available options in more detail. Even if you've superimposed clips before, look through this section to pick up tips and shortcuts. If you're using Premiere 3.0, also keep an eye out for several new twists the latest version adds to the process.

▶ **Essential Steps**

You can superimpose movies, animations, or still-images over any other visual clip in Premiere. The superimposing process requires five steps.

1 In the Construction window, drag a clip into an S track in Premiere 3.0 (or the sole Super track in Premiere 2.0). The clip will play on top of overlapping clips in tracks A and B—including filters, transitions, motion and other effects you've slapped onto those clips. **3.0** Premiere 3.0's S tracks also superimpose over lower number S tracks—so material in the S2 track, for example, will play on top of S1 clips.

Here, the king of the hill is at the bottom. The S2 track clip at the bottom of this window will superimpose on top of all overlapping material in the other tracks shown.

☞ *Create up to 97 S tracks in Premiere 3.0 by choosing "Add/Delete Tracks..." in the Project menu (see page 62).*

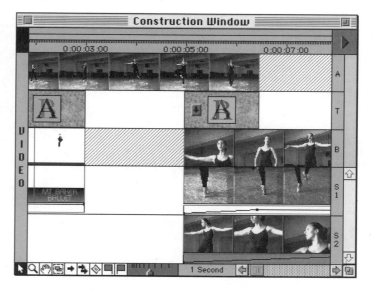

2 Click the clip in the superimposing track to select it. Then choose "Transparency..." in the Clip menu (Command T) to call up the Transparency Settings dialog box—your superimposing control center.

Premiere 2.0 and 3.0 share the same Transparency Settings dialog box design, with one exception—3.0 has five icons sitting under the Sample box (shown) that adjust your view.

☞ *To avoid slowdowns from CPU-intensive filters (such as Radial Blur or Mesh Warp), always try to superimpose clips before adding such filters.*

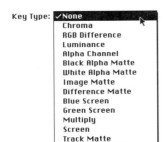

Now specify what portion of the superimposed clip's image you want to become transparent.

3 From the Key Type pop-up menu in the middle of the dialog box, select a key type. A "key" is simply a transparency-creating method. Eleven key types are available in Premiere 2.0; fourteen in Premiere 3.0. The last three key types in the menu at left are the new ones in Premiere 3.0. (Hang on—there's much more about each key type later in this chapter.)

4 Look in the Sample box to see which areas of your clip become transparent based on the key type you select. The Sample box shows the clip's first frame. If the clip is a sequence, you can drag the slider under the image to view other frames.

To help you see transparent areas in dark or light clips, in Premiere 2.0 you can click the image to toggle between black and white for the transparent areas. That no longer works in Premiere 3.0, but the five new icons below the window do the equivalent plus much more (as we'll soon see).

In either Premiere, you can drag the handle at each corner of the Sample box frame to further limit the superimposed portions of the clip. That creates a "garbage matte" which we'll also explore a few pages ahead.

Dragging handles in the Sample box creates a garbage matte. Garbage mattes are one way to form insets and split screens.

5 Use the lower half of the Transparency Settings dialog box to fine-tune the transparency. The available options depend on your selected key type.

The Chroma key type, for example, activates all sliders plus the Smoothing check box. Other key types use fewer or no sliders.

☞ *Switching to a different key type will erase your slider settings. Consider jotting down the numerical values (low-tech!) or copying the clip before switching.*

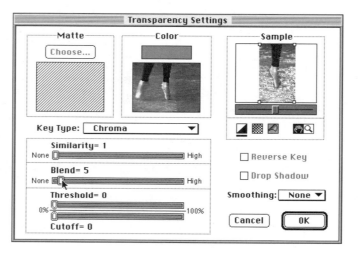

While adjusting options, watch the Sample window to see how the clip's transparency changes. When you achieve the desired effect, click OK in the dialog box to have Premiere carry out your transparency instructions.

☞ *Premiere 2.0 users must preview to see the background image under the super clip.*

That's all of the steps. The only other task is to preview the segment from the Construction window to see it in action. If necessary, re-visit the Transparency Settings dialog box to make further adjustments.

3.0 Premiere 3.0 has a new shortcut for quickly re-visiting the key options or switching to a different key type. In the Construction window, hold down the Control and Option keys and your mouse button on the superimposed clip to see a pop-up menu of key types.

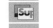

This 3.0 shortcut is similar to the fast way you can access Premiere filters by holding down the Option key.

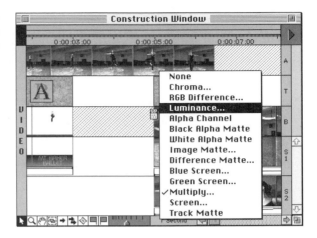

 Keys with an ellipsis (...) after their names in the above menu have adjustable sliders.

If the key type you choose in this manner offers adjustable sliders, the Transparency Settings dialog box will appear so you can fine-tune those options.

Those are the essentials of the transparency process. Not bad, eh? Now let's find out more about those useful icon controls under the Sample box in Premiere 3.0.

▶ Sample Box Views

3.0

In Premiere 3.0, new icons under the Sample box help you to see more clearly the transparent areas in your clip. On a clip of a light-colored sandy beach, for example, transparent areas shown in black will be easier to recognize.

The first three icons determine which image represents the transparent areas.

The icons do not alter the clip's transparency—just the appearance of transparent areas in the Sample box.

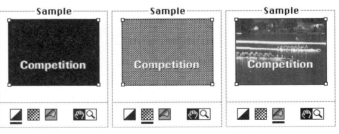

Click this icon to choose black or white to fill the background. Click again to toggle between these two basic choices.

Click this icon to see a checkerboard pattern in the background. Click again to reverse the checkerboards.

Click the peeling icon to see the actual background clip(s) in your project—often the most useful (but slowest) view.

The other two buttons in the collection—the Zoom and Hand tools—work together to give you a close-up view of your clip's pixels. They operate like the Zoom and Hand tools in the dialog box of well-endowed 3.0 filters.

To zoom the image larger, choose the Zoom tool and click in the image where you want to zoom. You can zoom up to 10x size. To zoom back towards the original scale, Option-click with the Zoom tool.

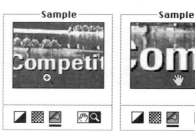

Use the hand to shift the zoomed image portion that appears in the Sample box. Double-click the Hand tool icon to return the image to its original size.

Here are two more zooming caveats.

• Double-click the Zoom tool *icon* to see the image at *actual* size within the box—the size of the source clip. To clue you in that you're at true size, Premiere 3.0 outlines the plus or minus sign in the cursor.

• Press the spacebar while using the Zoom tool to switch temporarily to the Hand tool. Press the Command key while using the hand to switch temporarily to the zoom.

▶ Drawing the Fade Line

☞ *If you already know how to manipulate the fade line of audio clips, you can breeze through this section because the two faders operate similarly.*

So far, we've ignored one of the most important features of superimposed clips—the fade line. Every clip in an S track (or the one and only Super track in 2.0) has a fade control sitting under it in the Construction window. You can shape the fade line to alter the superimposed clip's opacity. For example, you can fade in to make a clip gradually more visible or fade out to make it disappear.

Initially, Premiere sets the fade line at the top of the control—100% opacity—full intensity. Dragging the handle at either end of the clip creates a diagonal fade line which will fade the clip at a constant rate.

This clip gradually fades in from 0% to 100% over the A track clip. The steeper the angle, the more rapid the fade.

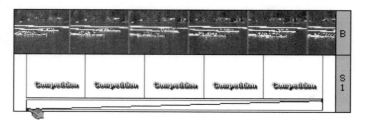

For a more complicated fade profile, however, you must add extra handles. Here's how in three quick steps.

1 Place the Selection tool's arrow cursor over the fade line where you want to change the clip's opacity. The cursor will turn to a pointing hand. Then click to create a handle—a black dot—which acts as a hinge point for the clip's fade line.

Clicking on the fade line creates a handle you can drag to shape the line.

2 Drag the handle down to reduce the clip's intensity. Refer to the Info window for the precise fade level as you drag. 100% is opaque; 0% is transparent.

Drag the handle while keeping an eye on the bottom of the Info window.

Fade Level: 50%

Cursor at: 0:01:36:03

3 Add as many other handles as desired. To delete a handle, just drag it off the fade control.

Before we fade away from this topic, try the following two keyboard shortcuts to fading that will save time:

Shift a Segment

To shift a fade *segment* up or down between two handles, hold down the Shift key as you drag the segment. That's faster than dragging two handles independently. In fact, if you haven't added extra fade handles to a clip, it's the quickest way to change the opacity of an entire clip.

Using the Shift key, you can quickly adjust a clip's opacity between two handles—even if it's an angled fade line. The cursor icon reflects the Shift control.

3.0 Scissors

In Premiere 3.0, holding down the Command and Control keys while the cursor is in a clip's fade area produces miniature scissors. Use the scissors to "cut" the superimposed clip's fade line. The fade line doesn't actually break, but you get two handles that you can drag to create abrupt fade changes. The handles sit on adjacent frames of your superimposed clip.

See page 89 for more about superimposing insert shots over other clips.

Clicking the scissors creates two adjacent handles which you can drag to any level.

▶ Key to the Keys

Now that you know the basic process, let's get our first look at the different key types. Premiere 3.0 carries fourteen key types; Premiere 2.0 has eleven. The key you select determines what portion of the superimposed image will become transparent, revealing the underlying image. Television veterans refer to transparent areas as *keyed out* (as in looking through a key hole). The film industry speaks similarly of *matting*—as in using a matte to block out portions of an image. We'll use the two terms and their derivatives interchangeably here.

The chart on the next page presents the "big picture"—the main purpose of each key type so you can choose the right one at a glance. It organizes the keys into four categories—a slightly different order than Premiere offers them—to help you to understand and compare them. In later pages, we'll find out more about each key.

While looking over the chart, don't forget about the default key choice Premiere gives you:

None

None doesn't key out anything in the superimposed image. Stick with this default choice when you *only* want to create a garbage matte or use the superimposed clip's fade line controls to adjust opacity.

For more about garbage mattes, see page 264.

Now for the keys to the transparency door…

Summary of Premiere Keys

Color-Based Keys

Use these keys to define by color what becomes transparent in your superimposed image. See page 265 for details.

Chroma

This is the most sophisticated color key—offering the most options for fine-tuning. You can blend transparencies and adjust shadows (or other greys) independently.

RGB Difference

Here's a simpler, but less flexible color key than Chroma—a good choice for color keying when shadows aren't an issue.

Blue Screen

This key is optimized for clips with pure *blue* backgrounds—the same technique used in televised weather broadcasts.

Green Screen

For clips with pure *green* backgrounds, this is the best choice.

Keys on Brightness

These keys use brightness— the grey values—in your superimposed clip to define what becomes transparent. See page 267 for details.

Luminance

Use this key to see background greys under the superimposed clip's colors—a great way to add subtle textures and imagery.

`3.0` Multiply

With this new key in Premiere 3.0, you can cast the superimposed clip onto the *bright* areas of the underlying image.

`3.0` Screen

This 3.0 key complements Multiply. It lays the superimposed clip onto *dark* areas of underlying clips—like a double-exposure.

Alpha Channel Mattes

Rely on these to superimpose Premiere titles, Illustrator images and other clips that contain an alpha channel. See page 269 for details.

Alpha Channel

Choose this key for alpha channel-endowed clips that do not have a black or white background.

Black Alpha Matte

If the alpha-channel clip has a *black* background, select this key.

White Alpha Matte

If the alpha-channel clip has a *white* background, select this key.

Separate Mattes

With these mattes, you select a separate clip (a matte) that defines what's transparent in the superimposed clip. See page 270 for details.

Image Matte

This key shapes your superimposed clip with a *still-image* matte—like a cookie-cutter. It's a good choice when using still-images that lack an alpha channel.

Difference Matte

Premiere compares the selected still-image matte and the superimposed clip—different (or similar) color pixels become transparent. You can use this to key out complex backgrounds.

`3.0` Track Matte

Unlike the above mattes, this new key in Premiere 3.0 can turn an entire movie clip into a *moving mask* (or "traveling matte").

▶ Quickly the Key Options

Here's one other quick course. This one summarizes the options in the lower half of the Transparency Settings dialog box that are available for each key. No key activates all options, as you can see from the chart below. In fact, some options show up for only one or two key types.

Key Type Options

	Similarity	Blend	Threshold	Cutoff	Reverse Key	Drop Shadow	Smoothing
• None					•		
Color-Based Keys							
• Chroma	•	•	•	•			•
• RGB Difference	•					•	•
• Blue Screen			•	•			•
• Green Screen			•	•			•
Brightness Keys							
• Luminance			•	•			
• Multiply				•			
• Screen				•			
Alpha Channel Keys							
• Alpha Channel					•		
• Black Matte							
• White Matte							
Separate Mattes							
• Image				•			
• Difference	•			•	•		•
• Track				•			

In a nutshell, here's the purpose of each control.

Similarity Slider

Dragging this slider right broadens the range of transparent pixels from what was initially selected. For example, with the Chroma or RGB Difference key types, it can widen the range of colors that become transparent.

Blend Slider

This slider is only available for the Chroma key type. Moving it right increasingly turns opaque colors in the superimposed image *partially* transparent—blending them in with the fully transparent areas you define.

Threshold and Cutoff Sliders

These two sliders work together to set the transparency of shadows (or other greyscale areas) in your superimposed clip. Their specific effect depends on the selected key type (as we'll see shortly). The Cutoff slider alone also appears in 3.0's new Multiply and Screen key types. There it adjusts the superimposed clip's overall transparency— the same function that the clip's fade line serves.

Reverse Key

This check box reverses which pixels are transparent or opaque in the superimposed clip.

These are examples of the Reverse Key check box turned off (left image) and on (middle) using the Alpha Channel key. The original superimposed title is the far right image.

 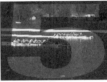 

Drop Shadow

This option adds a 50% grey, 50% opaque shadow four pixels below and to the right of the opaque clip areas. It can be effective with simple shapes, such as titles and graphics.

Smoothing

Smoothing: ✓None / Low / **High**

Use this pop-up menu to soften, or anti-alias, *contrasting edges* between the superimposed clip and the background image. It doesn't smooth other parts of the composite image. You have a choice of None, Low or High settings.

From left to right, here's None, Low and High settings on the same combination of clips.

That's all of the transparency options. At this point, you should understand Premiere's transparency powers well enough to get through many projects. If you're interested in stepping deeper into the transparency goo, take a break and then walk into the next section.

Transparency Revealed

This section plunges deeper into tips and techniques that turn each key type into a transparency-generating powerhouse. The pages are organized by the same key type categories we witnessed in the previous section. Let's take out the garbage mattes first.

▶ More About Garbage Mattes

☞ *To see the garbage matte handles in Premiere 3.0's Sample box, the image has to be at original size—not zoomed.*

The Sample box provides a simple way to define transparent areas in your superimposed clip. For any key type, you can drag the four corner handles in the Sample box to create a *garbage matte*. A garbage matte allows you to

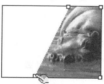

block out an unwanted region of a clip (the garbage) so the underlying image can peek through. It works independent of any additional transparency produced by a selected key type.

A garbage matte becomes even more potent when used with other Premiere features. For example, turn on the Reverse check box in the Transparency Settings dialog box to switch transparent and opaque areas in the clip.

Reverse keying switches transparent and opaque areas. In this case, one way is clearly preferable.

You also can apply Premiere's motion settings to better position a superimposed clip in (or out) of the garbage matte area. Keep in mind that a garbage matte *does not* roll, spin, tumble or move with a superimposed clip's motion. A garbage matte is always stationary.

☞ *To create a matte that moves, use 3.0's new Track Matte (see page 272).*

The garbage matte that defines the square above the title remains stationary as the superimposed clip moves upward due to its motion settings.

One last garbage matte tip: To smooth, or anti-alias, the edges of the matte without creating additional transparent areas, select the RGB Difference key in the Key

Key Type: | RGB Difference ▼ |

Type pop-up menu of the Transparency Settings dialog box. Be sure to keep the Similarity slider at None (far left) and don't select a color in the Color box. Then use the Smoothing pop-up menu to anti-alias the edges.

Without anti-aliasing, the matte may stand out harshly against the background clip. Angled garbage matte edges will be noticeably jagged.

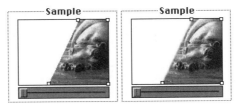

Here's the same clip with the Smoothing pop-up menu set to High.

▶ Color-Based Keys

Premiere's color-based key types allow you to define *by color* (and in some cases greys) which areas are transparent in the superimposed clip. Let's recap the four choices.

Chroma

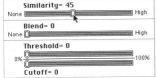

The Chroma key type is the most flexible (and most complex) of the four. It uniquely offers the Blend slider for blending transparencies within the image. And with the Threshold and Cutoff sliders, you can independently adjust the transparency of greys—such as shadows.

RGB Difference

This simpler version of the Chroma key is useful when you don't need to adjust greys separately in the superimposed clip.

Blue Screen

☞ Televised weather broadcasts use this key to project the weather behind a forecaster standing in front of a blue screen.

Use this key to superimpose clips with a pure blue background. It's optimized for chroma blue—a pure blue similar to Pantone color #2735. This key is great for isolating skin tones, which typically have little blue (unless your subjects are holding their breath).

Green Screen

This key is set up for chroma green—a true green similar to Pantone color #354—in case you want to isolate reds and blues from your clip's background.

On the next page, let's resolve three issues that will help you to succeed (instead of bleed) with color keys.

On eight-bit color monitors, you may need to click a dithered color area more than once to get the most representative color.

For more about using color pickers, see page 241.

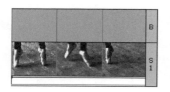

Moving the Threshold slider right increasingly retains shadows and greys in this clip. From left to right are 0%, 40% and 80% threshold values.

Clearing the Right Color

The first two keys, Chroma and RGB Difference, activate the Color box in the Transparency Settings dialog box. Use it to pick the color that will become transparent. You can place the cursor over the image to suck a color from the clip with an eyedropper. (Drag the Sample box slider if necessary to see later frames of a sequence.) Or you can click the rectangle above the image to choose a color from a color picker.

After choosing a color, drag the Similarity slider right if you want to broaden which colors will turn transparent.

Chroma Shadow Boxing

Threshold and Cutoff sliders for the Chroma key help you to retain greys—particularly shadows—in transparent regions of your superimposed clip. The sliders can be puzzling if you don't move them in the proper order. So let's go over the two-step process, using the two clips at left as examples. (The B track clip is a solid color matte.)

1 First push the Threshold slider right until shadows or other greys *in the transparent areas* of your superimposed clip are sufficiently visible.

2 Often you can leave the Cutoff slider alone. But if you want to darken the greys that are retained by the Threshold slider, drag the Cutoff right—but not past the Threshold.

Dragging the Cutoff slider *past* the Threshold slider's value produces an unusual effect: grey and transparent pixels *invert*. What was grey becomes adjustably transparent, and what was formerly transparent now shows a grey-scale version of the superimposed clip.

Turning Blue or Green

For the Blue Screen or Green Screen keys, you need to manipulate the Threshold and Cutoff sliders differently than for the Chroma key. The sliders start on opposite sides of the percentage scale.

1 Drag the Cutoff slider right until contrast *in opaque areas* of the superimposed clip remains unchanged.

2 Then drag the Threshold slider left until the blue or green background becomes fully transparent. You won't have to drag far if your clip's background color is true to the chroma standard.

3 To adjust the tightness of the key, shift the Cutoff and Threshold sliders *an equal distance* left. If the background clip then begins to bleed through the blue or green matte, push the Cutoff slider farther right.

▶ **Keys on Brightness**

These keys operate on the basis of a pixel's brightness—its grey value—regardless of whether the pixel is color or grey. All three keys are good choices for adding textures or shadowy images under a superimposed clip. In fact, the visual differences between these keys sometimes can be subtle—you may need to try all three before getting the exact effect you want.

Luminance

This keys out the grey values in the superimposed clip (within a range you define) while retaining the pixel's color. The end result is the superimposed clip's *color* appears on top of the background image.

Threshold and Cutoff sliders can modify the effect. Decrease the threshold value, for example, to make the background more subtle.

From left are threshold values of 100%, 60% and 20%. In the far right image, only the darkest areas of the superimposed close-up are transparent enough to reveal the mid-shot underneath.

Increase the Cutoff slider (but don't exceed the threshold percentage) to reduce the superimposed clip's color presence *in the transparent area.*

Cutoff values are (from left) 0%, 20% and 50%—all with a 80% threshold. Within transparent areas the threshold creates, the superimposed clip's color lessens as the cutoff value increases.

If you slide the Cutoff to a *higher* value than the Threshold slider, the transparent and color areas switch— it's similar to having a Reverse Key check box available for the key type.

3.0 Multiply

New to Premiere 3.0, this key type shows the superimposed clip strongest in the *brighter* areas of the underlying image. You can adjust the superimposed clip's intensity with the Cutoff slider.

The examples are (left to right) 100%, 60% and 30% cutoff values. The superimposed clip's strength decreases as the cutoff value drops.

Decreasing the cutoff value is the same as lowering the superimposed clip's fade line—both reduce opacity.

3.0 Screen

Choose this new 3.0 key type to make the superimposed clip more evident in *dark* areas of the underlying image— like a double-exposure. It's great for adding light elements, such as a lens flare, to an existing image. As with the Multiply key, the Cutoff slider is also available.

Dragging the Cutoff slider right decreases the opacity of the superimposed clip—just like the clip's fade line can do.

▶ Alpha Channel Mattes

If your clip includes an alpha channel, these keys are a sure bet for superimposing the images. Black areas in a clip's alpha channel—or white areas with the Reverse Key check box on—define where the clip will be transparent. Greys in the alpha channel create partial transparencies.

The left image has a gradient alpha channel (middle) created in Photoshop. When superimposing the clip in Premiere, dark areas of the alpha channel reveal more of the background clip.

Note that these mattes do not *create* alpha channels—you have to use clips that already have that information. Four sources for clips with an alpha channel are:

• type and graphics from Premiere's Title window

• imported Adobe Illustrator images—either a single file or a numbered series of files

• imported Photoshop files (if the alpha channel was saved in Photoshop)

For more about importing Illustrator or Photoshop files, see page 37 and 39. See page 148 for the Channel Map transition.

• virtual clips (in Premiere 3.0) or compiled clip segments that include a Channel Map transition that has assigned image data to the alpha channel

Remember that the Project window (by Name view) and Info window tell you if a clip has an alpha channel. And you can view the alpha channel of a still-image clip by clicking the Alpha button in the Clip window.

Choosing from Premiere's three alpha channel matte flavors is fairly simple.

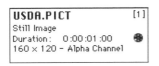

Alpha Channel

Generally, try this matte first for all alpha-endowed material—except clips with a black or white background.

Black Alpha Matte ("Black Matte" in 2.0)

Choose this key for superimposed clips that have an alpha channel *and* a black background. It removes the "halo" that can appear when a black background is keyed out, especially around anti-aliased titles and graphics.

If the Black or White Alpha Matte don't appear clean, try the Alpha Channel key type.

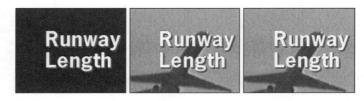

A title with a black background (left) is superimposed with the Alpha Channel key type (middle) and Black Alpha Matte (right). Note the difference around the top of the white characters.

White Alpha Matte ("White Matte" in 2.0)

This is the white background version of the Black Alpha Matte. It removes the "halo" that can appear when a white background becomes transparent around anti-aliased titles and graphics.

▶ Separate Mattes

The first two keys of this last group—Image Matte and Difference Matte—allow you to choose a *separate still-image* (the matte) which defines what becomes transparent in your superimposed clip. The third member of the trio, 3.0's new Track Matte, has the power to convert a separate movie into a dynamic *moving mask*. These keys provide an extra creative element to your visual composition besides the background and foreground clips.

If you select the Image Matte or Difference Matte, click the Choose button in the Matte box within the Transparency Settings dialog box. That will call up Premiere's Open dialog box from which you can select a clip that will become the matte. If you select a movie, only its first frame will become the matte. Either way, the chosen matte will appear in the Matte box.

Let's find out more about each matte.

Image Matte

This key is a good choice for creating a matte with imported still-images *that lack an alpha channel*—such as files from standard paint and draw applications or scanned images. Like an Alpha Channel matte, black pixels in the chosen matte (or white with the Reverse Key check box turned on) will act as a cookie cutter in your superimposed clip—showing the background. Areas of intermediate brightness will partially reveal the background.

Two common uses for the Image Matte are:

• isolating an effect (such as Premiere's filters) within an image —a technique we'll explore just ahead

• layering a texture or other superimposed image in a well-defined area on top of the background

To accomplish the second use, configure the Construction window and Transparency Settings dialog box like the example below.

The texture clip (a Crinkled Paper backdrop file from Premiere) is superimposed over the hippo scene. With the Image Matte key type chosen, the still-image selected in the Matte box limits the texture area to COOL. You can preview the results in the Sample box in 3.0 if you select the peel icon under the box. (In Premiere 2.0, preview from the Construction window to see the composite image.)

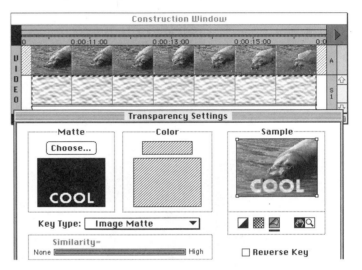

One other tip to keep in mind: select a *greyscale* image for the matte unless you want to alter the color of your superimposed clip. Colors in the matte will strip the same colors out of the superimposed clip. For example, red areas in a matte turn black pixels in the superimposed clip blue-green—the remaining RGB color components.

Difference Matte

This matte compares the superimposed clip with the selected image matte. Any pixels that are *different* become transparent—identical pixels are retained (or vice versa with the Reverse Key check box). The Similarity slider allows you to widen the range of affected pixels.

The Difference Matte is mostly useful for producing surrealistic composite images. But there is one other intriguing use. If you turn on the Reverse Key check box, you can key out complex backgrounds that have a moving subject—if you have an image of the same scene with the subject and without. Choose the one without as the matte for superimposing the clip with the subject.

The moving ballet dancer is superimposed over the marble texture by keying out the background. A clip of the room without the dancer serves as the matte. Fine-tuning with the Similarity slider will usually be necessary. Remember to turn on the Reverse Key check box before clicking okay.

☞ *The background cannot move or change in the frame for this technique to be successful. Steady tripod shots with static backgrounds are a must.*

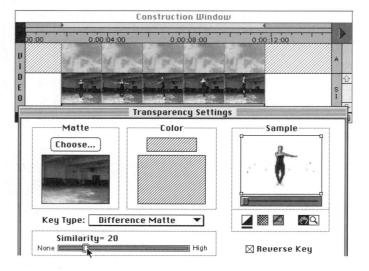

As a variation of the above technique, place a white matte in the A track instead of the other background clip. Then make a virtual clip of the segment in Premiere 3.0 (or compile the segment with the None codec in Premiere 2.0). Last, increase the virtual clip's contrast with the Brightness & Contrast filter. What do you get? An eye-catching silhouette of the moving element.

3.0 **Track Matte**

This new key in Premiere 3.0 operates like the Image Matte, with one intriguing difference—the matte can be an entire *movie*, not just a still-image. The matte can therefore change and evolve during the clip. All you have to do is place the clip that will act as the matte in the *next* S track in the Construction window. For example, if your superimposed clip is in S2, place the matte clip in S3. We'll examine this matte further one page ahead.

▶ **Isolating Effects**

📖 *For other ways to isolate filtered areas, see page 174.*

Premiere's filters normally apply their magic to the entire clip image. An important use of Premiere's Image Matte is to isolate filtered areas within a clip. To become a filter isolationist, follow the process on the next page.

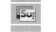
1 Drag the same clip into the A track and a superimposing track, aligning the clip's In and Out points.

Premiere 3.0's tracks are shown, but this page's three-step Image Matte technique is also viable in Premiere 2.0.

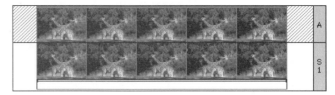

2 Select the clip in the S track and open the Transparency Settings dialog box (Command T). Select the Image Matte key type and then click the Choose button to select a still-image clip (or a movie clip's first frame). If you want to invert the masked area, turn on the Reverse Key check box. Then click OK.

A binocular-shaped still-image that's anti-aliased is selected for the matte. The Reverse Key check box is turned on to show the background clip within the masked area.

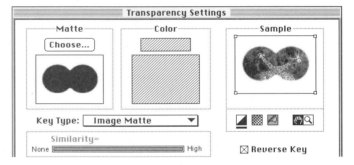

3 Apply filter(s) to the background clip in track A. Then preview the results. In this example, Posterize and Brightness & Contrast filters darken and simplify the background, highlighting the superimposed shape.

▶ **Moving Masks**

Let's culminate our super efforts by creating a *moving mask* (known in some circles as a "traveling matte").

A moving mask, or traveling matte, dynamically defines the portion of the superimposed clip that will become transparent.

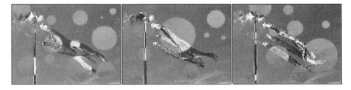

We'll first look at a terrific new way of doing this in Premiere 3.0 with the Track Matte. Then we'll cover the more lengthy process Premiere 2.0 requires.

[3.0] **3.0's Terrific Track Matte**

In Premiere 3.0, the easiest way to create a moving mask is to use the Track Matte. This new key type and 3.0's multiple S tracks save a tremendous amount of time over what Premiere 2.0 requires. Here are the steps:

1 Place the clip you want to superimpose in an S track, which will play on top of the image formed by lower number S tracks and tracks A and B. Then place the clip that will form the moving mask in the *next* S track. For example, if your superimposed clip is in S1, place the mask clip in S2. Align the two clips so they have the same starting time and duration.

In this example, the wind sculpture clip in Track A has been modified with the Posterize filter. The clip is aligned with an unaltered copy in the S1 Track. The bubbly moving mask in S2 will define where unaltered areas will be superimposed over the filtered image.

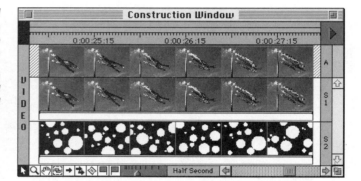

The moving mask clip can be a still-image clip with motion settings or a movie clip (with or without motion settings). The clip can even have filters and still work fine as a moving mask. In fact, since color in the mask affects your composite image, consider applying the Black & White filter if your mask is a color clip to eliminate any color intrusion. Also think about increasing the mask's contrast with the Brightness & Contrast or Levels filter to enhance the image's definition.

Like an alpha channel key, white pixels in the mask will be opaque and darker pixels will reveal the background image. That's why the Brightness & Contrast or Levels filter can be handy for prepping a moving mask such as this takeoff shot. The sky can be dropped out completely.

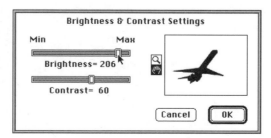

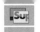

2 Select the clip you want to superimpose (in this example, the S1 clip) and open the Transparency Settings dialog box (Command T). Select the Track Matte key type. Turn on the Reverse Key check box if you want the background and superimposed areas to trade places.

Examples of the Reverse Key check box turned on (left) and off (right) with the Track Matte applied to the example clips.

Finally, click OK and preview the results.

Presto—a sophisticated moving mask in just two steps!

Note that the mask clip cannot have transparency settings of its own—Premiere will ignore them. The clip will only serve as a mask as long as the Track Matte key is active in the lower number S track. But you can drag another pair of clips in *two other S tracks* to add *another* moving mask that will combine with the first mask. This is your route to extremely complex composite effects.

Another pair of S tracks adds a second moving mask of bubbles to the composite scene. In this example, the S4 bubble clip has a different In point than S2's so the bubbles don't match. The S3 clip is filtered differently to provide further visual variety.

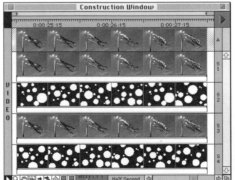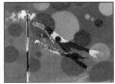

2.0 **Moving Masks in Premiere 2.0**

The next page shows how to create a moving mask with an alpha channel—a process that's accessible to 2.0 users.

1 Create an image with an alpha channel that will serve as the mask through which the clip will play. It can be a Premiere title, an imported Illustrator image or any other file with an alpha channel. In this case, we'll use a simple circle created in Premiere's Title window.

2 Place the clip you want to show *through* the mask in the A track. Then place the mask clip from Step 1 into the B track, aligning it with the A clip.

3 Drag the Channel Map transition between the two clips in the FX track. A dialog box will pop-up for you to map image components to the output.

The only pop-up menu you need to alter in the Channel Mapping dialog box is the last one. Set it to "Map Source B - Alpha to Alpha" as shown at right.

 For more about the Channel Map transition, see page 158.

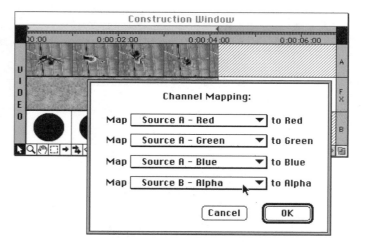

Then click OK and make sure the transition's Track Selector arrow points down. Finally, adjust the transition to extend the full length of the two clips.

4 Compile the segment using the "Make Movie..." command in the Project menu (Command K). Be sure to select the None compressor (to preserve the image's quality) as well as a color depth of "Millions of Colors+" (to retain the alpha channel in the movie). When compiling is done and the Clip window opens with the new clip, drag the clip into the Super track. Then drag the background clip you want into the A track.

The compiled clip with the alpha channel mask is in the Super track. The background clip is in position in track A.

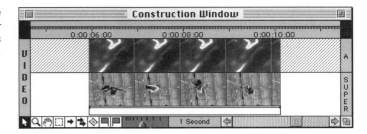

5 Select the masked clip in the Super track and open the Transparency Settings dialog box (Command T). Select the Alpha Channel key type. Turn on the Reverse Key check box if desired. Then click OK.

Key Type: [**Alpha Channel** ▼]

6 Now open the Motion settings dialog box (Command Y) for the masked clip in the Super track. Create any motion path desired, using the process described in Chapter 8. Before clicking OK, be sure "Transparent Fill" is unchecked in the dialog box.

In this example, a curving motion path will zoom the circle past the viewer's eye.

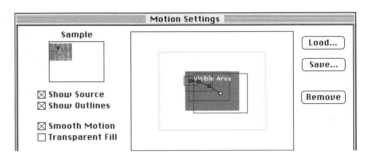

That's it—now preview your results.

The circular moving mask grows and zooms past the frame.

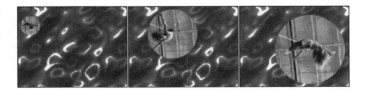

If you've persevered this far into the mysteries of superimposing, you're clearly a wizard with Premiere's transparency settings. Only one brief issue remains. Travel a few more pages to learn how to create background clips for your superimposed creations.

Background Sources

We've focused extensively in this chapter on superimposed clips while ignoring equally vital background image clips. Let's quickly meet the several background sources Premiere offers.

▶ Premiere's Texture Library

Superimposing title and graphics creates an insatiable demand for background textures. Before spending money on third-party clip disks—or devoting time to shooting your own textures—look in the Backdrops folder within Premiere's Libraries folder. Premiere ships with nearly a dozen textures—called backdrops—that you can quickly add and customize to your project.

Backdrops

Like any clip, use the "Open..." or "Import..." command in the File menu to bring a backdrop into your project. Or open the "Backdrop Library" to view thumbnails of all available background textures.

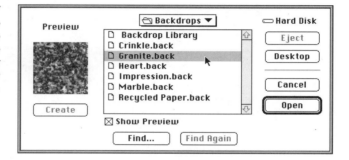

After opening a backdrop, a unique backdrop window appears. It shows a 256 x 256 pixel greyscale image of the selected texture. (If the file was previously modified, color may be evident.) Nine sliders sit to the left that you can use to tailor the texture's appearance.

Independently adjust highlights (the lightest areas), shade (medium greys) and shadows (blacks) in the backdrop. H stands for hue, S is saturation, and B is blackness. Default values for the sliders are shown.

☞ Click the large box to the left of each slider cluster to get a color picker. That's usually much easier than using the first two sliders in each group of three.

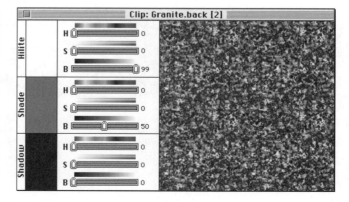

Note that on slower Macs, the sliders can be sluggish. For faster response, instead of *sliding* them left or right, *click* at the new slider location you want.

After manipulating the backdrop image to your liking, drag it into a video track in your Construction window. Although the size of textured backdrops that ship with Premiere are 256 x 256 pixels, they automatically *tile* to your movie's output size. So the backdrops retain full resolution in any project. In fact, Premiere's pre-made images are *seamless*—you won't see lines or abrupt texture changes along each edge in full-screen work.

☞ *Place your modified backdrop in a Library to use it in other projects. For more about Libraries, see page 34.*

▶ Roll Your Own Backdrops

You aren't limited to Premiere's pre-made backdrops. Roll your own backdrops using any clip image in your hip pocket. You can even customize the image with the backdrop's powerful image controls we just visited. Let's quickly step through the three-part procedure.

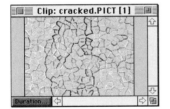

1 Display the frame you want to use for a backdrop in the Clip window. In case you're wondering, the cracked example at left was born by applying Mosaic, Crystallize, and Brightness & Contrast filters to a regular video clip. Then a PICT was created by selecting "Frame as PICT…" in the Export submenu of the File menu.

2 In the Export submenu of the File menu, choose "Frame as Backdrop…". Use the Save dialog box that appears to secure the new backdrop in a convenient place—such as Premiere's Backdrops folder.

Retaining the ".back" suffix that Premiere suggests for the file is a good idea so you can instantly recognize the file type.

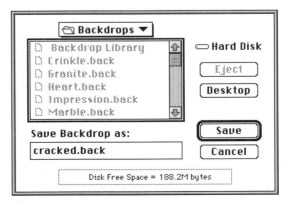

3 Now bring the backdrop into your project like any other clip—with the "Import..." or "Open..." command in the File menu. If you import the backdrop, double-click its thumbnail to open the backdrop window.

A greyscale version of the clip image will be waiting in the window for your adjustments.

☞ *The image area of the backdrop window is fixed at 256 x 256 pixels. If your backdrop is larger, you'll have to preview from the Construction window to see other portions of the image.*

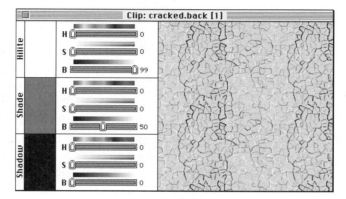

Your backdrop will *tile* at the size of the source clip you chose to make the backdrop. For example, look closely at the cracked image above—it's actually four 160 x 120 clips tiled together. If you don't want tiling to appear in your project, make sure the frame size of your backdrop source clip is as large as your final movie's frame. For example, if you're creating full-frame movies, select a full-screen Clip window to make the backdrop.

Now let's find out about the last kind of background clip Premiere can generate—a solid color matte.

▶ **Going to the Color Matte**

☞ *If you need black in the background, you may not need to create a black matte. Empty A and B tracks give the same result.*

Besides backdrops, Premiere also can create full-frame *mattes* of solid color. Mattes are handy for giving titles and other superimposed clips a color background. Like backdrops, color mattes are independent clips you can edit in the Construction window. This independence gives you creative flexibility. For example, you can fade a title into a constant color background. Or you can enhance one clip with different effects than the other.

Let's rapidly walk through how to create a color matte.

☐ *For more about color pickers, see page 241.*

1 Select "Add Color Matte..." from the Project menu (Command hyphen [-]). That calls up a color picker so you can choose a color. After clicking OK, a simple dialog box will appear for you to name the new matte.

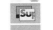

Name your new matte here.

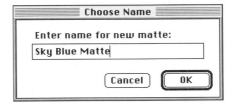

☞ *Color mattes are "pointer" files, so the memory required for each new matte is minimal.*

2 After clicking OK to the above dialog box, the matte deposits itself in the Project window. Then drag that thumbnail into a video track in the Construction window.

Note that the color matte is 640 x 480 pixels in size, so it should handle virtually all movie output needs. Like other still-image clips, the initial duration of the new matte is one second unless you change the default in the Still Images dialog box (accessible from the Preferences submenu of the File menu). You can also adjust a matte's duration by dragging its thumbnail edge in the Construction window—or by using any other editing technique covered in Chapters 3 and 4.

☞ *Alter a matte's color by double-clicking its thumbnail image to recall the color picker. Color changes will affect all places in your project where the matte is in use.*

Finally, if you want to save a spiffy color matte for use in other projects, throw it into a Library file. Premiere ships with a large Color Matte Library (tucked within the Libraries folder) that you can supplement with your custom mattes. Or create a new Library just for your special colors.

📖 *For more about Library files, see page 34.*

LIB.

Color Matte Library

One last tip: To retrieve your color matte from a Library, you'll need to use the "Open…" command in the File menu ("Import…" doesn't work). Then drag the matte from the Library window into your project.

▷ **The Output Step**

You have one more step to go to complete your editing voyage with Premiere. In the next chapter, we'll see how to wrap up your project successfully no matter what kind of output you seek—a QuickTime movie, a videotape recording, or an edit decision list. Soon you'll be able to make a perfect three-point landing.

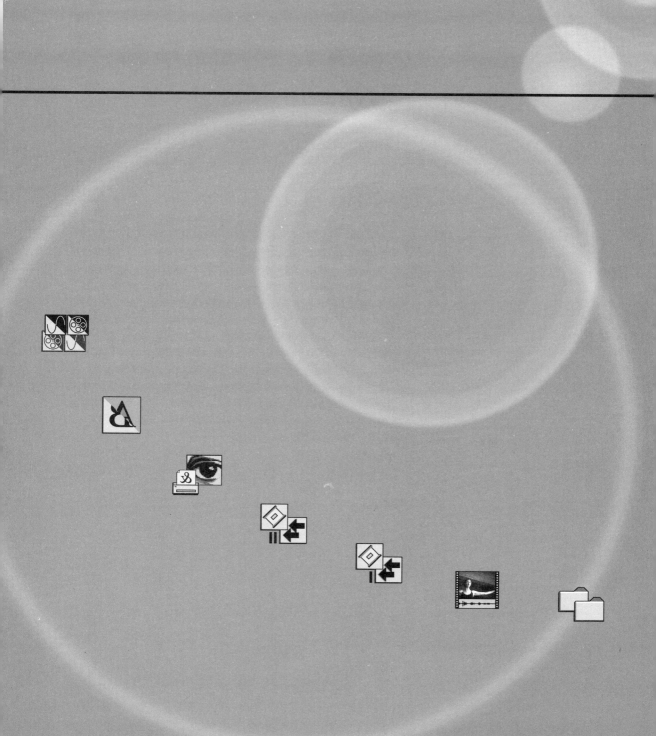

11

Optimizing
Your Output

Voilà! If you've put the finishing touches on your editing, Premiere gives you four ways to output the results. You can play it on your Mac as is or compile a movie so it plays on any QuickTime-capable computer. You also can output directly to videotape or build an edit decision list (EDL) for use with traditional post-production gear.

The first two parts of this chapter will show you how to accomplish all but the last approach (see Appendix B for more about EDLs). Then we'll visit a few remaining Premiere nooks that will help you get ready for more ventures and will save time while editing future projects.

Compiling the Final Movie

If your output goal is to create a QuickTime movie so your project can play from any QuickTime-capable hardware, this section is for you. We'll focus on Premiere's "Make Movie..." command and see how to wring the highest quality movie out of your hardware.

▶ The Compiling Process

Compiling builds a new QuickTime movie from your creative labors in the Construction window. The new movie is a separate file from your project, which holds source clip pointers and editing instructions for the movie.

It's always a good idea to save your Premiere project before compiling. After you save, follow these four steps to compile a sparkling new QuickTime movie:

1 If you edited your project with *miniatures*—a small copy of your source clips to speed up Premiere's performance—then bid farewell to those helpful files. Replace those smaller clips with the original source clips by selecting "Re-Find Files..." in the Project menu. (If you used Premiere 3.0's new *batch capture* abilities to grab a smaller set of source clips, you'll have to batch capture the final clips before doing this.)

For more about miniatures, see page 43. For more about batch capturing final clips in Premiere 3.0, see page 314.

In the dialog box that appears, show Premiere where to locate the original source files that will replace the miniatures. 3.0's new Find buttons at the box's bottom can help. Click Skip if you do not want to replace a requested file.

Premiere 3.0's dialog box is shown. 2.0's is similar but lacks the Find buttons and Control key option.

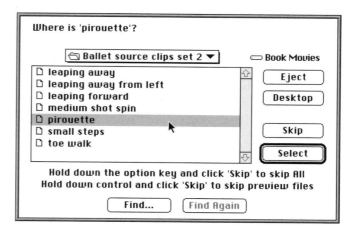

If your project's source files are all in the same folder, Premiere will automatically exchange them after you point the way to the first file. If the files are in different folders, Premiere will ask you to identify each location.

2 Choose "Movie…" from the Make menu (in 2.0, "Movie…" is in the Make submenu of the Project menu) or tap Command-K. Either action will pop-up the Make Movie dialog box.

Use this dialog box to name and save your new QuickTime movie. In the middle of the dialog box, Premiere summarizes the movie's output and compression settings.

Premiere 3.0's dialog box is shown. 2.0's is similar but has a single "Options…" button at the bottom and no "Disk Free Space" guidance.

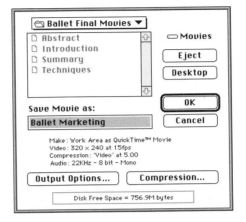

3.0

3 In Premiere 3.0, the preset you chose when starting your project should take care of most of the movie's settings. If you need to adjust the settings, click the "Output Options…" button or "Compression…" button. In Premiere 2.0, click the sole "Options…" button to see all movie settings at once.

Premiere 2.0's Project Output Options dialog box appears at the back. Premiere 3.0 splits the settings into two dialog boxes— and adds a few new controls.

📖 *More about each output option is just ahead. Appendix A (page 328) covers compression settings in detail.*

👉 *You also can reach these dialog boxes directly from the Make menu in Premiere 3.0. In 2.0, look in the Project menu.*

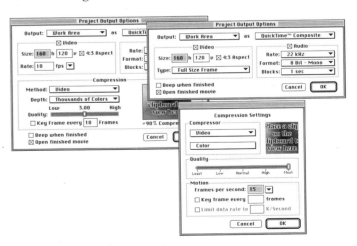

4 After you finish adjusting the settings and clicking OK to those dialog boxes, you'll be back in the Make Movie dialog box. Enter a name for your movie and select a save destination. Then click OK again.

Premiere will begin compiling your

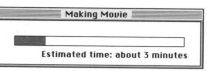

work, displaying a progress bar to show its status. Premiere 3.0 also will estimate the time remaining. If most of the special effects are toward the beginning of the movie, however, the time estimate will tend to be high.

Compiling usually takes *much* more time than a movie's playback. Premiere has to calculate each output frame. The process is especially slow for projects loaded with effects or multiple sound tracks. Premiere can't compile in the background, so forget about working simultaneously on other tasks with your Mac. Take a breather!

☞ Press Command-period [.] anytime to stop compiling. You'll end up with a movie file that's built as far as Premiere compiled.

3.0

Premiere 3.0 can dramatically cut down the compiling time, however, with its ability to re-use *temporary preview files*. The files may have been created when previewing your work, depending on your preview method and options. If the temporary files have the same settings as your new movie, compiling will be refreshingly fast.

📖 For more about how temporary preview files can save compiling time, see page 118.

Another nifty improvement in Premiere 3.0 (if you're running System 7) is that you can *pause* compiling. Simply switch to the Finder or another running application. Premiere resumes where it left off when you return.

One last caveat: Before compiling, make sure you have enough free disk space for the new movie—which can be huge depending on the project and compression settings.

In the Make Movie dialog box, Premiere 3.0 (with System 7) can show your available disk space.

Disk Free Space = 210.1M bytes

Premiere 3.0 also will pause compiling and warn you when available hard disk space drops below the "Low disk space warning level" set in the General Preferences dialog box. You can switch to the Finder and clear out disk space or stop compiling. Or you can continue (gulp) and risk running out of space before compiling finishes.

📖 For more about the "Low disk space" General Preferences setting, see page 298.

▶ Choosing the Output Format

Now let's step back and look at each output option you can adjust before compiling begins. In the Project Output Options dialog box, the first setting is a pair of pop-up menus for specifying the type of output (see next page).

Output: [Work Area ▼] as [✓QuickTime™ Composite
QuickTime™ Movie
Numbered PICT files
Filmstrip File]

For more about the yellow work area bar, see page 107.

With the left pop-up menu, you can choose to compile the entire project into a new movie or just the work area under the yellow bar in the Construction window. Pretty straightforward. The right pop-up menu requires more explanation, however. Let's review those options below.

QuickTime Composite

This is a good choice if your source clips have the same compression settings as your final movie, such as when using hardware compression boards. It's also a very fast compiling approach for cuts-only projects.

For many projects, this choice will save considerable compiling time. Premiere will compress only the portions of your movie that are *different* than your source clips. For instance, only segments where filters, transitions, motion settings or superimposed clips reside will be compressed. Other portions of your project will be left alone—even if the source clips were originally compressed differently. Your movie conceivably could end up with a smorgasbord of different quality levels and frame rates.

Compiling with a different frame size than your source clips forces re-compression of the entire movie, even if you select QuickTime Composite.

There are a few notable exceptions to QuickTime Composite's hands-off attitude. Premiere will always compress non-QuickTime clips, such as still-images or PICS animations, even if they're unaltered. And any source clip movies that were compressed with key frames (see page 334) will also face re-compression.

QuickTime Movie

This is a good choice for CD-ROM destined movies, since the entire movie should fit within a limited data transfer rate.

This option compiles the *entire* movie at the new output options and compression settings you select. Premiere even re-compresses source clips that are already compressed at the same settings. Although this approach takes more time than building a composite movie, it gives the movie a consistent playback frame rate and quality.

Numbered PICT Files

name.00000   name.00001

This option produces a series of numbered PICT files— one file for each frame of your movie. Premiere numbers the files sequentially with .00000, .00001 and so on, appended to their name. It can be useful for sending your production into Macromedia's Director or animation systems that do not accept the QuickTime movies. In Director, for example, you can step through each frame (and modify it if necessary) in the Score.

📖 *For more about the filmstrip file option, see page 98.*

3.0 Filmstrip File

Premiere 3.0 also can create a filmstrip file for Photoshop from this dialog box. This allows you to include effects and multiple clips in the filmstrip file without having to compile the segment beforehand.

▶ Frame Size & Type

After resolving the nature of the output Premiere will compile, you can more easily decide the frame size and type in the Project Output Options dialog box.

Size: `320` h `240` v ☒ 4:3 Aspect

Size

☞ *In Premiere 3.0, a General Preferences setting may limit the size. See page 297.*

Set the pixel height and width of your movie. To enter an odd movie proportion, turn off the check box. Movies in Premiere 3.0 can be from 60 x 45 pixels to a whopping 4000 x 4000 pixels (about 56 inches square!). That's up from Premiere 2.0's 2048 x 2048 pixel limit.

☞ *Typically, 240 x 180 or 320 x 240 is the largest movie size that doesn't play at single-digit playback frame rates on slower Macs or from CD-ROM.*

For playback on hardware compression-boosted machines, full-screen (640 x 480) compiling may be feasible. (Some boards produce better results when zooming a 320 x 240 image—check the board's documentation.) For CD-ROM or other slower playback environments, however, always balance the frame size with the desired frame rate.

Keep three other size-related issues in mind, too:

• *Have Enough RAM?*
The larger the movie, the more RAM Premiere will require for compiling. For example, Premiere needs at least 8 megabytes of RAM to build full-screen movies or you'll abruptly face an out-of-memory alert box.

📖 *For more about aspect ratio issues, see page 42.*

• *Respect the Aspect Ratio*
Your source clips and final movie should share the same aspect ratio or images will be distorted. If only a few clips have a different proportion, select each oddball in the Construction or Project window and turn on "Maintain Aspect Ratio" in the Clip menu. The clip will compile undistorted, showing black in residual areas of the frame.

☞ *Variable frame sizes are possible in a single movie with Premiere's Sequence window. See page 291.*

• *Stick to the Size Standards*
To squeeze the best frame rate from your Mac, stick with standard QuickTime movie sizes—unless your movie will stay on hardware compression machines. Standard sizes are 160 x 120, 240 x 180, 320 x 240 and 640 x 480 pixels.

Type

Leave this setting at its full-size frame default unless you're outputting full-screen movies to videotape. In that case, match this to how your QuickTime board outputs video. (Check the board's documentation, if necessary.)

If your project includes virtual clips and you choose "1/2 Horizontal" or "1/2 Vertical," some transitions or motion settings may distort. One solution is to temporarily set Type to "Full-Size Frame," select each virtual clip and choose "Replace with Source" in the Clip menu.

For more about the "Replace with Source" command, see page 91.

▶ Audio Output Options

The last output settings are three audio pop-up menus. Collectively, they determine your movie's sound quality.

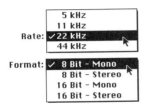

Rate and Format

The *Rate* pop-up menu sets the sampling rate of your movie's sound. Premiere gives you the standard kilohertz (kHz) choices. 44 kHz is CD-quality.

The *Format* pop-up menu establishes the movie's sound resolution and whether it will be mono or stereo. Consider stereo sound only if (a) your source clips are stereo, (b) the playback hardware supports stereo output, and (c) two speakers will be connected to that hardware. Otherwise, your audience won't hear a difference.

If your movie is for a wide range of hardware, generally set the sound quality as low as is feasible to preserve the movie's playback frame rate. Only hardware compression setups, audio-only movies, or RAM-based sound (see below) can escape this basic tradeoff.

Setting either option *higher* than your source clips will *not* coax higher quality sound into your final movie. All it will do is throw unnecessary data into your movie.

16-bit sound output (CD-quality) requires a suitable sound board and Sound Manager 3.0, which Premiere 3.0 ships with.

Refer to the chart on page 325 for a comparison of different sound quality levels.

Blocks

This determines the duration of sound that your movie will pre-load in RAM and play *interleaved* between blocks of video. The default of one second works well for most projects. If your movie suffers delays or has choppy audio, however, try a block of one-half second.

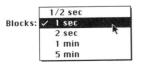

If you're *sure* sufficient RAM will be available for playback, selecting *a longer block than the movie's duration* can improve the movie's frame rate. That will leave less movie data to play on-the-fly from slower storage media.

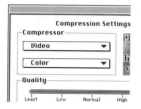

👉 *If the playback application lacks RAM for the sound block, the sound will drop out entirely.*

However, the movie won't start until all sound is loaded into RAM. This delay can be annoying—or completely unacceptable—depending on the nature of your project.

▶ Last-Minute Tips & Tricks

Here are a few last-minute issues you may need to address before your compiled movie is *truly* complete.

Compression Directions

What about Premiere's compression settings? Are pages missing from this book? No way! In case you overlooked an earlier note, turn to Appendix A on page 328. Since you must set compression while capturing clips *and* compiling final movies, those pages cover both at once.

3.0

Movie Psycho-Analysis

Consider using Premiere 3.0's Movie Analysis tool (in the Tools submenu of the File menu) to confirm the specs of your newly compiled movie. Particularly for CD-ROM-destined movies, it's a good way to verify the movie's average data rate—a critically important factor for movie playback on that relatively slow media.

📖 *For more about the Movie Analysis tool, see page 31.*

Flattening Movies For Windows and Unix

To play Premiere movies on Windows and Silicon Graphics machines, you have to "flatten" the movie file. No, your images do not turn into pancakes. A flattened movie file just adds indexing information to the file where the Windows and Unix operating systems expect it.

3.0 👉 *You can issue the "Flattened Movie…" command from other Premiere windows, but the Clip window is most direct.*

Premiere 3.0 has a command just for this purpose. With the movie's Clip window open, choose "Flattened Movie…" from the Export submenu of the File menu. You'll see the dialog box below for saving the new movie.

Make sure the name includes no more than eight characters plus the extension .MOV so other platforms can recognize the file.

2.0 👉 *Premiere 2.0 users can do the same thing with the Movie Converter utility in Apple's QuickTime Starter Kit.*

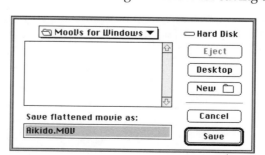

▸ A Potpourri of Output Issues

Compiling is often the last step in a Premiere project, but you also can stick with Premiere when presenting the movie or recording the show onto videotape. Synchronized MIDI playback is possible, too. You even can link several movies together into a more extensive sequence. Let's tackle that last topic first before learning about the other output opportunities.

▸ Splicing Movies into Sequences

Transitions or any other movie elements cannot run between movies in a Premiere sequence. So it will usually take careful planning to develop a single, smooth movie this way.

The Sequence window is a handy tool for playing several movies together. You can glue movies into a mega-movie or use the window as a palette to play movies one-by-one or in sequence. That's great for comparing movies, such as different comps for a client. There's no need to call up Premiere's formidable array of other windows on-screen.

Collaborative movies are also more feasible with the Sequence window. For example, different participants could develop a movie's introduction, middle and ending on different Macs. You could then use the Sequence window to assemble the movies quickly, review progress and perhaps even produce the final combined results.

To link movies into a sequence, follow these steps.

1 Choose "Sequence" from the New submenu under the File menu (Command semi-colon [;]). A small untitled Sequence window will materialize.

2 With the Sequence window active, use any Import command from the File menu to add movies. The movies can be new productions you've compiled with Premiere or any other QuickTime movie. You can also drag files into the Sequence window from any Project, Clip, Title, Library or other Sequence window.

Thumbnail icons of the selections appear in the Sequence window. Look under the window's title bar for the total number of items and their combined playing time.

Premiere 3.0's window is shown, but 2.0's is similar.

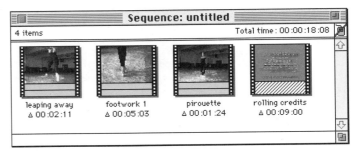

The Sequence window is intended for movies. But you *can* add still-images, animations or sound clips to the window. In fact, you can add any file Premiere normally accepts. To compile non-movie ingredients into a single movie, however, you'll have to use the "Movie…" command in the Make menu instead of the quicker "Composite…" command (as described in Step 5 just ahead).

(2.0) ☞ *In Premiere 2.0, "Movie…" and "Composite…" are in the Make submenu of the Project menu.*

3 Items appear in the Sequence window in the order that you brought them in. If desired, drag items around to change their order or delete any item with the Delete key. In Premiere 2.0, you can't select more than one item at a time as you drag or delete. Premiere 3.0 adds the normal Macintosh hold-down-the-Shift-key routine for making multiple selections.

☞ *Clear, Cut, Copy, Paste and Duplicate commands are also available in the File menu.*

3.0

You also can polish each sequence item further if the need arises. Since you're working with file pointers, the changes won't affect your original files. You can:

• *Trim*—Double-clicking a movie in the Sequence window opens a Clip window where you can adjust the movie's In or Out point. In 3.0, you also can select "Duration…" in the Clip menu to move just the Out point.

📖 *For more about the Speed command, see page 88.*

• *Speed*—The "Speed…" command remains available in the Clip menu to accelerate or slow the action of any movie in a sequence.

3.0

• *Re-name*—Premiere 3.0 offers a "Name Alias…" command in the Clip menu to attach a new name to any selected Sequence window item.

📖 *For more about the Name Alias command, see page 34.*

In 3.0, you also can adjust Sequence window icon sizes, much like the Project window. With the Sequence window active, select "Sequence Window Options…" in the Windows menu (Command 1) to see the box at left.

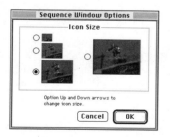

If you have so many files in the Sequence window that you can't find one, Premiere 3.0 can relieve any budding frustration with the "Go to/Search…" command in the Project menu. That calls up the simple dialog box at right for finding one or more files.

4 By saving a Sequence window, you preserve its contents and can call it back up later for further use. Choose "Save…" from the File menu (Command S) while the Sequence window is active. The standard Save dialog box appears for you to name and place the new file.

☞ *A saved Sequence window document has a small file size since it only holds pointers to the original movies.*

At this point, you have a few choices. You could:

• Play the entire sequence on your screen using the "Print to Video…" command (as described below)

• Use the "Print to Video…" command to output the sequence to videotape

☞ *You also can print Sequence window icons on paper in a quasi-storyboard format by selecting "Print Window…" in the File menu (Command P).*

• Double-click an item in the Sequence window to play just that segment in a Clip window

• Compile the items into a single new movie (see Step 5)

5 To compile sequence items into a single new movie, choose "Composite…" from the Make menu (in 2.0, it's in the Make submenu of the Project menu). Or tap Command-comma [,]. You'll get a Save dialog box for depositing the new movie in its proper place. After clicking OK, Premiere will build the new movie swiftly and retain full image quality since no re-compression occurs. You can then play the new movie in the Clip window or with the "Print to Video…" command.

☞ *A composite movie has a similar file size as the sum of its movie parts. To stop compiling, type Command-period [.].*

··

▶ **Printing to Video**

The "Print to Video…" command has two important roles—recording your movies to videotape and playing movies on your Mac's screen. The content will play in the center of a black screen with no menus, windows, cursors or other interface elements visible—just the image.

☞ *Sequences made of movies with different frame sizes will play centered in the screen.*

Here's the Print to Video process:

1 Open a Clip window or place movies in a Sequence window (as described earlier). In 3.0, you also can trigger Print to Video directly from the Construction window to preview uncompiled movies. Premiere 3.0 has a new mouse icon in the upper right corner of the Sequence window, too. If you turn on the icon, you gain the following *interactive* control over Print to Video playback.

• Print to Video will pause before each Sequence window item (and blink a mouse icon) until you click the mouse.

• During playback, you can tap the Right arrow key (or spacebar) to move forward among sequence items; tap the Left arrow key to move back.

• You can tap the Up or Down arrow key to pause in the middle of a movie's playback.

• You can use the Home or End keys on extended keyboards to move to the first or last Sequence window item.

Some QuickTime boards (such as SuperMac's DigitalFilm) ship with optimized plug-ins that improve on Premiere's Print to Video command. Look in the Export submenu of the File menu for that.

2 With the window that has the movie material active, choose "Print to Video..." in the Export submenu of the File menu (Command M). The Print to Video dialog box at right will then appear. Check below for advice about setting each Print to Video playback option.

Blank screen

This sets how long a blank (black) screen will appear before and after the material plays. If you're recording to tape, allow several seconds for the deck to get up to speed.

Zoom screen

Zooming ensures all line weights will be an even number of pixels thick, reducing flicker problems on NTSC displays.

This option will double the movie's frame size. A 320 x 240 pixel movie will play at full-screen, for example. Of course each pixel will double as well, becoming a blockier four pixels. Sometimes that's an acceptable approach.

For hardware zoom to be available, a zoom plug-in file for the board must be inside Premiere's Plug-ins folder.

If your video board offers hardware zoom, select the Hardware option. Without such a board, Premiere's software-based zooming is your only choice. The software zoom speed depends on your Mac's CPU speed. On slower Macs, expect a significant frame rate penalty.

Loop playback

This option will repeatedly play the material, momentarily pausing between loops. Any blank screen time will appear only before the first playback cycle. To stop playback, tap Command-period (.).

Activate Recording Deck

☞ For this option to be available, select the deck in the Device Control dialog box (accessed via the Preferences submenu of the File menu).

You can manually tap your deck's buttons to start or stop recording. However, Premiere can automate that if you have a controllable deck linked to your Mac. Turning this check box on will start the tape deck when you click OK. When playback is finished, recording will stop.

☞ Set your Mac's monitor to at least your movie's color depth for the smoothest playback.

☞ On slower Macs, there can be a brief lag in playback between Sequence window items. Compile the sequence to get rid of that delay.

3 Click OK and away you'll play. No matter what options you select, you can tap Command-period (.) to stop playback at any time. If you're recording to video-tape, whatever frame rate you see on your monitor when using Print to Video will appear on tape. If your Mac isn't sufficiently powerful for a fast frame rate with Print to Video playback, you have three (more costly) options.

• You can acquire a hardware compression board for faster real-time playback and recording, or

• You can record in non-real time (frame-by-frame at a much slower rate) with a third-party machine controller and frame-accurate controllable recording deck. Diaquest, Videomedia and others offer such solutions.

📖 See Appendix B (page 337) for more about creating EDL's in Premiere.

• If your movie's source material is on videotape, Premiere can generate an edit decision list (EDL) you can use with traditional post-production equipment to record a new master videotape.

▶ **From Mac to Tape**

If you will be recording movies directly onto videotape with the "Print to Video..." command, follow this advice.

• Make sure your Mac can output NTSC-compatible signals. Many, but not all, QuickTime boards provide such output (check the specs). Other video boards—and the built-in video of most Macs—produce a NTSC-compatible scan rate but lack an encoder to convert the Mac's non-interlaced signal into the interlaced NTSC format. In that case, a separate encoder box is required. RasterOps, VideoLogic and others offer such products.

• If you're using more than one computer monitor, place the window with your movie(s)—such as the Sequence window—on the screen run by the fastest video card. Premiere will use that card to output the movie.

• Unless you have a third-party sound card (such as Digidesign's *Audiomedia II*) or sound capabilities built into your QuickTime board, outputted sound will have to run from your Mac's single sound jack. Recording stereo sound from there—assuming your Mac can output stereo—requires a cable that will split the signal into left and right channels (a $5-10 Radio Shack special).

▶ Premiere's MIDI Connection

Premiere can send a start and stop MIDI signal at the beginning and end of a movie's playback. This capability is ideal for kiosks or other individual presentations that will include high-quality background music. By pulling the music data off of QuickTime's shoulder, the playback Mac can be more devoted to displaying images at the fastest frame rate it can manage.

☞ To time your movie to MIDI playback while editing, create a low-quality recording of it as a reference clip and temporarily place that in an audio track.

To put Premiere's MIDI signal in synch with your sound source, select "MIDI Setup..." in the Preferences submenu under the File menu. To access the dialog box, you'll need Apple's *MIDI Manager* and *Patch Bay* software installed on your Mac (both are typically provided or available from the manufacturer of your MIDI instrument or from most MIDI software packages).

Click the first check box to have MIDI start/stop commands sent with your movie's playback. Click the second check box to send MIDI clocks signals out of the serial port. The MIDI device will synch to the tempo you set in the Tempo box.

After you activate the settings in this dialog box, simply play the sequence with the Clip Window's play button or by using the "Print to Video..." command from the Clip window, Sequence window or (in Premiere 3.0) the Construction window.

A final MIDI note: The MIDI signal originates entirely from Premiere's bag of tricks—nothing extra is embedded into the QuickTime movie file. So if your movie will later play in an application other than Premiere, it will lose the MIDI playback capabilities.

Getting Ready for More

Well, it's a wrap. We've traveled through the entire project process (except capturing clips in Premiere—the following chapter). All that's left is to set a few preferences for the next project and clean up your hard drive—in other words, get ready for more. (Premiere 2.0 users note: You can move on to the next chapter. This entire section covers juicy items that are only available in Premiere 3.0.)

▶ 3.0's General Preferences

3.0

The General Preferences dialog box opens with fewer options on display than shown here. Clicking the More Options button at the box's bottom reveals the box's entire contents. Default settings are at right.

☞ *Want to restore Premiere 3.0 to its original settings? Trash the Adobe Premiere Prefs file (in the Preferences folder of your Mac's System Folder) after closing Premiere.*

Now that you've experienced most of Premiere's powers, this is a good time to select "General Preferences…" in the Preferences submenu of the File menu. You'll see a dialog box that controls many of 3.0's niftiest features.

General Preferences

Maximum image size: `2048 x 2048 ▼`
Size changes take effect on restart.

Window at startup: `New Project ▼`
Clip window shuttle control: `Jog Control ▼`
Method for choosing colors: `Premiere Picker ▼`

Low disk space warning level: `1024` K

☒ Deactivate Appletalk when recording
☒ Maintain virtual clip source areas
☐ Open QuickTime clips 'collapsed'
☒ Allow zooming in clip samples
☒ Enable 'Find File' when opening files
☒ Show disk free space when saving files
☐ Don't accelerate previews
☐ Prevent disappearing cursor

[Fewer Options…]   [Cancel] [OK]

Officially, "More Options…" items should only be adjusted at the direction of Adobe's tech support crew. But let's briefly look at *all* preference items in order, anyway. Maybe this will save you a phone call.

Maximum image size

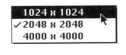

☞ *Changes will apply the next time you start Premiere.*

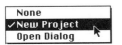

This sets the upper size limit of any clip Premiere will handle. If you don't need larger than 1024 x 1024 pixel clips, choosing that frees up 128K of Premiere's RAM for other uses. Selecting 4000 x 4000 (near motion-picture resolution) eats up 256K more of RAM than the default.

Window at start-up

This setting determines what you face after double-clicking Premiere's icon to start the application.

Jog   *Shuttle*

Clip window shuttle control

Choose between first seeing 3.0's new Jog Control or the Shuttle Control after opening a Clip window. The other remains available by Option-clicking the visible control.

 *See page 241 for a color picker comparison.*

Method for choosing colors

Pick your preferred color picker—Premiere's or Apple's.

Low disk space warning level

When compiling a movie, Premiere will warn you if the free space on your destination hard disk drops below the level set here. You'll have a choice of stopping compiling, switching to the Finder to clear out space, or continuing. If you like early warnings, boost this setting upwards.

Deactivate AppleTalk when recording

When capturing clips, this option ensures your Mac won't skip a frame or two from network activity. Premiere will turn AppleTalk back on after your digitizing session.

Maintain virtual clip source areas

Leaving this on protects virtual clips in your project. When (a) you use the Track or Multi-Track tool in the Construction window, and (b) select a region that includes a virtual clip's source area, this ensures *all tracks that form the virtual clip* will be selected.

Open QuickTime clips 'collapsed'

Turn this on to have video Clip windows always open with just their controls. Images will appear in the Preview window, saving screen space. Clicking the collapse button on the right side of the window's control bar toggles between a collapsed state and the entire window.

Allow zooming in clip samples

Many Premiere 3.0 filters have a Zoom and Hand tool next to their built-in preview window so you can take a closer look at the effect. The Sample Box image in the Transparency Settings dialog box also has such tools. There's really no reason to turn this feature off.

Enable 'Find File' when opening files

This puts handy new Find buttons in the bottom of the Open and Import dialog boxes of 3.0. Turn this off only if you have a super-duper dialog box utility that conflicts.

Show disk free space

Disk Free Space = 210.1M bytes

At the bottom of Save dialog boxes, this shows how much free disk space is available on the destination volume. Again, turn this off only if a dialog box utility conflicts.

Don't accelerate previews

Keep this off. Turning it on *prevents* Premiere from doing a trick behind QuickTime's back to smooth previews.

Prevent disappearing cursor

This fixes a cursor problem with some DigitalFilm boards. Turn it on only if Adobe or SuperMac give a thumbs up.

▶ **Multiple Sets of Plug-Ins**

Premiere 3.0 has another neat preference setting we haven't seen. You can create plug-in folders for different editing situations and tell Premiere which one to use for a particular session. Select "Plug-Ins..." in the Preferences submenu of the File menu to see the box below.

Select the Plug-Ins folder you want to activate for your Premiere session. Your choice takes effect the next time you start Premiere. The folder can have any name and can be stored anywhere on the disk volume.

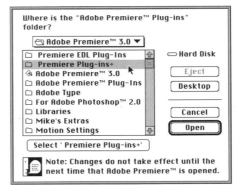

 You also can use this to select a combined folder of Premiere and Photoshop-compatible plug-ins when a wider range of filters is desired.

A great use of this feature is to create folders with *different* sets of transitions. For EDL work you could select a plug-ins folder with only "valid" transitions. When later working on multimedia, you could then use the command to switch to Premiere's original Plug-Ins folder.

▶ **Assigning Function Keys**

3.0

If you use an extended keyboard, check this out. Premiere 3.0 arrives with several of your keyboard function keys already assigned to commands. But you can insist on your own F-key assignments. To do that, select "Function Keys..." from the Preferences submenu of the File menu.

The Function Key dialog box shows your currently assigned commands. Click the Shift check box to see commands that require the Shift key.

Function Keys		
F1: **Undo**	**Load...**	
F2: **Cut**		
F3: **Copy**	**Save...**	
F4: **Paste**		
F5: **Multiple...**		
F6: **Folder...**	☐ **Shift**	
F7:		
F8:		
F9: **Title**		
F10: **Movie Capture**		
F11: **Batch Capture**		
F12: **Audio Capture**		
F13: **Movie Analysis...**	**Cancel**	
F14:		
F15:	**OK**	

To assign a new command to a function key, select the function key's box and then pull down any menu in Premiere and choose the command you want to assign. To clear a function key of a command, drag-select the command in its box and press the Delete key. With the Save and Load buttons in the dialog box, you can even create multiple F-key sets (i.e. for capture, editing, titles).

Note that some corners of Premiere, such as the Title window and Movie Capture window, display their own unique menus. To assign a command from such menus, be sure to activate the window that shows the menu *before* opening the Function Keys dialog box.

▶ Spring Folder Cleaning

3.0

Now that you've finished your Premiere project, let's unclutter your hard disk. Odds are that scratch movies, unused clips, temporary files and other residual files from your effort are taking up precious megabytes. However, we don't want to trash your project's original source clips (or the separate Premiere project file) if you believe your final movie may need further editing later.

For complicated projects, weeding out unneeded files while maintaining the integrity of projects would be a nuisance. Fortunately, Premiere 3.0 has a new "Folder Cleaner" that can search a folder or disk volume for unused files and (with your approval) delete them. Any Premiere file it finds that is not referenced by a project, sequence or library is targeted for spring cleaning.

The folder cleaner doesn't identify non-Premiere files, such as text files, for deletion.

There's one catch, however. It only analyzes the files in a selected folder or disk volume (including any embedded folders). If the selected folder or volume also includes files you want to keep from a project, library or sequence that's *located outside the selected folder or volume,* Premiere will identify those files as deletion candidates. You'll have to carefully deselect them from the hit list. The folder cleaner is therefore most useful if you already segregate files from different projects in separate folders.

The cleaner requires that all Project, Clip, Sequence and Library windows are closed. If any are open, you'll first see a dialog box for closing them.

To tidy up, select "Folder Cleaner…" from the Tools submenu of the File menu. An Open dialog box will appear for you to select a folder to clean. After you click Open, Premiere will take a moment to analyze the folder contents before showing the large dialog box below.

Files in the top half of the box have been moved since they were originally created. In the bottom half of the box are files that projects, libraries or sequences in the folder or volume do not reference. These are the more likely deletion candidates.

```
┌──────────────────── Folder Cleaner ────────────────────┐
│ These files were not in their original locations, but a file with the │
│ same name was found. (Selected files will be deleted).                 │
│ crop barn                                          21.5K ▲             │
│ jet takeoff                                         1.1M               │
│ owl.moov                                           79.3K               │
│ rowing teams                                        2.0M               │
│ URL PICT new                                        9.1K ▼             │
│                                                                         │
│ These files are not being used and are scheduled to be deleted.        │
│ (Selected files will be deleted).                                      │
│ aikido Diff PICT.00001                            150.4K ▲             │
│ Aikido title 3.PICT                               142.3K               │
│ Aikido Title 4.PICT                               145.7K               │
│ Aikido title 5.PICT                               140.2K               │
│ Aikido.Blue Title gradient                          3.5K               │
│ Aikido.Title gradient low                           3.5K ▼             │
│ Total selected size = 1.3M        ( Cancel )  ( Delete )               │
└─────────────────────────────────────────────────────────┘
```

Click Cancel if you're unsure about going ahead and possibly removing some important files. Or go ahead and select or deselect items in both lists, then click Delete to have Premiere delete very selected file. Premiere will give you one last warning before doing this.

▶ **Thanks for Traveling!**

Congratulations! In our long journey together, you've earned a license to fly Premiere solo anywhere you would like to go. It's truly a pleasure to travel with you.

If you always get source clips from other resources or applications, you can stop here. To capture *new* material in Premiere, however, tackle one more chapter. 3.0 in particular has capture abilities that are worth a long look.

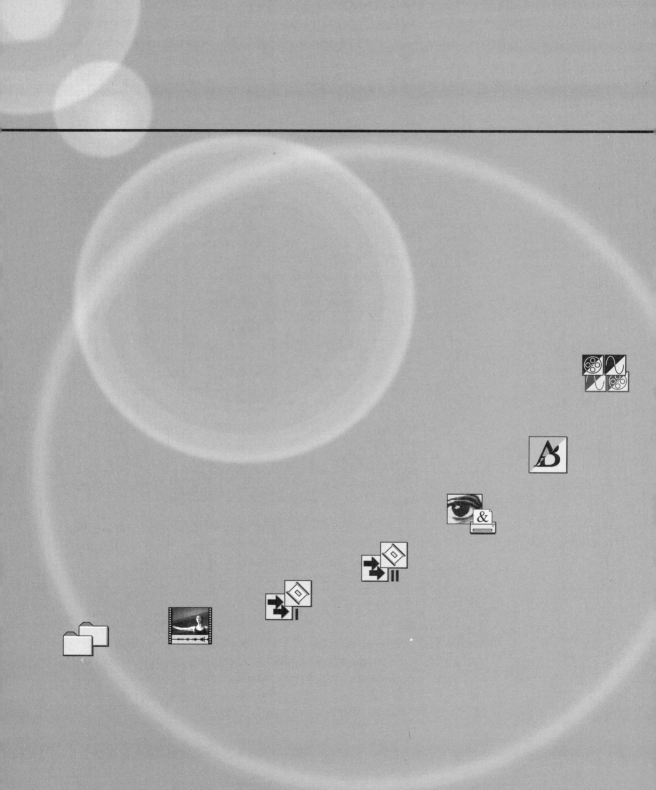

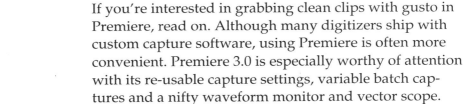

12

Capturing
Video & Sound

If you're interested in grabbing clean clips with gusto in
Premiere, read on. Although many digitizers ship with
custom capture software, using Premiere is often more
convenient. Premiere 3.0 is especially worthy of attention
with its re-usable capture settings, variable batch captures and a nifty waveform monitor and vector scope.

In this chapter, we'll first walk through the steps of
digitizing video and audio clips, discovering many tips
and shortcuts along the way. Then we'll maneuver
through dozens of capture settings—making the right
tradeoffs for your hardware setup and creative goals.

The Digitizing Process

Premiere's digitizing process varies depending on the type of clip you want to grab and your hardware setup. Ahead we'll see how to digitize video without—and with—device control hardware as well as how to capture audio-only clips. That should cover all of the bases. Before we begin, though, let's optimize your setup for digitizing.

▶ Capture Preliminaries

With a few simple clicks, you can dramatically improve the digitizing performance of Premiere. Chapter 1 detailed several ways to fine-tune Premiere's *overall* performance. Here's a recap of the items that boost movie capture—plus a few tips not covered earlier.

Free Up RAM

☞ *If you have hardware compression or a controlled-capture setup, capturing to RAM offers no advantage.*

Premiere can capture video to hard disk or to RAM. Since RAM is faster, it allows you to digitize movies at a higher frame rate, larger frame size or improved quality. The only limitation is each clip has to fit into the amount of RAM Premiere has available. Loading more RAM into Premiere therefore allows you to capture longer movies.

Memory

To maximize Premiere's RAM, visit page 17 to see how to tweak the System's memory, limit RAM-hungry extensions and controls panels, and turn off your Mac's file sharing. Then assign the RAM-goods to Premiere.

Reduce CPU Distractions

Anything that momentarily distracts your Mac may cause Premiere to skip a frame while capturing a clip. If you're aiming for a high frame rate that's as smooth as silk, keep your Mac on task with these steps:

3.0

📖 *For more about 3.0's AppleTalk preference setting, see page 298.*

• *Deactivate AppleTalk*
With the right preference setting, Premiere 3.0 can remind you about this before a movie capture session. A dialog box will give you the option of temporarily deactivating AppleTalk. Go ahead and do it. 2.0 users should, too—the old way—by selecting "Chooser" under the Apple menu.

• *Deactivate background utilities*
Deactivate any utilities that may suddenly come alive in your Mac's background. Common examples include screen savers, background compression utilities, alarm or clock programs and some send/receive fax software.

• *Fill your empty drives*
Last, restart your Mac with tape or CD-ROM drives turned off—or their extensions disabled. And place a disk in each floppy drive so your Mac doesn't compulsively check it every few seconds.

Hard Disk Hang-Ups
Hard drive performance is critical whenever you're capturing clips to disk instead of RAM. Be sure to take the next two steps to eliminate hard-disk hang-ups:

• *Select your fastest hard disk*
If you have more than one hard disk humming, make sure Premiere dumps captured movie data into your fastest drive. A disk array, hard drive or separate disk partition that's *dedicated to movie capture* is most ideal—particularly if your goal is full-motion clips. To point Premiere to your best storage volume, select "Scratch Disk…" in the Preferences submenu of the File menu. You'll see the dialog box below.

Unsure which drive is fastest? Larger hard drives tend to transfer and write data faster.

Use the top pop-up menu to specify the disk or partition for captured clips.

Premiere 3.0's dialog box is shown. 2.0's is similar but doesn't include the bottom two pop-up menus for temporary files.

Scratch Disks

Temp/Captured Movies: *Same as Application*
Video Preview Temps: *Same as Project File*
Audio Preview Temps: *Same as Project File*

Cancel   OK

• *Defragment or optimize the disk*
Before digitizing, use a utility such as Symantec's *Norton Utilities* to defragment—or better yet, optimize—the hard disk or partition for your new clips. QuickTime then won't miss a beat since it will be able to completely write each captured clip in one place on the hard disk platter.

One last check: Make sure your System Folder has the VDIG and/or sound driver for your capture hardware. See page 16.

▶ **Calibrating the Video Image**

3.0

There's one other preliminary adjustment that Premiere 3.0 alone offers. Turn on your video source and step into the new Waveform Monitor and Vector Scope, which you can use to improve the color and brightness of your incoming video signal for capture. To see these terrific new tools, select "Waveform Monitor" from the Capture submenu of the File menu.

Your source video appears in the top center window. The left side of the window has sliders to adjust the image (available sliders depend on your digitizer's capabilities). The Intensity slider in the lower right corner adjusts the strength of the readings.

The tapedeck control buttons and frame indicator at the bottom of the window appear only if you have a device control setup.

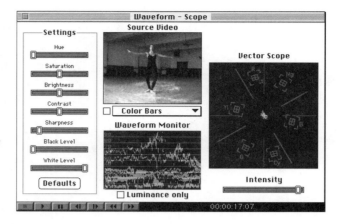

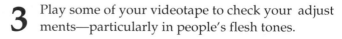

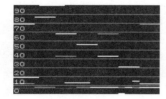

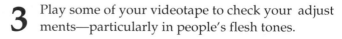

The primary purpose of this window is to correct, or *calibrate,* for any bias that your equipment (or even cables) may introduce to the video signal. To do that, you must have *standard color bars* recorded on your videotape. Then follow these steps:

1 Play your recorded color bar segment. As it plays, turn on the pop-up menu under the Source Video window to see Premiere's *reference* color bars for comparison. Then watch the Vector Scope. If your recorded bars produce a different pattern, use the Hue and Saturation sliders to adjust the video to match the reference results.

2 Next, turn on the "Luminance only" check box under the Waveform Monitor to isolate the brightness levels in the color bars. Is there a difference between your source video and the reference bars? If so, use Brightness, Contrast, Black Level and White Level sliders to match the two readings as closely as possible.

3 Play some of your videotape to check your adjustments—particularly in people's flesh tones.

🖙 3.0's Goodies folder (in the Third Party Stuff folder) has a full-screen PICT of color bars you can record onto videotape. Use Premiere's "Print to Video..." command (see page 293).

Tah dah! That's all it takes to calibrate your incoming clips. There's one hitch, however. What if you *don't* have standard color bars available on your videotape? You can still use the Waveform Monitor and Vector Scope as informative helpers to adjust the video image *subjectively.* For that, you'll need to understand better what the readings represent. Let's focus on the Waveform Monitor first.

The Waveform Monitor charts the luminance and color saturation of the source video. Vertically, the top of the Monitor represents white (essentially "100 IRE" for users with prior waveform monitor experience) and bottom is black (0 IRE). As each incoming scan line of video arrives in Premiere (via your digitizer), it's charted from left to right on the monitor as a series of *vertical* lines.

Each vertical line's height on the Monitor represents the color saturation of a pixel in the video scan line. Brighter image areas plot towards the top. Scanning is so fast that you see several lines at once on the Monitor.

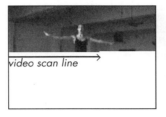
video scan line

values for that video scan line

☞ *Pure black shadows and white areas can help QuickTime's compression efficiency. So you may need to balance that factor with aesthetics. See page 322.*

A well-balanced image with moderate contrast will plot mostly in the middle areas of the Waveform Monitor. A Monitor dominated by extreme readings at its top or bottom, however, may be cause for slider adjustments. Perhaps too much shadow or glare is in the image.

The Vector Scope radially plots dots for the hue and color saturation of the source video. Each primary color bar we saw earlier appears at a different "clock" position.

To color-correct the redness shown by this Vector Scope reading, adjust the Hue and Saturation sliders (or if you're shooting live, perhaps the lighting) until the dots are more balanced around the center.

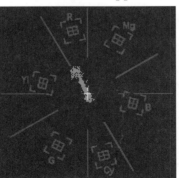

For example, if your video has a subtle red tinge (perhaps from warm indoor lighting or poor white balance in the video camera), most dots will plot towards the red box (eleven o'clock). The more saturated the colors, the farther the dots fall from the center.

☞ *The hue abbreviations are magenta (Mg), blue (B), cyan (Cy), green (G), yellow (Y) and red (R).*

The pop-up menu in the dialog box's center holds three other reference images (besides color bars). It also has a very useful "Clipboard clip" item that allows you to compare your source video to any copied clip—to gain image consistency between clips. That can be important, for example, for multiple-camera shoots. If the cameras weren't calibrated and matched in the field, color and brightness differences of different shots of the same scene could be noticeable. Here you can correct the differences.

📖 *For more about Video Input settings, see page 321. For more about saving capture settings, see page 317.*

Finally, keep in mind that your slider adjustments will also appear in the Video Input dialog box—so you won't have to adjust sliders twice. Best yet, you can save and re-use your slider settings (more about that ahead).

▶ Steps for Grabbing Video

Premiere should now be ready to capture movies. Let's first see how to digitize video clips in Premiere the "regular" way—without extra device control hardware that gives Premiere control over your video source. Then we'll discover the elements that device control adds.

Capturing *without* device control takes four steps:

1 Select "Movie Capture" from the Capture submenu of the File menu. (In 2.0, it's in the New submenu.) A simple Movie Capture window appears, from which you can record and monitor the video. A Movie Capture menu also shows up in the menu bar.

Premiere 3.0's window is shown. 2.0's includes a box to enter the reel name. Ignore that unless you're building an edit decision list.

☞ *If the window doesn't open but your digitizer's VDIG is loaded properly, the digitizer may require a certain color depth setting on your monitor.*

In the lower corner, you can drag the size box to adjust the frame size of the captured clip. As you drag, the frame snaps to QuickTime's standard sizes (160 x 120, 240 x 180, 360 x 240 and 640 x 480 pixels on large monitors). Shift-drag to get in-between sizes with a 4:3 aspect ratio. Or Option-drag to resize to any proportion.

2 Before clicking the Record button, browse through the Movie Capture menu. You'll often find fault with the defaults, so they're well worth checking.

Select "Recording Settings..." to check capture settings. See page 319 for advice.

Select "Video Input..." and "Sound Input..." to review compression, quality and source settings. See page 321 for guidance.

3.0 *Premiere 3.0 can load and save capture settings, saving time. See page 317.*

To record video without sound, select "Sound Off." Leaving it unchecked and piping in silent video during capture may cause your Mac to devote processing time to the "empty" sound signal.

3 After confirming the various capture settings, the Movie Capture window should still be visible. If you're digitizing from tape or videodisc, cue up to several seconds before the desired segment. Then play the video.

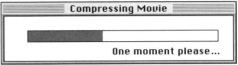

Premiere may take a few seconds before capture begins, so click the Record button *well* before the desired material. (This also will give you more editing flexibility.)

4 To stop recording, press the mouse button for a second or two. (The cursor temporarily disappeared during capture.) If you turned on "Post-Compress Video" in the Recording Settings dialog box earlier, Premiere will now take extra time to compress the captured file.

Compressing Movie

One moment please...

☞ *To import your new clips more easily into a Premiere project (or create miniatures for speedier editing), save the clips in one folder as they're captured.*

5 Finally, the captured movie will appear in an untitled Clip window. Select "Save…" in the File menu to save the new clip. Give the file a descriptive name (such as "Car leaving", not "Clip # 4") to ease later searches for the clip. If you have a project open, you can then import or drag the clip into your project.

The Clip window appears with your captured sequence.

3.0 ☞ *If you haven't turned on "Report dropped frames" in the Recording Settings dialog box, consider triggering 3.0's Movie Analysis tool to assess the captured clip. See page 31.*

One last capture note: Do you lack device control but plan to create an edit decision list from these clips? If so, manually adding time code to each clip *now* may be a good idea—the clip and its source are both at hand. Choose "Timecode…" from the Clip menu.

📖 *For more about the "Timecode…" command, see page 338.*

▶ **Differences for Device Control**

If you're using device control hardware from Diaquest, Videomedia, ARTI or others that let you control a frame-accurate tapedeck from your Macintosh, Premiere's video grabbing talents can greatly expand. With device control and Premiere, you can:

☞ *No device control gear? You can skip ahead to "Digitizing Only Decibels" on page 315.*

• capture video with frame-accurate precision while controlling the entire process from your Mac

• instantly advance to a selected video frame, including the in or out frame of your desired segment

• record automatically between the in and out frames

• embed time code automatically into the captured clip if your deck can read time code

• capture clips in slow motion on decks that can run at variable speeds, later increasing the frame rate with Premiere's "Speed…" command—a sneaky (but effective) way to capture a higher frame rate

3.0 • log in several video segments in Premiere 3.0 and then batch capture them automatically

To activate Premiere's device control talents, make sure your controller's plug-in file or control panel is in Premiere's Plug-Ins folder or the System Folder, respectively. Then select "Device Control…" in the Preferences submenu of the File menu. Choose the device in the dialog box that appears. (You may then see another box with further settings.) Click OK—restart Premiere if necessary.

Now you can use the same five-step capture process outlined earlier. The only difference is you'll encounter a more complex Movie Capture window similar to below.

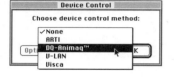

Premiere 3.0's window (shown) adds a Log In/Out button and a slightly different Reel Name box. Otherwise, 2.0's and 3.0's window are similar.

☞ *This window is designed for device control, but you can still click the Record button after manually triggering your deck.*

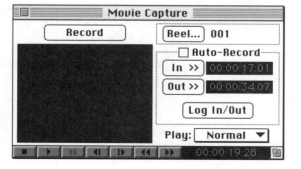

Let's see what each doodad in this window does.

Reel… ("Reel Name" in 2.0)

If you're building an edit decision list, enter the name of the source tape reel here. Otherwise, don't bother. In 3.0, click the Reel button and use the text entry box that appears if you dislike the numerical name (001) Premiere handed you by default.

Tapedeck Buttons

Along the bottom of the window are several buttons for controlling your deck from Premiere. The following keyboard shortcuts for these buttons are available in 3.0:

- Tap the spacebar or "P" to play or pause.

- Press Right or Left Arrow keys to advance one frame forward or back.

- Type "F" to fast-forward the deck, "R" to rewind.

- Press "G" to start recording, "S" to stop the deck.

In either Premiere, the time code at the window's bottom shows your deck's current frame. In 3.0, you can cue to a specific location by clicking that box, entering a new SMPTE figure and tapping the Return key.

Auto-Record

Turn on this check box to have Premiere automatically capture a video segment. You can specify the desired frames in two ways. Play the tape and click the In and Out buttons to set the start and end frames of a segment. Or click the adjacent boxes to enter time code directly. Use 3.0's new Log In/Out button to add the specified clip to a batch capture list (more about that shortly).

Play

The Play pop-up menu is active if your deck can play at 1/5th or 1/10th speed. Either choice will give QuickTime more time to grab a higher frame rate on Macs that lack hardware compression. Later, you can increase the clip to normal speed with Premiere's "Speed…" command.

Now that you know the window's gizmos, here's the device control process in brief: Turn on the Auto-Record check box, specify your desired frames, then click the Record button. Your tapedeck will automatically seek and grab the segment. Afterward, the deck will pause and the clip will sit in an untitled Clip window. Easy!

3.0 ☞ *In Premiere 3.0, adding a "+" or "−" before the entered time code advances or rewinds the deck by that value.*

3.0 ☞ *More 3.0 shortcuts: To set the In point, press Shift-I or the "1," "4," or "7" key. To set the Out point, tap Shift-O or the "3," "6," or "9" key. To advance the deck to the In or Out frame, type "I" or "O" or Option-click the In or Out button.*

📖 *For more about the Speed command, see page 88.*

☞ *You can skip setting the Out point—only the In point is necessary to capture a single clip with device control. Just click the mouse button when you want to stop auto-recording.*

▶ **Batch Capturing:
The Process**

2.0 *Premiere 2.0 users can jump ahead to page 315.*

Batch capturing is a great convenience for 3.0 users with device control hardware. You can log several clips at once and have Premiere capture all of them automatically. You can even specify different capture settings for each clip.

Follow these steps to complete a batch capture:

☞ *If there's not an open Batch List window, you can also create a new one by clicking the "Log In/Out" button in the Movie Capture window.*

1 Open a new Batch List window—the center of the batch capture process—by selecting "Batch Capture" from the Capture submenu of the File menu. You'll see an empty version of the window below.

☞ *Use this window to generate a list of the clips you want to capture. After constructing your list, click the Sort button to sort items alphabetically by reel name and numerically by In times.*

☞ *Keep in mind you can create or open several Batch List windows at once.*

✓ Reel Name	In	Out	File Name	Settings
◆ 001	00:00:26:00	00:01:12:00	001 – 00;00;26;00	320x minimal
◆ 001	00:01:24:20	00:01:47:10	001 – 00;01;24;20	320x 22/8bit
◆ 001	00:02:24:12	00:02:28:00	001 – 00;02;24;12	320x 22/8bit
◆ 001	00:02:36:16	00:02:48:00	001 – 00;02;36;16	320x 22/8bit
◆ 001	00:03:31:00	00:03:44:13	001 – 00;03;31;00	320x 22/8bit
◆ 001	00:04:02:00	00:04:11:12	001 – 00;04;02;00	320x minimal
◆ 001	00:06:12:00	00:06:33:16	001 – 00;06;12;00	320x 22/16bit
◆ 001	00:07:14:15	00:07:33:12	001 – 00;07;14;15	320x 22/16bit

Batch List: Bicycle Comp

[Add...] [Delete]   [Sort]   [Capture]

☞ *A clip's Out point may not be captured exactly as specified— some extra frames are likely.*

2 Generate the batch capture list, using the techniques described in the *Generating the Batch* section ahead. Then choose "Save" in the File menu to keep the list.

3 Make sure a black diamond appears to the left of each clip in the list you want to capture (as shown in the window above). Clicking the diamond toggles capture on or off for that clip.

☞ *Click the top check mark in the batch list window to toggle all batch items on or off at once.*

4 Click the Capture button. A dialog box will appear for opening a new or existing Library file to hold the captured clips. Be sure the library you create or open rests on your fastest hard disk because Premiere will use that disk for batch capture (despite any preference settings).

Once you identify the library file, Premiere will request that you place the reel in the tapedeck and click OK. After you do that, Premiere will automatically record the clips you specified. Press Command-period (.) if you need to abort the batch capture process.

As Premiere successfully captures each clip, a check mark will replace each diamond. If for some reason an error occurs, a red X will loudly mark the affected clip (so you can try to grab it again later). After all clips are digitized, your tapedeck will stop automatically.

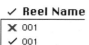

✓ Reel Name
✗ 001
✓ 001
✓ 001
◆ 001

5 Save the Library that holds the new clips. From that window, you can then drag the clips into a Project window or Construction window. Then edit away!

▶ **Generating the Batch**

Now that we've overviewed the entire batch capture process, let's go back and find out more about how to generate a batch list of clips for Premiere to capture.

There are three ways to enter items in the batch list:

[**Log In/Out**]

• Use the Movie Capture window. Set the In and Out point of a particular clip and then click the Log In/Out button in the window. A small dialog box will appear to enter a file name for the segment. Although Premiere will suggest a combination of the reel name and In point, a descriptive name is often better. After you click OK, the segment will appear in your batch list.

File Name

File Name: | 001 - 00;00;24;18 |

[Cancel] [OK]

Clip Logging

[Reel...] 001

[In »»] 00:00:36:06
[Out »»] 00:00:49:00

[Log In/Out]

00:00:32:00

Use this dialog box as another way to establish capture segments for the batch list. The disadvantage of this approach is you cannot interactively view the video to set the In and Out times.

• Use the Clip Logging window. It's basically the right half of the Movie Capture window and is intended for users with video on an external monitor. Open the window by selecting "Clip Logging" in the Capture submenu of the File menu. A new "Settings..." command also will appear in the menu bar that controls whether Premiere uses a reel name/In point combo for the file name.

Clip Capture Parameters

Reel Name: | |

File Name: | |

In Time: | 00:00:00:00 | is 00:00:00:00

Out Time: | 00:00:00:00 | is 00:00:00:00

Frame Rate: | 30 fps ▼ |

Format: | Non Drop-Frame ▼ |

[Cancel] [OK]

• The third way to add items to a batch list is to click the "Add..." button at the bottom of the Batch List window. That opens the dialog box at left.

☞ Shift-click to select clips between two clicks. Option-click to select all clips from one tape. Or use "Select All" in the File menu to choose all batch entries.

After adding clips to the list, you can manipulate the list further to suit your recording needs. For instance, double-click a listing to re-visit its capture parameters. Or sort or delete items with buttons at the window's bottom.

▶ The Batch Capture Menu

As you prepare your batch list, take advantage of the Batch Capture menu. Let's look over its powerful tricks.

Attach/Remove Settings

As mentioned earlier, you can specify a *capture settings file* that Premiere will use to digitize each clip (see page 317 for more about saving capture settings).

```
Batch Capture
  Recording Settings...
  Video Input...
  Sound Input...

  Attach Settings...
  Remove Settings

  Handles...

  Import from text file...
  Export to text file...
  Import/Export Settings...

  Send In/Out to Movie Capture
```

You can assign *different* capture settings to different clips in the batch list! Clips that do not require top-notch sound, for example, can use a capture settings file with low quality sound, saving hard disk space.

```
Settings
320x minimal
320x 22/8bit
320x 22/8bit
320x 22/8bit
320x 22/8bit
```

To assign settings to selected clips in the list, choose "Attach Settings...". Use "Remove Settings" to clear attached settings. Keep in mind that if you don't specify a capture settings file for a clip, Premiere will grab the clip with the *currently active* capture settings. If there's a prior clip in the list, capture will occur with its settings (if any).

Handles

☞ *This doesn't affect the listed In and Out times in the Batch List window.*

This produces a simple dialog box that directs Premiere to add a specified amount of extra time before and after the In and Out frames when it digitizes the clip.

Import/Export

☞ *To print Premiere's batch list, make sure the window is active and then select "Print Window..." in the File menu.*

Use the first two commands of this trio to import a text file as a batch list or to export Premiere's list as a text file. Select "Import/Export Settings..." to determine the proper order of items in the incoming or outgoing list.

Send In/Out to Movie Capture

Use this command to send a clip's time code to the Movie Capture window so you can digitize an individual clip in your batch list. For instance, you can re-digitize a clip that ran into an error during batch recording.

▶ Recapturing the Final Batch

☞ *This is similar in concept to using Premiere's "Miniatures..." command. See page 43.*

Take note—Premiere 3.0's batch capturing opens up a new opportunity. At first, you can grab small, low quality clips so Premiere's editing performance will be zippy and require less hard disk space. Before compiling your movie at the end of your editing, you can then *easily* and *precisely* re-digitize your project's clips at *final* quality! Look on the next page for how to do this nifty final step.

1 Open a new Batch List window by selecting "Batch Capture" in the Capture submenu of the File menu.

☞ Select "Remove Unused" in the Project menu to rid the Project window of unused clips so they aren't captured needlessly.

2 Click your Project window to make it active and choose "Select All" in the Edit menu (Command A). Then drag the selected clips into the Batch List window. Premiere will generate a batch list from this action.

3 Attach capture settings to the clips as desired by perusing the Batch Capture menu (as described in on the prior page). Then click the Capture button at the bottom of the Batch List window and go through the remainder of Step 4 on page 312.

[Capture]

4 Premiere will place the newly captured clips in the folder that includes the Library (the Library itself contains the clip pointers). If that folder is a different one than where your initial set of smaller clips are hiding, you'll need to issue the "Re-Find Files..." command from the Project menu to tell Premiere to substitute the final clips for the inferior set of clips you used for editing.

📖 For more about the Re-Find Files command, see page 284.

▶ Digitizing Only Decibels

We've covered every angle of capturing video clips. Now let's see how to capture audio-only material. In Premiere, you can capture sound as a QuickTime movie or as an AIFF (Audio Interchange File Format) file.

☞ Make sure you have a sound digitizing device connected or built into your Mac. A sound driver is also required in your System Folder if you aren't using built-in digitizing.

Each has distinct advantages. If you capture sound as a movie, Premiere 3.0 can save the digitizing settings you use so you don't have to reset them again later. With the AIFF approach, saving settings isn't possible but you can keep an eye on the volume level as you record.

To digitize sound as a *QuickTime movie*, travel along the five-step path for capturing video that we explored earlier (page 308), with two exceptions.

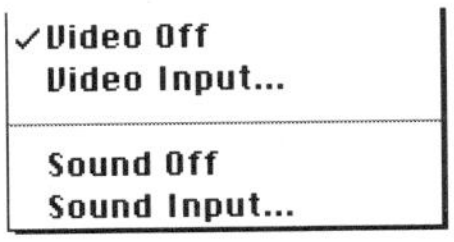

```
✓ Video Off
  Video Input...

  Sound Off
  Sound Input...
```

• Check "Video Off" and uncheck "Sound Off" in the Movie Capture menu, as shown at left. Depending on your digitizer and source, leaving video on may result in a sound movie with a continuous black video image.

📖 For more about the Sound Input dialog box, see page 322.

• You only need to inspect the "Sound Input" dialog box. Other capture settings do not affect audio digitizing.

To grab sound as an *AIFF file*, instead follow these steps:

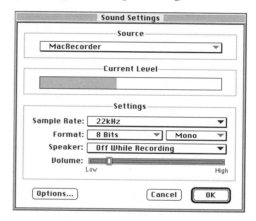

1 Choose "Audio Capture" in the Capture submenu of the File menu. (2.0's is in the New submenu.) An Audio Capture menu appears as well as an Audio Recorder window. The window has an icon of your capture device, a Record button, a volume meter, and time code at the bottom to show the recorded duration.

2 Before pressing that tempting Record button, check your sound settings. Select "Sound Input..."—the only Audio Capture item in your Mac's menu bar. You'll get a large one-stop clearinghouse for all audio controls.

Refer to page 324 for guidance on these AIFF sound settings. Clicking the Options button at the bottom of the box may reveal additional options, depending on your digitizing hardware.

☞ *When you close the Audio Recorder window (shown at the top of this page), these settings return to default values. Premiere 3.0's new ability to save capture settings doesn't apply here.*

☞ *Watch the Level meter and adjust the source volume to stay out of the red. "Clipping" is a sure sign of distortion.*

Level: ▮▮▮▮▮▮▮▮▮▮▯

3 Click OK after adjusting the settings. Back at the Audio Recorder window, get your recorded or live sound source ready. Then click the Record button in the window to begin digitizing.

4 Click Stop (the former Record button) or anywhere outside the window to halt the flowing audio bits. The new sound clip will then appear in an untitled Clip window.

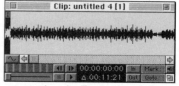

Note that when capturing narration in Premiere 2.0, grabbing brief clips rather than a giant audio clip makes sense—they'll be easier to synchronize with video clips in the Construction window. In 3.0, however, a monster narrative clip is okay. Just Option-drag copies of its Clip window into your project with different In and Out points!

📖 *For more about 3.0's* *Option-drag technique with the Clip window, see page 65.*

5 Finally, select "Save…" in the File menu to keep the sound clip for your Premiere projects. You can then import or drag the clip into any open project.

▶ More Capture Process Tips

Here are three additional tips that can assist your capture efforts. Only the first tip is exclusive to Premiere 3.0.

Saving Capture Settings

Hooray! Premiere 3.0 can save recording, compression and input settings for movies. Select "Save Settings…" in the Movie Capture menu. A Save dialog box will appear to name and place the file (your capture settings). The next time you want to capture with those settings, choose "Load Settings…" in the Movie Capture menu.

☞ *You cannot save Sound Input settings for digitizing AIFF files (see prior page).*

Note that if "Video Off" or "Sound Off" are on (checked) in the Movie Capture menu before saving, Video or Sound Input settings will not be part of the file.

Cropping the Movie Image

You can crop the video image in the Movie Capture window, although it may reduce the captured frame rate. Just draw a rectangle in the image box with your cursor before digitizing. Only the cropped portion will continue to preview. To return to a full image, click in the box.

This technique isn't precise, however, and maintaining a consistent aspect ratio is difficult. Also, many capture boards can't crop at top speed. Premiere 3.0 offers two better cropping approaches that you can use later while editing. For accurate cropping of edge noise, apply 3.0's *Crop* filter to the clip in the Construction window. For more extensive cropping, try 3.0's *Image Pan* filter.

📖 *For more about the Crop filter, see page 199; for the Image Pan filter, page 198.*

Capturing Less is More

To gain at least a frame or two per second in real-time video captures on slower Macs, record sound in a *separate* pass from the video images. Your Mac will then be able to devote more of its power to grabbing images. In Premiere 3.0, you can later create a *soft link* between such clips to keep the clips synchronized in the Construction window.

☞ *For more about 3.0's new soft links, see page 85.*

With the capture *process* behind us, let's sort out the capture *settings*. Along the way, we'll highlight strategies that apply to a wide range of digitizing situations.

Capture Settings

Capture settings are the key to grabbing the cleanest, smoothest clips possible from your Mac. Since they're one of the most technical areas of a project, many users shy away from challenging Premiere's default settings. With this section, however, you can now boldly run through the settings—and even get comfortable with them.

▶ Understanding the Tradeoffs

As you evaluate each capture setting, remember that increasing a digitized clip's frame size, frame rate, image quality or sound quality creates *more movie data per second*. That has three implications:

• It increases the clip's *file size*, which may be a factor depending on how you'll store and distribute your movie.

☞ *Even most hardware compression boards slow a bit when capturing at full-frame size and "Most" image quality.*

• Increased size or quality may reduce *the maximum frame rate you can capture*—unless you have hardware compression or a controlled-capture setup.

• On slower Macs, movies made from heftier clips will *play at a slower frame rate*.

These fundamental QuickTime tradeoffs should encourage you to acquire the following two capture habits.

Prioritize

Before digitizing, decide what's most important for your final production. Then give those factors priority over other settings. For example, maybe your movie can live with a choppier frame rate to get higher quality images from CD-ROM. Other times, reducing the image quality may make sense to push up the frame size or frame rate.

Think Playback

Always base your decisions on the anticipated *playback hardware* (which may be different than *your* Mac). For example, if you can grab full-screen, full-motion clips but you will distribute the final movie on CD-ROM, only quarter-screen or smaller movies will be feasible. If you're using the same setup to produce a videotape with Premiere, however, then you can go for the max.

📖 *Guidance to all compression settings is in Appendix A. See page 328.*

With these habits in mind, let's begin our travels through the many capture settings of Premiere. We'll start at the top of the Movie Capture menu.

▶ Recording Settings

As your first destination, select "Recording Settings…" in the Movie Capture menu. If you do not have device control, you'll receive the half-empty dialog box below.

The dialog box is humble-looking on the surface, but carries far-reaching implications for your digitizing success.

3.0 *"Report dropped frames" is a new check box in 3.0.*

2.0 *Premiere 2.0 has a "Show preview while recording" check box that Premiere 3.0 doesn't include—most digitizers ignore this setting anyway.*

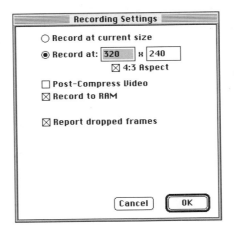

Let's look over each recording setting in order.

Record at...

The two "Record at" radio buttons offer a simple choice—digitize at the size of the image in the Movie Capture window or record at entered pixel dimensions (regardless of the Movie Capture window's size). The latter is useful if you want to drop below 160 x 120 pixels or capture full-screen (640 x 480) on a standard monitor.

☞ *60 x 45 pixels is the smallest possible movie size.*

Generally, capture source clips at *your intended final movie size*. For the best frame rate, stick to standard QuickTime sizes whenever possible. Standard sizes are the same ones the Movie Capture window snaps to: 160 x 120, 240 x 180, 320 x 240 and 640 x 480 pixels.

Post-Compress Video

If you have hardware-compression or a controlled-capture setup, leave this check box off. Otherwise, for small-frame clips—such as 240 x 180 pixels or less—post-compression may help. Your Mac can grab more frames per second because compression occurs *after* the entire clip is digitized (instead of as each frame is captured).

☞ *Post-compressing large format clips produces a low frame rate since current Macs can't transfer the enormous uncompressed data fast enough. A SCSI-2 board with a fast disk array can partially solve this on Quadra-level Macs.*

Make sure you have sufficient hard disk space for each temporarily uncompressed movie file, though. Otherwise, post-compression will cut your captured clips too short.

☒ Record to RAM

☞ Again, if you have hardware compression or a controlled-capture setup, leave this check box off.

The beginning of this chapter (page 304) highlighted the speed advantages of digitizing directly to RAM rather than QuickTime's usual hard disk approach. Slower Macs can especially benefit from this. The key is to load enough RAM into Premiere to fit each clip. If memory is scarce, all but postage stamp-size clips will have to be brief.

Sometimes the only way to be sure you have enough RAM is to try RAM-recording first. If you cannot fit a clip, then drop back to disk-based capture. Or consider detouring to dedicated digitizing software such as SuperMac's *ScreenPlay* or RasterOps' *MediaGrabber*. Such smaller applications have less memory overhead than Premiere, potentially leaving more RAM for your captured clip.

☒ Report dropped frames

📖 For more about the Movie Analysis window, see page 31.

Turn this on if your goal is smooth full-motion clips. Skipped, or dropped, frames can produce very obvious jitters and jerks in clips with significant motion in the scene. After capturing a clip, Premiere 3.0 will show a Movie Analysis window if frames were dropped. The window will inform you of the precise details.

▶ Extra Settings For Device Control

For device control setups, additional recording settings are available towards the bottom of the dialog box.

The last check box, "Use Reel Name..." is new to 3.0.

If your Mac is connected to device control hardware, the lower half of the Recording Settings dialog box will contain a few additional options, as shown below. Let's quickly check out these extra recording settings.

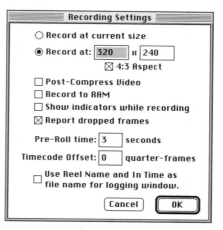

☒ Show indicators while recording

Turn this on to see the current time code in the lower corner of the Movie Capture window while digitizing. If you're capturing in *real-time*, though, you may pay for being informed. Leave this off to maximize the frame rate.

Pre-Roll time

This sets how long the video will play before digitizing starts. Most decks need a few seconds to reach full speed.

Time Code Offset

Is the time code in your captured clips consistently offset from the source's time code? Some device controllers produce this problem, depending on the capture settings. Use this option to correct, or *calibrate*, the difference. If the time code in the captured clip's Clip window is greater than the source, enter a positive number in the box. If the Clip window's figure is less, enter a negative number.

☞ *The entered number represents quarter-frames, so if your clips are offset by whole frames (which is most common) enter a multiple of four.*

3.0 ☒ Use Reel Name and In Time...

Turn this on to have Premiere use the reel name and In time as the file name of a logged clip (for batch captures).

▶ Video Image & Source Setups

Let's move to the next group of capture settings: Video Input. After you select that item in the Movie Capture menu, a QuickTime-standard Video dialog box appears. It has three panels—Compression, Image and Source—that you can access with a pop-up menu in the upper left corner. Since Appendix A (page 328) covers compression settings for captured clips, let's view the Image options.

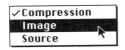

Available sliders depend on your video digitizer. Play your source video to preview adjustments in the image box. Click the Defaults button to return to original values.

3.0 ☞ *You can skip this panel if you already calibrated the video with 3.0's Waveform Monitor and Vector Scope (see page 305). Those settings are reflected here.*

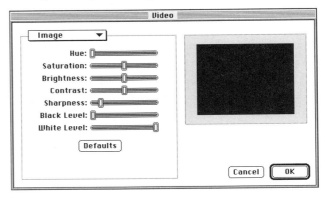

Most of the sliders are familiar to any television user. Use the Hue slider like the tint control on a TV, for example. And shift the Saturation slider if color bleed is evident. Black Level and White Level sliders are less familiar—they control the extent of black or white in the image, independent of Brightness and Contrast sliders.

Besides the usual aesthetic and clarity adjustments, keep a less obvious goal in mind for QuickTime movies: *Reduce noise*. Lessening the "dancing pixels" in a clip can help QuickTime's compression since there will be fewer different pixels from frame to frame. It also improves the clip's visual coherency—particularly on 8-bit or less displays. To reduce noise, use Brightness, Contrast, Black Level and White Level sliders (if available) to purify the very black and white regions in your scene—without reducing the image's dynamic range *too* far.

Do you have dialog box fatigue yet? Fortunately, the Source panel of the Video Input dialog box takes no more than a glance and very little brain power. Select "Source" in the top pop-up menu to view the panel below.

Choose your capture weapon if you have more than one.

Many digitizers offer composite and S-Video input. Some also support RGB video or a second Composite input. Select the best one available for your project.

Choose between the NTSC, PAL and SECAM standards your digitizer may offer.

Select your type of video source to improve the image.

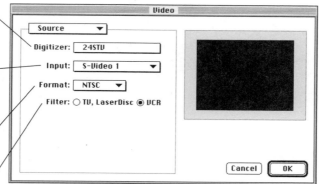

▶ Sound Input Settings, Part I

Earlier we saw how you can select "Sound Input…" from the Movie Capture menu or Audio Capture menu. The choice depends on whether you want to digitize sound as a QuickTime movie or AIFF file, respectively.

Sound input settings are nearly the same no matter which path you choose. You don't have to be a recording engineer to tackle them, but a little sound advice can go a long way. Let's use the three-part Sound Input dialog box for capturing movies to review the possibilities.

When you first open the Sound Input dialog box, you'll most likely see the Compression panel. The right side of the dialog box remains unchanged in all panels.

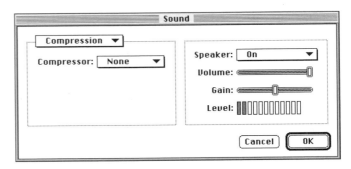

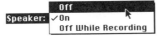

Compressor

QuickTime 1.5 and later supports 3:1 and 6:1 MACE compression (MACE is Macintosh Audio Compression Expansion). Premiere can accept and create such compressed sound files, *but doesn't retain the file size savings* when compiling a movie. So always stick with None—this audio compression provides no real benefit.

Speaker

This setting doesn't affect the digitized audio—it only determines whether you can monitor the incoming sound over your Mac's speaker. Any changes will be heard after you OK the dialog box.

Volume

The volume slider only affects your Mac's speaker, too—not the digitized sound. It overrides the similar setting in your Mac's Sound Control Panel.

Gain

If your digitizer supports it, this slider adjusts the *digitized* sound volume. Increase the captured amplitude by dragging the slider to the right, or decrease it by sliding left.

☞ *As a general strategy, set the sound source to a relatively high volume (but not to the point of distortion). Then moderate it with other sound volume controls, starting with those closest to the sound source.*

Instead of (or in addition to) the Gain slider, you may be able to control the sound volume at two other places: the sound source (such as a tapedeck's controls) or the digitizer (i.e. MacRecorder's thumbwheel).

Level

Watch the Level meter while previewing your soon-to-be-captured audio. If the level is too high (in the red), sound peaks will be clipped—producing distortion. Too low a sound level may not be heard clearly—and any digital noise in the sample will be proportionately louder.

☞ *Narrating at your Mac? To avoid picking up fan and hard drive whine, record to tape away from your Mac and then digitize the audio with line-output jacks.*

▶ **Sound Sample & Source**

The Sample panel of the Sound Input dialog box contains three key settings that affect sound quality. To see these controls, select "Sample" from the pop-up menu in the top left corner of the dialog box.

The left half of the dialog box holds the Sample settings. The available options depend on the sound quality levels supported by your audio digitizer.

```
═══════════════════ Sound ═══════════════════
┌─────────────────────┐  ┌──────────────────────────┐
│  Sample        ▼    │  │ Speaker:  Off        ▼   │
│                     │  │                          │
│  Rate:  22.255 kHz ▼│  │ Volume: ▭▭▭▭▭▭▭▭▭▭▯      │
│                     │  │                          │
│  Size: ◉ 8 bits ○ 16 bits │ Gain: ▭▭▭▭▭▯▭▭▭      │
│                     │  │                          │
│  Use: ◉ Mono ○ Stereo │ Level: ⅀⅀⅀⅀⅀⅀⅀⅀⅀⅀     │
└─────────────────────┘  └──────────────────────────┘

                              [ Cancel ]  [[ OK ]]
```

Rate

Use the *Rate* pop-up menu to determine how many sound samples per second your Mac will record. Premiere gives you the standard kilohertz (kHz) choices. If your capture hardware supports it, 44 kHz is also available. Of course, higher rates more accurately capture the original sound.

Size

Sound Manager

The *Size* buttons set the captured sound's resolution and dynamic range. Note that 16-bit sound (CD-quality) capture requires a suitable sound board. 16-bit *output*, however, also requires Sound Manager 3.0 or later (which ships with Premiere 3.0). Otherwise, the playback Mac will internally dither the 16-bit sound to 8-bits.

Use

Consider stereo sound clips only if your final movie is intended for stereo-capable hardware with two speakers. Otherwise, your audience won't hear a difference.

Look over the chart on the next page to help you decide upon the most appropriate sound quality target. Unless you're creating audio-only movies (and have hard disk space to burn) or will play the final video/sound movie only with hardware compression, you'll generally want to aim for one of the moderate sound quality levels in the middle of the chart.

If you aren't sure which way to go after looking over this chart, try a potential choice on a small clip and let your ears decide.

☞ *If you have MacRecorder and seek 11 kHz, 8-bit sound, you can get better results with SoundEdit than Premiere. First capture in SoundEdit at 22 Khz. Then paste the file into a new Sound Edit document set to 11 kHz. That will downsample— you'll get better quality than directly digitizing at 11 kHz. Finally, save in AIFF format and import the file into Premiere.*

Pick Your Sound Quality

Sample Rate	Sample Size	Megs/ Minute*	Best Movie Use
5 Khz	8 bits	.32	Voice-only clips when frame rate or storage size is a top priority.
7 kHz	8 bits	.44	Rough voice demos when frame rate and storage are important.
11 kHz	8 bits	.65	Voice-only informal movies. Low quality background music. Off-line editing reference.
	16 bits	1.30	Good for voice or background music. Slightly grainy, but nearly AM radio quality.
22 kHz	8 bits	1.30	Reasonable for many multimedia uses, especially when outputted on high-quality speakers. Very good for voice. Good for background music and effects.
	16 bits	2.60	Excellent for high-quality narration. Very good for background music.
44 kHz	8 bits	2.60	Overkill for voice. Near CD-quality music.
	16 bits	5.20	CD-quality for music.

* Megabytes per minute (mono and without MACE compression). Double the figures for stereo sound.

To tap into the built-in sound digitizing of a recent Mac, choose "Built-in." Otherwise, select your third-party device.

Some digitizers may offer a choice of QuickTime sound channels. Otherwise, move on.

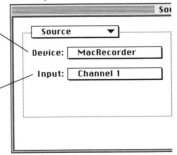

After you're done with the sound quality settings, select "Source" in the top pop-up menu. Yeah! The last panel! Like before, only the left side changes. This one's a snap. Adjust where needed, click OK and then take a deep breath—you're now truly ready to capture clips in Premiere.

▶ **Signing Off**
It's been great flying together. Good luck on all of your future digital editing adventures. I hope that you too will enjoy Premiere…with a passion!

P.S.: Still ahead are two useful appendices and a *very* detailed index. Have fun!

A   B

Appendices

These last pages address topics that are important but not of interest to all readers. Appendix A holds the essentials to properly setting a movie's QuickTime compression. The settings are central to successfully capturing clips and compiling movies. If you need a refresher course or are new to QuickTime, be sure to look there.

Appendix B will help you to build an edit decision list in Premiere so you can link your project to traditional post-production suites and output top-quality videotape. This capability is one of the unique strengths of Premiere that makes the program especially valuable for video professionals. Have fun on the EDL Express!

A. Choosing Compression Settings

📖 If you need a refresher on basic QuickTime tradeoffs, see page 318 before moving ahead.

Use the Video Input dialog box (top) to set the compression of captured source clips. The same controls appear again in the Compression Settings dialog box (bottom) for compiling your Premiere movie. Although the same settings are in two dialog boxes, they are completely independent of each other.

Properly setting a movie's compression is an important element of successful Premiere authoring. The right settings can mean smoother playback, higher quality images and smaller movie files. Unfortunately, you usually can't have all three at once. So, much of the art of setting compression is balancing variables to reflect your priorities.

You can set compression in two corners of Premiere:

• For capturing source clips—use the Video Input dialog box accessed from the Movie Capture menu.

• For compiling Premiere movies—use the Compression Settings dialog box. Select "Compression…" in the Make menu (the Project menu in 2.0). Or reach the dialog box indirectly via the "Movie…" command in the Make menu. (Again, that's 2.0's Project menu. Beep!) In 3.0, choosing "Presets…" in the Make menu also does the job.

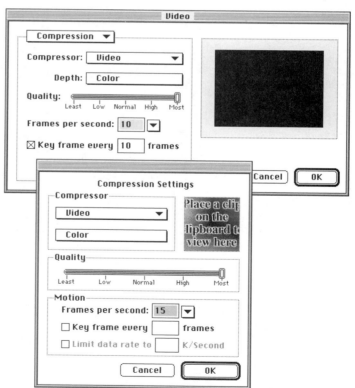

Let's look at each compression setting in order and determine the best settings for your project.

▶ Inspecting the Codecs

Codecs—short for *compressor-decompressors*—are the heart of QuickTime. Codecs rapidly compress data when you capture a clip, and quickly decompress it on-the-fly during a movie's playback. They're the pump that enables your Mac to handle the enormous amount of data in every second of a movie.

There are two broad families of codecs—*software-based* and *hardware-based*. All codecs built into QuickTime are software-based; they perform their magic entirely in software. Currently, QuickTime includes six varieties, although Apple may add more over time. Such codecs automatically appear in Premiere's Compressor pop-up menu. Apple's software codecs are useful because any Mac with QuickTime automatically has those codecs available for the movie's playback.

Hardware-based codecs that ship with hardware compression boards (such as SuperMac's *DigitalFilm* or RasterOp's *MoviePak*) provide a much higher level of performance. They typically can capture and play full-screen, full-motion, 24-bit movies. The latest generation can even grab 60 fields of video per second, more closely approaching broadcast quality.

With the growing family of codecs, what's your best choice? The decision becomes more complex when you realize what may be best for *capturing* source clips may not be so ideal for *compiling* Premiere movies.

If you have a hardware compression board installed, picking a codec is usually easy—select the hardware-based codec for the best capture, compiling and playback—at least on *your* Mac. This approach makes good sense, for example, if you're editing video on-line and will output your work directly to videotape.

To play your movie with equal zip on *other* computers, however, the same hardware compression board must be installed in *those* machines. Some manufacturers offer less expensive playback-only versions of their boards for this purpose. So hardware compression-only movies can be viable for kiosks, special presentations or other limited quantities of playback stations.

If you only have QuickTime's software-based codecs on hand, choosing a codec isn't so easy. Different codecs are suitable for different uses—to date, there's no magic

RasterOps MoviePak™

☞ *Drop third-party codecs (they're extensions) into the System Folder to have them appear in Premiere's menu.*

☞ *Several hardware compression boards provide more than one custom codec. Check the board's documentation for the best codec choice.*

☞ *To play hardware compressed clips on a wide range of computers, compile with a software-based codec (reducing frame size, rate or other variables as necessary).*

elixir that meets all needs. Look at the chart below to see how Apple's software-based codecs compare.

Generally, slower-working codecs do a better job of preserving image quality. The actual compression you achieve varies from clip to clip—that's why the ratings are general.

☞ This comparison applies to 8-bit or greater movies (256 or more colors/greys). For mono-chrome clips (anyone doing that?), try the Animation codec at a Black & White color depth for all types of material.

QuickTime Software Codec Comparison

Codec	Image Quality	Playback Speed	File Size	Compile Time
None	**Best**	Poor[1]	Poor	**Best**
Video	Good	Good	Good	Good
Animation	VGood	Good	Good	Good
Cinepak[2]	Good	**Best**	**Best**	Poor
Photo–JPEG	VGood	Poor	VGood	Poor
Graphics[3]	VGood	Poor	Good	Good

1. Playing small-frame movies from hard disk on Quadra-level hardware is better.
2. Cinepak before QuickTime 1.6 was called "Compact Video."
3. The Graphics codec is evaluated only for 8-bit movies.

To further help you decide, let's look at the movie situations that call for each software-based solution.

Apple's Video/Animation Duo

For software-only compression, the Video or Animation codec is usually the best choice for *capturing* source clips. The Video codec is designed for "natural" video images. The Animation codec is better for animated graphics and other computer-generated "noise-free" visuals.

Both are fast-working, smooth-playing and tight-compressing. Image quality, particularly at higher quality settings, is fine for informal movies. Stick with these codecs for compiling your final movie too unless you have a reason to switch to Cinepak (see below).

☞ If you plan to switch to Cinepak for the final movie, capture with Video's Quality slider set high to minimize any image loss from switching.

The Slick Cinepak

Cinepak has many virtues over the Video codec—particularly for 16- or 24-bit productions. Movies can double in size or frame rate, CD-ROM playback improves and higher quality images are possible. But Cinepak has one big drawback: it's very "asymmetrical." It typically requires thirty seconds to two minutes to compress *each frame* in order to perform so well upon playback.

☞ Before QuickTime 1.6, Cinepak was called "Compact Video"—it's the same codec. Apple licenses it from SuperMac.

Capturing clips with Cinepak isn't recommended unless you can afford to wait an eternity for all but the briefest clips. (If you masochistically do use it, turning on the "Post-Compress Video" check box in Premiere's Recording Settings dialog box is a must.) Generally consider Cinepak only for *compiling* your final Premiere movie. Even then, with its long compression times, Cinepak is primarily suitable for commercial or corporate productions distributed on CD-ROM.

For more about post-compressing clips after capture, see page 319.

None is for Some

If you have *abundant* hard disk space to store uncompressed files, None can be a feasible capture choice for two categories of authors: (1) Those with controlled-capture setups that can grab every frame slowly, and (2) authors with Quadra-level Macs who only need small-frame clips. In either case, the images will be optimal in quality because there will be no compression. To play your movie on other hardware, switch to a different codec for final compiling.

A rule of thumb to calculate from: One minute of uncompressed, quarter-screen, 16-bit video without sound requires about 12 megabytes of storage space.

For Premiere 2.0 users, None has another important purpose. Use it to create *intermediate* clips for adding extra layers of effects to a clip—a technique this book demonstrates in several places (look in the Index under *None*). Compiling with the None codec—at the same color depth as the source clips—ensures that the source clip's image remains untouched.

3.0 *Premiere 3.0 users can avoid this time-consuming step with the wonders of virtual clips now available.*

Photo-JPEG

The JPEG-based Photo codec works too slowly for anything other than slide show-style sequences. However, it provides *excellent* quality natural images *and* tightly compressed files—a great combination for archiving 16- or 24-bit source clips (especially if you have a frame-by-frame controlled-capture setup). Spin the files through a different codec later for improved playback.

Graphics

This is the runt of the group. On 8-bit displays, the Graphics codec can produce slightly better-looking images than the Video codec. But its decompression slowness requires hard disk playback for a decent frame rate. Therefore, save this for 8-bit *still-images*.

▶ The Depths of Color

☞ *"Best Depth" is a choice only when capturing clips. It uses the optimal color depth for the codec. For Apple's Video codec, it's thousands of colors.*

The color depth pop-up menu determines the *maximum* number of colors in your movie's image. What actually is displayed depends on the monitor. The range of choices varies. For example, the Animation codec offers all possible color choices, but the Video codec only allows "Color" (the same as "Thousands of Colors") or "Grayscale" (256 grays).

Best Depth
Black and White
4 Grays
4 Colors
16 Grays
16 Colors
256 Grays
256 Colors
✓Thousands of Colors
Millions of Colors
Millions of Colors+

Here's the key concept: Select the color depth of *your source material or your final movie's display—whichever is lower.* For example, if your animation only contains 16 colors, there's no need to capture or compile with more. Likewise, if your audience only has eight-bit (256 color) monitors, there's little reason to create deeper clips. *More color data simply forces other performance tradeoffs.*

Video at "256 Colors" is grainy but suitable for many small, informal movies. "Thousands of Colors" (about 32,000) is similar to the color range on television and is satisfactory for almost all multimedia. Reserve "Millions of Colors" (approximately 16 million—"true" color) for broadcast-level output. Use "Millions of Colors+" (32-bit color) when you must preserve a movie's alpha channel.

▶ Is Quality Number 1?

Lower quality images are progressively more blurry, blocky (small blocks of similar pixels) and streaky. The bottom close-ups are magnified by 200%.

The Quality slider controls *how much* compression is applied to your movie. The higher the image quality, the less compression you get—which increases the movie's file size. Worse yet, a larger file size may slow the movie's frame rate without hardware compression help. So the Quality slider plays an important role.

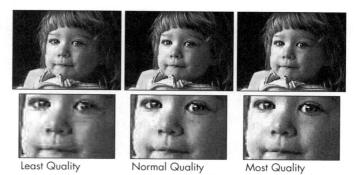

Least Quality   Normal Quality   Most Quality

The deciding factors depend on your source material, output goals and hardware setup. To capture 30 fps full-screen clips, for example, moderate quality levels may ensure smooth motion in action-oriented clips. Many current hardware compression boards tend to skip a few frames when the Quality slider is pulled past "High."

In less active clips, image detail may be more crucial. Compression artifacts are generally more noticeable in large-frame movies. But nondescript backgrounds often can take more compression than close-up shots of people.

For audiences watching 8-bit or less displays, mid-quality images are indistinguishable from higher settings.

For most off-line editing and multimedia purposes (quarter-screen size or less), it's hard to go wrong with the slider's mid-point. For both capture and final compiling, it's a reasonable balance between all factors.

If image quality is a priority and disk space is less important, consider capturing at higher quality to establish a better visual basis for your clips. You can always compile at less quality later if necessary.

If you're tempted to slide to extremes with the Video codec, though, think twice. "Most" typically produces files twice as large as "High" but doesn't look much better at small-frame sizes. "Least" displays much worse than "Low" but only compresses about 10–20% tighter.

The Animation codec (at 256 colors or less color depth) always uses "Most" quality even though you can move the slider.

Extreme settings for the Animation codec are less of a problem. If you use the color depth of the source material and set the quality to "Most," the codec is *lossless*. QuickTime completely preserves the original image data.

▶ Targeting the Frame Rate

Can your Mac setup capture 30 frames per second (fps) clips? Will you record the final movie on videotape or play it exclusively on 30 fps-capable computers? If the answer to both is yes, then go for full-motion. Otherwise, aim for the frame rate *your audience's hardware* will run. The playback speed of their hardware will depend on many factors—such as CPU speed, hard drive or CD-ROM performance, data-transfer limits, compression abilities, video board and the color depth setting of their monitor. Of course, your movie's specs also matter, such as frame size, color depth and the selected codec. Whew!

"Best" shows up only for capturing clips. It tells Premiere to capture at the highest frame rate your Mac can handle.

✓Best
8
10
12
15
24
30

☞ *Even with the fastest Macs, you may need to lower the frame rate to reduce the movie's file size—to ensure it fits on a particular storage media or transfers quickly by modem.*

Generally, if your movie is for a wide range of Macs, aim for 10–15 fps. This middle-of-the-road rate will gradually increase as faster Macs become more predominant. To optimize for specific machines, test sample movies on equivalent setups to find a better rate.

Extra frames will only increase the file size (and digitizing or compiling time) of your clips unnecessarily. Your audience will not see any improvement in the final movie because QuickTime will merely skip the extra frames during playback to keep pace. In fact, with software-based codecs, capturing at an unnecessarily high frame rate may force you into other tradeoffs up front.

Consider three related issues when setting the rate:

• Anything lower than about 15 fps no longer tricks our eye into perceiving the show as a smooth, continuous image. But an acceptable frame rate also depends on the movie's content. If there's lots of motion or close-ups of people, for example, a higher rate is noticeably better.

• If you're aiming for less than full-motion, try to use an *even multiple* of your source format. Otherwise, the clips may not translate as cleanly when you edit and compile them. From 30 fps NTSC video, for example, lean towards a 5, 6, 10 or 15 fps frame rate for capture and compiling.

• If you set the compiled frame rate lower than your source clip's frame rate, Premiere will selectively *drop* frames to build the new movie. If you set the frame rate higher than your source clips, Premiere will insert *duplicates* of existing frames. Playback smoothness won't improve, but the movie's file size will mushroom.

▶ The Key to Key Frames

☒ Key frame every [12] frames

Key Frame	Compress Changes	Compress Changes	Key Frame

The images in most sequences typically do not change much from frame to frame. Activating the Key Frames check box tells QuickTime to compress only the *changes* from frame to frame, while periodically storing an entire frame's data—a "key frame"—as an anchor point. This approach is known as *frame differencing* or *temporal compression*. It's a step further than QuickTime's usual "spatial" compression of each frame's data. The benefit: smaller movie file sizes and faster frame rates.

If your movie doesn't have much motion or will always play on fast hardware without interruption, key frames can be less frequent. You'll reap greater file space savings.

For video movies with sound, you can often get good results with one key frame per second. For example, if your movie will play at about 12 fps, enter 12 in the key frame box. Animations can often have fewer key frames—perhaps once per five to ten seconds.

Too few key frames can create problems, especially on slower hardware. Images and sound may not synch as well. Images also may retain small blocks or streaks of pixels from previous frames. And users may face slower random access with the movie's playback slider.

Frame differencing is not available for the Photo–JPEG or None codecs.

Turning on the check box but leaving the box blank also is inadvisable. QuickTime will not insert a new key frame until more than 90% of the image has changed from previous frames. Unless there is constant action in the movie, several seconds may pass between key frames.

Note that you also may adjust *how much* temporal compression occurs—with the Quality slider. Normally, the slider sets spatial and temporal quality levels together. You can independently change temporal quality by holding down the Option key (if Key Frames is turned on). The slider's name changes to "Temporal."

If you later change the spatial quality, be sure to check temporal quality again, because it may slide too.

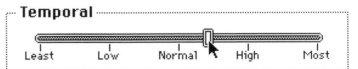

Why bother? For most situations, there's no reason to—keeping both compression levels the same is fine. If your clip is unusual enough to have either vast (or very few) differences between frames, independently tuning the temporal quality may be advantageous.

▶ Limiting the Data Rate

If you select the Cinepak codec, a compression setting for limiting a compiled movie's *data rate* becomes available. That's the flow of data per second that your movie produces. Limiting the data rate is very useful for CD-ROM-destined movies because it eliminates momentary "spikes" of data (such as from a rapidly changing, highly-detailed scene) that can slow playback.

For playback on a wide variety of old and new CD-ROM drives, enter 90–100 K/second. The latest crop of

☞ *As CD-ROM drives add more zip, this higher data rate target will change.*

CD-ROM drives provides double-speed or better playback. If you're not concerned about backward compatibility, consider aiming for 180–250K per second.

If your movie has video *or* sound, you can target the *maximum* data rate of CD-ROM drives (150K/second on older units, 300K/second or more on the new drives). That's also true if your movie's sound loads into RAM before playback (from Premiere 3.0's Audio Block pop-up menu in the Output Options dialog box—see page 289).

▶ More Compression Tips

Here are four more compression-related tips to consider:

Optimizing Each Clip

You don't have to stick with the same compression settings for all captured source clips in your project. If you want to spend the time, you can optimize the settings for each clip. Then compile the final movie as a *composite movie* in Premiere which preserves the individual clip settings—at least where there are no effects or other changes.

📖 *For more about making composite movies, see page 287.*

Previewing the Compressed Image

Place a clip on the clipboard to view here

In Premiere's Compression Settings dialog box, you can see your compression settings applied to the colorful default image. Or you can copy a clip to the clipboard to view the first frame of that material in the window. Either method can help you to decide the most appropriate image quality level for your movie.

Making Two Versions of a Movie

If your movie is for a wide variety of hardware, consider creating a couple of movies, each optimized to a particular playback environment. This approach is especially well-suited to roomy CD-ROMs.

Tune-ups at the MovieShop

☞ *The QuickTime Developer Kit is available from APDA (call 1-800-282-2732 in the U.S.; 1-800-637-0029 from Canada).*

If you're using Premiere to create corporate or commercial movies for CD-ROM distribution, Apple's *MovieShop* application is a superior tool for optimizing your movie's data to CD-ROM. MovieShop and several other interesting QuickTime goodies are available on Apple's *QuickTime Developer's Kit.*

B. The EDL Express

If you're working with frame-accurate source videotape, Premiere can generate an *edit decision list* (EDL) of your project. The EDL records and translates your editing work into a specially-formatted text file. Traditional video post-production systems can then use that file (and your source tapes) to output a top-quality master tape of your production. But you can happily do almost all editing beforehand in Premiere *off-line*, avoiding much of the stiff expense and complexity of the more expensive gear.

Premiere can export EDLs to several systems, including CMX 3400 and 3600, Grass Valley, and Sony BVE. Use this appendix to get your EDL in shape for their tape.

☞ *Other systems can be supported if they offer a plug-in file for Premiere's Plug-Ins folder.*

▶ EDL Preliminaries

Many EDL exporting problems can be avoided if you check three preliminary issues beforehand.

1. Full Motion or Bust

To produce a frame-accurate EDL, your source tapes must have time code *and* your project's source clips must be captured from the tapes at 30 frames per second. With many QuickTime capture boards (including those with hardware compression), that means staying away from a "Most" Quality setting for QuickTime compression and capturing at half-frame size (320 x 240 pixels) or less.

3.0 ☞ *To check for dropped frames during capture in Premiere 3.0, turn on the "Report dropped frames" check box in the Recording Settings dialog box. See page 320.*

2. What's Your Reel Name & Time Code?

The next hurdle is to assign accurate time code information to each clip in the Construction window. Otherwise, Premiere will give the clips an erroneous starting time of 00:00:00:00. Every clip also must carry the correct tape reel name so the post-production gear can find the segment.

The easiest way to embed this data in a clip is *during capture*. Premiere's Movie Capture window can perform the task well if you have a device control setup. If the necessary data isn't branded into the clip during capture, add it to the clip later (see *In the Nick of Time Code* ahead).

☞ *For more about capturing clips in Premiere with time code and a reel name, see page 309.*

3. Editing Within Limits

With Premiere's digital power, you can easily compose the impossible for traditional post-production systems. So be sure to restrict your Construction window work to edits that will translate correctly—or at least be recognized—by the system you're exporting to.

For example, Premiere's filters and motion settings cannot be replicated at the analog high-end. They're purely for QuickTime's digital realm. Also, many of Premiere's fancier transitions translate to simple wipes or dissolves (see *Transition Translations* a few pages ahead). Superimposing is more limited, too. And forget about using Macintosh still-image PICTs or disk-based sound clip files. Everything must sit on videotape.

☞ Transitions between two clips captured from the same tape aren't possible either. But you can dub the source tape that holds the affected segments (be sure to correctly revise the time code for the affected clips).

Checking your project for EDL suitability would be fairly straightforward if all high-end systems had similar capabilities and limitations. Wishful thinking! Like most other video technologies, high-end editing hardware is in a constant state of flux (or chaos depending on your viewpoint) amidst competing standards.

You'll therefore need to work closely with a post-production house to achieve the best results. If you haven't used such facilities before, contact the service provider *early in your project process* so you can get the latest scoop on what's allowable or not in Premiere for their systems. They can suggest work-arounds to problems and make the process smoother and more efficient.

☞ Premiere also includes a "Generic EDL" that is only marginally useful for other systems. Check with your post-production house before counting on it for your Premiere project.

▶ In the Nick of Time Code

You can add time code and reel name information belatedly to project clips if it wasn't done during capture. First open a clip's Clip window—or select the clip in the Project or Construction window. (Opening the Clip window is preferable in Premiere 3.0, as you'll see.) Then choose "Timecode…" from the Clip menu (Command plus [+]) to see the dialog box below.

Use the Clip Timecode dialog box to embed time code and reel name information into a clip, both of which are necessary for exporting an edit decision list.

```
════════════ Clip Timecode ═════════════
┌─────────────── Timecode: ───────────────┐
│  ┌──────────────┐                        │
│  │              │  is  00:00:00:00       │
│  └──────────────┘                        │
│  Frame Rate: │ 30 fps          ▼│        │
│     Format:  │ Non Drop-Frame  ▼│        │
└──────────────────────────────────────────┘

                      ● File beginning
   Set timecode at:   ○ Current frame

┌──────── Reel Name / Description: ─────────┐
│  ┌────────────────────────────────────┐  │
│  │                                    │  │
│  └────────────────────────────────────┘  │
└──────────────────────────────────────────┘

  ( Revert to Original )   ( Cancel )  [ OK ]
```

To fill in the Clip Timecode dialog box with success, consider the advice that's offered below.

Timecode

If time code was previously embedded in the clip, it will appear in the top text entry box. Otherwise, the box will be blank. Simply enter the clip's start time that's on the source tape. (See *Set Timecode at:* below for an alternative that's available in Premiere 3.0.)

Frame Rate

Select the appropriate frame rate for your exported media. It should match the time base of your project.

Format

If you select 30 fps for the frame rate, you can choose "Drop-Frame" (29.97 fps) or "Non Drop-Frame" (30 fps) time code formats. Most editing systems handle both. For the most accurate results, select the time code format used on your source videotapes.

Note that if your source tapes are in drop-frame format, the Clip window's time code indicator may not exactly match the tape's true time code. By selecting "Drop-Frame" in this menu, Premiere will adjust the EDL's time code to precisely match the source video.

Set Timecode at:

Premiere 3.0 allows you to enter the time code for *the currently displayed frame* in the Clip window, instead of only the first frame. First open the clip's Clip window and display a frame—perhaps a change of scene or particular action point. Then open the Clip Timecode dialog box. Two radio-style buttons will be active in the middle of the box. Turn on "Current frame" and then enter the time code for the frame the Clip window displays.

Reel Name/Description

Enter the reel name of the clip's source tape. You also can add a short description, although the EDL formats retain only a limited number of characters.

Revert to Original

Click this button to revert the clip to the previous time code and name settings, if any.

You can enter time code in abbreviated form, skipping unnecessary zeros and colons. For example, 1007 will correctly become 00:00:10:07.

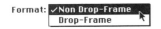

Premiere 3.0's Clip window can display either time code format. See page 52.

Set timecode at: ○ File beginning ● Current frame

Revert to Original

☞ *Editing a clip later (such as changing the In point) is no problem. Premiere will adjust the clip's time code data.*

That's all of the elements. After you give the Clip Timecode dialog box your OK, Premiere will embed the information in *all copies* of the clip in your project. You'll only need to set the time code for *other* clips in your project that lack the necessary or correct data.

Unfortunately, there's no way to tell at a glance which clips in your project, if any, lack time code and/or a reel name. If you're unsure, you may need to open this dialog box to check *every* clip in your project. Humph!

▶ The EDL Export Dialog Box

☞ *You don't have to first compile your project into a movie to generate an EDL.*

After taking care of the three issues mentioned earlier, you can go ahead and export your project's edit decisions. With the Construction window active, select the desired EDL format in the Export submenu under the File menu. The dialog box you'll then see depends on your EDL selection. CMX, Grass Valley and Sony all share this box.

Locate a home on your hard disk for the new EDL file.

Name the EDL file here. Grass Valley EDLs should be named LSTxxx.EDL where xxx is a number from 000 to 999.

Enter a descriptive title for the EDL's header.

Enter the time code that recording should begin on the record reel.

The frame rate shown matches the project's time base. Turn on drop frame time code format if that's the format of your tapes.

```
┌─────────────────────────────────────┐
│      🖴 EDL Files ▼                   │
│  ┌──────────────────────┐ ⬆  ⬜ Hard Disk │
│  │                      │ ┌──────────┐   │
│  │                      │ │  Eject   │   │
│  │                      │ └──────────┘   │
│  │                      │ ┌──────────┐   │
│  │                      │ ⬇ │ Desktop  │   │
│  Save EDL as:             ┌──────────┐   │
│  ┌──────────────────────┐ │   Save   │   │
│  │ LST124.EDL           │ └──────────┘   │
│  Title for this EDL:      ┌──────────┐   │
│  ┌──────────────────────┐ │  Cancel  │   │
│  │ Zoo News EDL 12.4    │ └──────────┘   │
│                                           │
│  Start Time Code: ┌───────────┐ 01:00:00:00 │
│                   │01:00:00:00│            │
│  Frame Rate: 30 FPS (NTSC)                │
│       ☐ Drop Frame  ┌─────────────┐       │
│                     │ Wipe Codes...│       │
│  Audio Processing: ┌──────────────────┐   │
│                    │ Audio Follows Video ▼│ │
│      Level Notes: ┌──────────────────┐    │
│                   │ None            ▼ │    │
└─────────────────────────────────────┘
```

3.0 *Click this button to assign wipe codes used by your post-production facility (see next section).*

Consult your post-production house for the suggested Audio Processing setting.

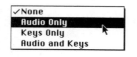

✓None
Audio Only ⬅
Keys Only
Audio and Keys

Audio and/or superimposed clip (key) fade levels can be displayed as notes in your EDL. The notes can be used to adjust key levels during the on-line editing session.

▶ Transition Translations

For your convenience, the next page summarizes how Premiere's transitions are interpreted by standard EDLs. This information is unabashedly taken straight from Adobe. The EDL's interpretation heads each list.

Transition Translations in Standard EDLs

☞ *For the few Premiere transitions that are not listed, check with your post-production house for the translation.*

Barn Door Wipe
Band Slide
Band Wipe
Barn Doors
Doors
Sliding Bands
Spin Away
Split

Box Wipe
Iris Cross
Iris Diamond
Iris Point
Iris Square
Iris Star
Multi-Spin
Spiral Boxes
Swirl

Circle Wipe
Clock Wipe
Iris Round

Cross Split Wipe
Center Merge
Center Peel
Center Split

Diagonal Wipe
Page Peel
Page Turn
Radial Wipe

Dissolve
Additive Dissolve
Channel Map
Cross Stretch
Cross Zoom
Curtain
Displace
Dither Dissolve
Fold Up
Funnel
Luminance Map
Non-Additive Dissolve
Paint Splatter
PICT Mask
Random Blocks
Texturize
Three-D

Horizontal Split Wipe
Venetian Blind

Horizontal Wipe
Checkerboard
Zig-Zag Blocks
Wedge Wipe

Inset Wipe
Inset

Wipe
Cube Spin
Pinwheel
Push
Random Wipe
Roll Away
Slide
Sliding Boxes
Stretch
Swing In
Swing Out

▶ **Cracking the Wipe Codes**

|3.0|

Different video switchers use different codes to interpret wipe patterns. In Premiere 3.0, you can specify the wipe codes that apply to your post-production facility. Neat! To do that, click the "Wipe Codes…" button in the EDL Export dialog box to see the box below.

Click in a box and enter a new wipe code as necessary. A small animation of each wipe will play.

The bottom left buttons are icing on the cake. Load and save different wipe code sets for different switchers!

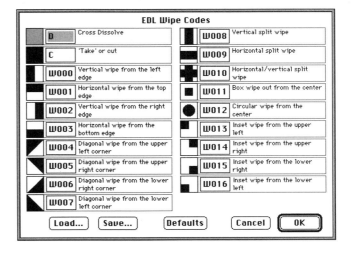

▶ Reading the EDL File

3.0

With this window, you can double-check the data and even edit it further if desired. Revisit the file anytime in 3.0 by using the "Open..." command in the File menu.

☞ *For CMX or Grass Valley systems, you'll also need to get the file onto a compatibly formatted floppy. Check out Alba EDL Pro software. Call Alba at (803) 853-3677.*

☞ *Unnumbered lines directly under each event are notes or comments.*

Here's the last EDL-creation step: Click the Save button in the EDL Export dialog box we saw a few pages back. Premiere will quickly create an EDL file on your hard drive. If you're using Premiere 2.0, you can open the file with a word processor (be sure to select a mono-spaced font). Within 3.0, however, a text editing window will arise with your edit decision list when you open the file.

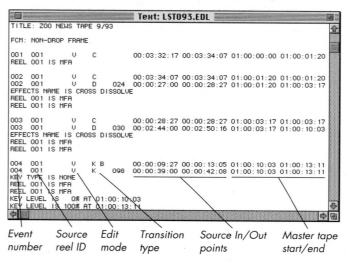

Event number / Source reel ID / Edit mode / Transition type / Source In/Out points / Master tape start/end

To help you understand and review your EDL text file, here's a brief guide to what each column represents.

• The first column is the *event number*—a single edit—numbered consecutively from 001 for each edit decision in your project.

• The second column is the *source reel ID*. If this data is missing for a clip, you'll see a non-number code.

• The third column is the *edit mode*—where the edit takes place. "V" stand for video track only, "A" is audio track only and "B" is both.

• The fourth column is the type of *transition* for the clip. "C" is a cut, "W" is a wipe, "K" stands for a superimposed key and "D" is a dissolve.

• Remaining columns have time code. The first two are the In and Out points for the clip on the source tape. The last two figures are the start and end frames for the segment that will be recorded on the master tape.

☞ **Four tips to using this Index:**

- All Premiere menu commands are included (except for the obvious, such as Undo, Cut, Save). Look up a menu item by the *main* menu name that appears at the top of your screen.
- All charts in this book can be found under "summary charts."
- Just about everything else is listed several ways—by name, associated task, window, category, etc. Industrial-strength!
- 3.0-only items show a (3.0); 2.0 stuff gets (2.0).

Numbers

About the Author

Michael Feerer had his start in video by taping his junior high school's productions back in the days when video recorders were the size of refrigerators. His eye for the visual continued through an award-winning early career as a planner of civic centers. More recently, he's been a certified Macintosh multimedia maniac (whatever that means) in the Pacific Northwest. He enjoys hiking, bicycling, reading (of course) and exploring the wilds with his family in and around Bellingham, Washington.

# Order Form

to order, call:
(800) 283-9444 or (510) 548-4393 or (510) 548-5991 (fax)

#	Title	Price	Total
	Desktop Publisher's Survival Kit	22.95	
	Everyone's Guide to Successful Publications	28.00	
	Four Colors/One Image	18.00	
	The Illustrator 5 Book	29.95	
	Illustrator Illuminated	24.95	
	The Little Mac Book, 3rd Edition	16.00	
	The Little Mac Word Book	15.95	
	The Macintosh Bible, 4th Edition	32.00	
	The Mac is not a typewriter	9.95	
	Photoshop 2.5: Visual QuickStart Guide (Mac Edition)	18.00	
	The Photoshop Wow! Book (with disk)	35.00	
	Premiere with a Passion	34.95	
	The QuarkXPress Book, 3rd Edition (Macintosh)	29.00	
	QuarkXPress 3.2: Visual QuickStart Guide (Mac Edition)	15.00	
	Real World FreeHand 3	27.95	
	Real World Scanning and Halftones	24.95	
	Silicon Mirage	15.00	
	The Underground Guide to Laser Printers	12.00	

SHIPPING:	First Item	Each Additional			
UPS Ground	$ 4	$ 1	Subtotal		
UPS Blue	$ 8	$ 2	8.25% Tax (CA only)		
Canada	$ 6	$ 4	Shipping		
Overseas	$14	$14	**TOTAL**		

Name		
Company		
Address		
City	State	Zip
Phone	Fax	
❑ Check enclosed	❑ Visa	❑ MasterCard
Company purchase order #		
Credit card #	Expiration Date	

Peachpit Press, Inc. • 2414 Sixth Street • Berkeley, CA • 94710
Your satisfaction is guaranteed or your money will be cheerfully refunded!

More from Peachpit Press. . .

Desktop Publisher's Survival Kit
David Blatner

Provides insights into desktop publishing on the Mac, including a disk with 12 top desktop-publishing utilities. *(176 pages)*

Everyone's Guide to Successful Publications
Elizabeth Adler

Everything you need to know to produce effective marketing materials. *(412 pages)*

Four Colors/One Image
Mattias Nyman

Step-by-step procedures for reproducing and manipulating color images using Photoshop, QuarkXPress, and Cachet. *(96 pages)*

The Illustrator 5 Book
Deke McClelland

Every tool and feature of Illustrator 5 is thoroughly explained along with tips and hints for new and experienced users. *(648 pages)*

Illustrator Illuminated
Clay Andres

A full-color book that shows how professional artists use Illustrator. Examples of illustrations from concept through completion. *(200 pages)*

The Little Mac Book, 3rd Edition
Robin Williams

This best-seller covers the basics of Mac oper–ation and provides useful reference information and charts. *(336 pages)*

The Little Mac Word Book
Helmut Kobler

Provides concise and clear information about working with Microsoft Word 5.0. *(240 pages)*

The Macintosh Bible, 4th Edition
Arthur Naiman and a cast of thousands

It's more than just a book—it's a phenomenon. Three free updates included. *(1,248 pages)*

The Mac is not a typewriter
Robin Williams

Our elegant best-seller is a classic guide to typesetting on the Mac. *(72 pages)*

Photoshop 2.5 for Macintosh: Visual QuickStart Guide
Elaine Weinmann and Peter Lourekas

A thorough but quick visual reference guide that moves you from a beginner to an intermediate-level user without much reading. *(264 pages)*

The Photoshop Wow! Book
Linnea Dayton and Jack Davis

A full-color, detailed tutorial in Adobe Photo-shop techniques. Comes with a disk of filters and other goodies. *(200 pages)*

The QuarkXPress Book, 3rd Edition
David Blatner

This best-selling guide is required reading for any serious XPress user. New edition includes a handy chart of keyboard shortcuts. *(728 pages)*

QuarkXPress 3.2 for Macintosh: Visual QuickStart Guide
Elaine Weinmann

This award-winning book is often used as a textbook by DTP educators, thanks to its simplicity of style and clarity. (240 pages)

Real World FreeHand 3
Olav Martin Kvern

The ultimate insider's guide to FreeHand, this authoritative and entertaining book covers the basics and advanced techniques. *(528 pages)*

Real World Scanning and Halftones
David Blatner and Steve Roth

Master the digital halftone process and learn about image sharpening, application settings, gamma, OCR software and more. *(296 pages)*

Silicon Mirage
Steve Aukstakalnis and David Blatner

At last—a book that explains how virtual reality works and how it's used. *(336 pages)*

The Underground Guide to Laser Printers
The Editors of FLASH Magazine

Save money on printer repairs and toner as you follow the advice in this book. *(180 pages)*